C000175352

Thinking Critically About Law

So you've arrived at university, you've read the course handbook and you're ready to learn the law. But is knowing the law enough to get you the very best marks? And what do your lecturers mean when they say you need to develop critical and analytical skills? When is it right to put your own views forward? What are examiners looking for when they give feedback to say that your work is too descriptive?

This book explores what it means to think critically and offers practical tips and advice for students to develop the process, skill and ability of thinking critically while studying law. The book investigates the big questions such as: What is law? and What is 'thinking critically'? How can I use critical thinking to get better grades in assessments? What is the role of critical thinking in the workplace? These questions and more are explored in Thinking Critically About Law.

Whether you have limited prior experience of critical thinking or are looking to improve your performance in assessments, this book is the ideal tool to help you enhance your capacity to question, challenge, reflect and problematise what you learn about the law throughout your studies and beyond.

A. R. Codling has over a decade's experience studying and teaching law at the Universities of Cardiff, Leeds, Reading and Sussex and is currently a tutor in problem-based learning at York Law School.

Thinking Critically About Law

A Student's Guide

A. R. Codling

Routledge
Taylor & Francis Group

LONDON AND NEW YORK

First published 2018
by Routledge
2 Park Square, Milton Park, Abingdon, Oxon OX14 4RN

and by Routledge
711 Third Avenue, New York, NY 10017

Routledge is an imprint of the Taylor & Francis Group, an informa business

© 2018 A. R. Codling

The right of A. R. Codling to be identified as author of this work has
been asserted by her in accordance with sections 77 and 78 of the
Copyright, Designs and Patents Act 1988.

All rights reserved. No part of this book may be reprinted or reproduced
or utilised in any form or by any electronic, mechanical, or other
means, now known or hereafter invented, including photocopying and
recording, or in any information storage or retrieval system, without
permission in writing from the publishers.

Trademark notice: Product or corporate names may be trademarks
or registered trademarks, and are used only for identification and
explanation without intent to infringe.

British Library Cataloguing-in-Publication Data
A catalogue record for this book is available from the British Library

Library of Congress Cataloging-in-Publication Data
A catalog record for this book has been requested

ISBN: 978-1-138-12536-0 (hbk)
ISBN: 978-1-138-12537-7 (pbk)
ISBN: 978-1-315-64756-2 (ebk)

Typeset in Joanna
by Apex CoVantage, LLC

www.MichaelCarltonArt.com

The Monkey Mind

by Michael Carlton

The artwork on the cover by Michael Carlton is called 'Monkey Mind' and refers to the
confused little monkey part of the brain that tries hard to figure out things that it is
unable/not designed to figure out or comprehend. It tries, but then ends up
getting lost and overwhelmed in its own processes of thought.

Dedicated to my brother Thomas Patrick Jackson

Contents

Figures

Tables

Task list

Chapter 1: Introduction

Chapter 2: What *is* 'critical thinking'?

Chapter 3: What *is* 'law'? Thinking critically about legal perspectives

Chapter 4: Putting critical thinking into legal practice

Chapter 5: Thinking critically about assessments

Chapter 6: Thinking critically in the workplace and beyond

Chapter 7: Conclusion

Table of treaties, statutes and cases

English statutes

Constitutional Reform Act 2005
Coroners and Justice Act 2009
Criminal Damage Act 1971
Education Act 1996
Equality Act 2006
Further and Higher Education Act 1992
Homicide Act 1957
Human Rights Act 1998
Law Commission Act 1965
Law Reform (Year and a Day Rule)
    Act 1996
Marriage Act 1949
Offences Against the Person Act 1861
Protection from Harassment Act 1997
Sexual Offences Act 2003
Theft Act 1968

English cases

A v Head Teacher and Governors of Lord Grey School
    [2006] 2 WLR 690
Airedale Hospital Trustees v Bland [1993] 2
    WLR 316
Attorney General for Jersey v Holley [2005] 3
    WLR 29
Caparo Industries v Dickman [1990] 2 AC 605
Director of Public Prosecutions v Morgan [1976]
    AC 182
Donoghue Stevenson [1932] AC 562
Haughton v Smith [1975] AC 476
Lau v Director of Public Prosecutions [2000] 1
    FLR 799
Oxford v Moss (1979) 68 Cr App Rep 183
R (on the application of Begum) v Headteacher and
    Governors of Denbigh High School [2007] 1

AC 100; [2006] UKHL 15; [2006] 2
    WLR. 719; [2006] HRLR 21
R v Adomako [1994] 3 WLR 288; [1995] 1
    AC 171
R v Ahluwalia [1992] 4 All ER 889
R v Barnes [2005] EWCA Crim 3246
R v Bateman [1925] 19 Cr App R 8
R v Bow Street Magistrate ex parte Pinochet
    (No 3) [2000] AC 147
R v Bree [2007] EWCA Crim 804
R v Dudley and Stephens (1884) 14 QBD 273
R v Duffy [1949] 1 All ER 932
R v G [2004] 1 AC 1034
R v Ghosh [1982] 3 WLR 110
R v Humphrey's [1995] 4 All ER 1008
R v Ireland; Burstow [1997] 3 WLR 534
R v Litchfield [1998] Crim LR 507
R v Miller [1983] AC 161
R v Misra & Srivastava [2005] 1 Cr App R
    328
R v R [1991] 3 WLR 767
R v Thornton (No 2) [1996] 2 All ER 1033
R v Woollin [1998] WLR 382
Re A (Children) (Conjoined Twins: Surgical Separation)
    [2000] 4 All ER 961; [2001] 2 WLR
    480; [2001] Fam 147

European treaties

European Convention on Human Rights
    and Fundamental Freedoms 1950
Treaty on the European Union 2007

European cases

Dahlab v Switzerland [2001] Appl. No.
    42393/98

Acronyms

BPTC	Bar Professional Training Course
BSB	Bar Standards Board
CAB	Citizen's Advice Bureau
CEDAW	Convention for the Elimination of Discrimination of Women
CLS	critical legal studies
CPE	Common Professional Examination
CPS	Crown Prosecution Service
CRTs	critical race theories
CV	curriculum vitae
ECHR	European Convention on Human Rights and Fundamental Freedoms 1950
ECtHR	European Court of Human Rights
EHRC	Equality and Human Rights Commission
GBH	grievous bodily harm
GLD	Graduate Diploma in Law
HE	higher education
HRA	Human Rights Act 1998
LLB	Bachelor of Laws
LPC	legal practice course
MCQs	multiple-choice questions
NHS	National Health Service
OAPA	Offences Against the Person Act
OSCOLA	Oxford University Standard Citation of Legal Authorities
PBL	problem-based learning
PGCAP	Postgraduate Certificate in Academic Practice
QAA	Quality Assurance Agency
QC	Queen's Counsel
QLD	Qualifying Law Degree
SRA	Solicitor's Regulatory Agency
TCAL	*Thinking Critically About Law*
UK	United Kingdom
UN	United Nations
US	United States

Glossary

Analysing	Taking things apart.
Application	The ability to apply or use information in new situations.
Argument	The identification of one or more claims supported by logical reasoning and evidence which leads to a justified conclusion.
Assess	Evaluate the nature, ability or quality of an argument or situation.
Assumptions	A statement that is accepted without proof or a belief that is supposed or taken for granted.
Audience	Whoever receives the message being conveyed by being a viewer, reader or listener either through conversation, books, television or other medium.
Authority	Evidence to support arguments, reasons, opinions or beliefs. (An example of a legal authority is legislation, such as the Theft Act 1968). *See also 'Hierarchy of Legal Authorities'.*
Bourgeoisie	A Marxist term meaning those that own the means of production (the middle classes).
Communitarianism	In comparison to liberalism, communitarians argue that a person's identity is partly defined by their communities, thus highlighting the importance of civic duty and social solidarity.
Consequentialism	The consequences of any action are the only standard of right and wrong.
Creative thinking	Involves 'synthesising' (see what follows) information to create a new or original argument or answer to a question.
Critical analysis	Once taken apart (see 'analysis'), examine, scrutinise and question the validity of information and weigh up the strengths and weaknesses, pros and cons, of an argument.
Critical legal studies (CLS)	The CLS movement provides a direct attack on the inequalities of doctrinal customs of law. Key proponents include Duncan Kennedy and Costas Douzinas.
Critical legal theories	Legal perspectives that essentially doubt the prospect of universal foundations of law.
Critical race theories (CRTs)	A perspective that provides a critical examination of the intersection of race, law and power. Key proponents include Patricia Williams and Tariq Modood.
Critical reading	Understanding the meaning of a text as well as recognising how each text is unique.

Critical reflection	Requires consideration of whether an answer or argument works as well as recognising one's own limitations and areas for improvement (otherwise known as self-reflection).
Critical thinking	There are numerous ways to describe the phrase 'critical thinking'. The aim of this book is to encourage you to generate your own definition. To achieve this, it provides a working definition of thinking critically, to be 'an intellectually disciplined process of thought whereby you develop your own informed legal opinion or argument(s) on a particular issue' (see Chapter 2).
Critical writing	Refusal to accept the conclusions of others by undertaking an evaluation of the arguments and evidence they provide.
Describing	Setting out in simple terms the definitions of key terms or ideas.
Dialectical	Relating to the logical discussion of ideas and opinions.
Discourses	A formal discussion of a subject in speech or writing, such as a dissertation or sermon *etc.*
Enlightenment	A broad intellectual and philosophical movement that took place in Europe in the eighteenth century comprising the ideals secularism, liberalism, democracy and an interest in the natural sciences.
Evaluation	An assessment of the validity of an argument.
Evidence	Information such as facts, authorities and studies used to support arguments, reasons, opinions or beliefs.
Fake news	News stories on the internet that are untrue.
Feminism(s)	Adopting Margaret Davies's term, feminism(s) are philosophical, political and social perspectives that are united only by the commitment to take seriously the distinct experiences of women. Key proponents include Simone de Beauvoir and Catharine MacKinnon.
Groupthink	A term coined by Irving Janis to describe people's tendency to reach a collective agreement at the cost of individual thought. Critical thinking is essential to overcome the pitfalls of group thinking.
Hierarchy of legal authorities	The hierarchy of legal authorities works as follows: ● First, how the wording of legislation ● Second, is interpreted by judges their decisions of cases and ● Finally, scrutinised by academic opinions found in journal articles.
Historicism	The notion that social evolution is explained in terms of inevitable historical forces.
Knowledge	Knowledge comes from being aware of and remembering previously learned material.
Legal pluralism(s)	A legal perspective which asserts that law is a multi-sited social phenomenon. Different legal pluralism(s) include institutional; cultural and religious; critical and subjective legal pluralism(s).
Legal positivism	A legal perspective whose main proponents are Jeremy Bentham, H.L.A. Hart and Ronald Dworkin. The main characteristic of positivism is the separation of law and morals. Also known as 'doctrinal' or 'black-letter' law.

Legal subjects	People subject to the rules of normative orders.
Liberalism	A political philosophy founded on the key principles of liberty and equality. Compare with communitarianism (earlier).
Logic	A set of rational considerations that support a justification for any belief.
Marxism	A perspective that claims that human actions and institutions are determined by the law of economics and that change is about class struggle. Notable proponents include Karl Marx and Frederick Engels.
Modernism	A literary period (1890–1930) which marked the search for aesthetic unity, order and universality.
Natural law theory	A legal perspective that supports the close relationship of law and morality. Its proponents include Saint Thomas Aquinas and Thomas Hobbes.
Nihilism	The belief that nothing in the world has real existence.
Normativity	Normative statements make claims about how things should or ought to be.
Objectivity	The quality of being objective by not being influenced by personal feelings or considerations when representing facts, as opposed to being 'subjective' (see what follows).
Outline	Give only the main points, showing the main structure.
Philosophy	The critical study of basic principles and concepts of a particular branch of knowledge (law, for example), particularly with the view of improving or reforming them.
Postmodernism	A multi-disciplinary perspective which aims to attack the values of the Enlightenment, particularly the notion that objective human knowledge can be achieved through the attainment of universal truths.
Problematising	Problematising a question or issue requires you to turn it into a problem requiring a solution.
Proletariat	A Marxist term for the class of wage earners in capitalist society who are forced to sell their labour (the working classes).
Rationality	Using reasons to solve problems.
Reasoning	The mental process of reason, processing arguments, conclusions, judgments *etc*.
Reflection	Considering whether an answer or argument works as well as recognising one's own limitations and areas for improvement and further development (or self-reflection).
Scepticism	Doubting the truth of something. Used to the extreme, doubt as to whether knowledge of anything is possible.
Sociological perspectives	Regard law as merely one feature of society.
Sophistry	The use of clever but false arguments with the intent to deceive.
Strategic learning	Learning on a 'need to know' basis.

Strong critical thinking	The consistent pursuit of fair and just arguments.
Structuralism	An intellectual approach to the question of how language relates to the world and how meaning works.
Subjectivity	The quality of being subjective, when arguments are influenced by personal feelings or opinions, as opposed to ones that are 'objective' (see earlier).
Synthesis	The combination of components or elements to form a connected whole.
Thinking	All those things going through our minds: thoughts.
Utilitarianism	An ethical theory that supports the belief that the best action is the one that maximises 'utility' in society. An example of utility is the well-being of all people.
Weak critical thinking	Lacks fair-mindedness: characterised by fair judgment, impartial and unprejudiced thinking.

Preface

Thinking *creatively* (and *self-reflectively*) about law

I believe in the importance of demystifying the learning process for students. This is because, today, whilst starting to carve out their future careers, many students are working in part-time jobs while simultaneously settling into new educational and social cultures. Legal skills have always been a topic that has interested me, from my own personal development to those of my students. This interest has led me to increasingly contemplate the question: what is 'critical thinking'? I think that there are several important and under-investigated sub-questions that surround the notion of thinking critically for law students in higher education (HE) institutions in the United Kingdom (UK) today. These include: what do law students think the phrase 'critical thinking' means? What do law teachers think? Are the views of what critical thinking 'is' held by law students and teachers the same, or do they differ? Are graduates of law expected to think critically in their roles? I discuss these questions and more in the following pages of this book entitled *Thinking Critically About Law* (TCAL).

> [The] teaching of skills in the mystified context of legal reasoning about utterly unconnected legal problems means that skills are taught badly, unselfconsciously, to be absorbed by osmosis as one picks up the knack of 'thinking like a lawyer'.[1]

TCAL draws on my first-hand experiences of studying and teaching law for now more than a decade: initially, whilst studying for my A-Levels at Sixth Form College in Bristol; then as an undergraduate on the Bachelor of Laws (LLB) degree with European studies programme at the University of Reading, England, and University of Uppsala, Sweden, respectively; followed by postgraduate study at the University of Sussex; to undertaking my doctorate, back at the University of Reading. To date, my teaching experiences include tutoring both undergraduate and postgraduate students at the Universities of Cardiff, Leeds, Reading, Sussex and York in a variety of approaches (from traditional to problem-based learning methods) and subjects including (legal) research and writing skills, jurisprudence, feminism and international human rights to criminal and land law. As part of my Postgraduate Certificate in Academic Practice (PGCAP) – an important teaching qualification for those working in universities – I was inspired to conduct my project on the topic of critical thinking due to colleagues' concerns about final-year law students' lack of ability to think critically. Reflecting upon my own

---

1   Duncan Kennedy (1982) 'Legal Education and the Reproduction of Hierarchy'. 32 *Journal of Legal Education*, 591–615, p. 595.

experiences of studying law, I wondered where in the curriculum, exactly, it was that students were encouraged to learn the skill. In the following chapters I draw upon the findings from studies I conducted. Initially, for my PGCAP project, through discussions with six law students and seven members of staff at the School of Law, University of Reading; then conducting further studies for TCAL (in the form of an online question-naire) with both staff and students at Cardiff Law School and the School of Law at the University of Leeds, as well as with graduates who are pursuing a legal career. The findings from these studies underpin my theoretical and practical guide for how law students can engage with the ideas, concept and skills of thinking critically prior to, during and following graduation from the LLB law degree.

From my time studying and teaching law, I have found the subject to be a worth-while academic pursuit for several reasons. As well as being a highly regarded subject both educationally and professionally, law is a dynamic subject always open to change and the impact of issues of current affairs, and its transferable skills open the career paths for students from being a vocational profession to a good grounding on many other pro-fessional career paths. I, personally, pursued the academic route. From my studies, I have established a subjective legal pluralist perspective, which purports that law 'like, religion, is whatever we believe' it to be.[2] The approach is influenced by Roderick Macdonald's statement that 'rules are only as good as the *reasons* behind them'[3] and based on the narra-tive premise of Martha-Marie Klienhans and Macdonald's critical legal pluralist approach on the relationship between law and society.[4] A subjective pluralistic perspective requires the narrative accounts of 'legal subjects' (people subject to the rules of normative orders) to be captured and analysed for elucidations of normativity. For me, thinking critically about law requires 'creative'[5] as well as 'self-reflective'[6] thinking.[7]

For TCAL, I have read numerous books and articles on the topic, putting together statements and extracts from these in the following pages so that today's busy student does not have to – they are all conveniently collected together in one accessible, com-plementary textbook. Practical tasks are also included in the following pages, as active learning is required to develop these skills by empowering students in their own learning process. The essential questions to consider in the process of thinking criti-cally about law are: what do the phrases 'critically thinking' and 'law' mean to you?[8]

Amy R. Codling
Yorkshire
2017

2 Amy Codling (2015) 'What do You Believe? Taxonomy of a Subjective Legal Pluralism' in Russell Sandberg (ed.) *Religion and Legal Pluralism*. Farnham: Ashgate, 199–212, p. 210.
3 Roderick A. Macdonald (2002) *Everyday Lessons in Law*. Montreal & Kingston: McGill-Queen's University Press, p. 86. Emphasis added.
4 Martha-Marie Kleinhans and Roderick A. Macdonald (1997) 'What Is a Critical Legal Pluralism?'. 12(2) *Canadian Journal of International Law and Society*, 25–46.
5 See Elizabeth Gruenfeld (2010) 'Thinking Creatively Is Thinking Critically'. 125 *Innovative Practices for Leadership Learning*, 71–83.
6 See Carol M. Lerch et al. (2012) 'Reflection: A Key Component to Thinking Critically'. 3(1) *The Canadian Journal for the Scholarship of Teaching and Learning*, 1918–2902.
7 Creative in the sense of producing work that is original and unexpected, and self-reflective in acknowledging one's own position and limitations.
8 Take part in the latest TCAL survey at www.surveymonkey.co.uk/r/J7QRKW2.

Chapter 1

Introduction

Is there such a thing as a 'dumb question'? Is asking such a question 'dumb' itself? Scientist and philosopher Carl Sagan reassuringly states that there is no such thing as a dumb question. This is because if we do not ask questions, however 'dumb' they may first appear, how could we know anything?

> There are naive questions, tedious questions, ill-phrased questions, questions put after inadequate self-criticism . . . But every question is a cry to understand the world.
>
> There is no such thing as a dumb question.[1]

Two key questions for those looking to or already studying law that this book Thinking Critically About Law (TCAL) explores are: first, how do you 'think critically' about 'law'? Second, how can you demonstrate that you have thought critically about law while undertaking an English Bachelor of Laws (LLB) degree and beyond? These questions may appear to be 'dumb' ones at first because they are so basic. Yet they are fundamental to the attainment of a first-class degree for an undergraduate. To achieve such results you need to, first, acquire a clear understanding of your own answer to questions such as what is 'thinking critically' and what is 'law'? Once achieved, second, you can demonstrate your understanding and ability in your assessments. These elements do not happen in isolation from one another; as the old saying goes, 'what came first, the chicken or the egg?' By thinking theoretically, philosophically and creatively as well as reflecting upon your thoughts and study skills, you will find that you develop your own understanding of what it is to think critically about law. Once developed, this ability will stand you in good stead over the course of your professional career (whatever you decide to do) and, generally, for the rest of your life.

I. TCAL's aims

TCAL aims to provide you with essential theoretical and practical guidance for how to engage with thinking critically prior to, during and following graduation from an LLB. It provides advice on how to overcome or avoid receiving the following feedback on your assessments such as:

> 'Too descriptive'.
> 'More critical analysis required'.
> 'Your lack of critical commentary has let you down'.[2]

TCAL is an essential textbook to have while studying law for several reasons. It complements your core law subject textbooks,[3] as well as those on legal

---

1 Carl Sagan (2008) The Demon Haunted World: Science as a Candle in the Dark. New York: Ballantine Books.
2 Lisa Cherkassy et al., (2011) Legal Skills. Basingstoke: Palgrave Macmillan, p. 109.
3 Such as Mark Thompson and Martin George (2017) Thompson's Modern Land Law. Oxford: Oxford University Press; Mark Elliot and Robert Thomas (2017) Public Law. Oxford: Oxford University Press and Jeremy Horder (2016) Ashworth's Principles of Criminal Law. Oxford: Oxford University Press, etc.

skills.[4] It also complements books on the topic of thinking critically that do not specifically focus on law.[5] In comparison to books that do consider thinking critically and legal reasoning together (which can be complex to read and lack practical guidance)[6] TCAL provides a holistic approach to the theory and practice of thinking critically about law. The following pages provide an accessible account of critical thinking and legal theories as well as guidance on how to develop and refine your research and writing skills. In comparison to other legal textbooks, TCAL begins by thinking philosophically and theoretically about critical thinking and law. It contains helpful statements, extracts and activities that have been put together from a range of sources to demystify the process of thinking critically about law.

Note on studies

TCAL also draws upon the findings from original research.[7] Initially, the survey was conducted by discussions with six law students (two from each year group) as well as seven members of staff at the University of Reading. Further studies (in the form of an online questionnaire) were also conducted with approximately one hundred students and members of staff at Cardiff Law School and the School of Law at the University of Leeds, as well as with professional practitioners in the legal field. The findings from these studies underpin TCAL's theoretical and practical guide for thinking critically about law.

The difficulty of thinking critically about law

Although critical thinking is a desirable transferable skill to attain at university, it is something 'that even PhD students often fall short in'.[8] One reason, asserted by first-year student, for this is that:

> I am like: 'critical thinking, what is that? I have never heard of that.'[9]

Some students explain that their difficulty in thinking critically about law is that they were not given the chance to develop such skills prior to starting at university

---

4   The following do not consider thinking critically about law or discuss it in only one chapter: Lisa Webley (2016) Legal Writing. London: Routledge; Emily Finch and Stefan Fafinski (2015) Legal Skills. Oxford: Oxford University Press and Cherkassy, supra note 2.

5   Such as Martin Cohen (2015) Critical Thinking Skills for Dummies. Chichester: John Wiley & Sons Ltd; Richard Paul and Lisa Elder (2014) Critical Thinking: Tools for Taking Charge of Your Learning and Your Life. London: Pearson and Stella Cottrell (2011) Critical Thinking Skills: Developing Effective Analysis and Argument. Basingstoke: Palgrave Macmillan.

6   See Wade Mansell, et al. (2015) A Critical Introduction to Law. London: Routledge and Michael Head and Scott Mann (2009) Law in Perspective: Ethics, Society and Critical Thinking. Sydney: UNSW Press.

7   Other empirical studies on critical thinking have been conducted in the UK (Jennifer Moon (2008) Critical Thinking: An Exploration of Theory and Practice. London: Routledge); Australia and New Zealand (Jeffrey McGee, Michael Guihot and Tim Connor (2013) 'Rediscovering Law Students as Citizens: Critical Thinking and the Public Value of Legal Education'. 38 Alternative Law Journal, 77–81 and Archana Parashar and Vijaya Nagarajan (2006) 'An Empowering Experience: Repositioning Critical Thinking Skills in the Law Curriculum'. 10 Southern Cross University Law Review, 219–241). These, however, do not specifically capture the views and opinions of law students, teachers and those in the profession.

8   Cohen, supra note 5, p. 2.

9   First-year student, Reading.

(whether undertaking law as an A-level subject or not). A cynical response, provided by another student in their first year, is that critical thinking is simply

> a vague phrase that is thrown around by lecturers and tutors. Something that is constantly asked of students, yet never taught to them.[10]

Others contended that they are expected to demonstrate their critical thought in their assessments without being adequately taught what it means or how to demonstrate it in their work. A student in their final year of study even responded that

> I still do not fully understand what exactly is required of me when I am asked to critically analyse an essay.[11]

To overcome these difficulties and gain an appreciation of thinking critically about law before your final year of study, the key aim of TCAL is to help you move from a descriptive style of work to an analytical approach that is 'critical'. This is an essential part of the transition from leaving school (or a working environment) to the expectations at university: the place to develop your reflective, creative and critical thinking abilities. Similar to Michael Head and Scott Mann's book *Law in Perspective*, TCAL's aim is to encourage '*critical, responsible and creative thinking* about law'.[12] It aims to focus on stimulating your thought processes to get you away from the idea that there is a 'right' or 'correct' answer for legal problems to one that is personal, creative and well reasoned.

The importance of critical thought

When asked the question: 'is thinking critically important to attaining a first-class degree'? ninety-eight per cent of students who took the study thought that it is important to do so, as shown in Figure 1.1.

One of the key reasons that thinking critically is considered to be essential in the attainment of a first-class degree is because it forms part of governmental strategy.[13] In 2008 the Quality Assurance Agency (QAA) – an independent body that checks the standards and quality of HE in the UK – indicated that those obtaining an honours degree should be able to

> [c]*ritically* evaluate arguments, assumptions, abstract concepts and data (that might be incomplete) to make judgments and to frame appropriate questions to achieve a solution . . . to a problem.[14]

In line with this, many universities include reference to the importance of students' abilities to demonstrate critical thinking in their institutional strategies. The

---

10 First-year student, Cardiff.
11 Final-year student, Reading.
12 Head and Mann, *supra* note 6, p. ix.
13 Ron Dearing (1997) *Higher Education in the Learning Society (Report of the National Committee of Inquiry into Higher Education)*. London: HMSO.
14 QAA Publication. 'The Framework for Higher Education Qualifications in England, Wales and Northern Ireland'. August 2008. Available at www.qaa.ac.uk.

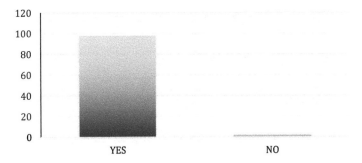

Figure 1.1 Question: Is thinking critically important to attaining a first-class degree?

University of Reading's 'Learning and Teaching Strategy' (2013–2018), for example, references the importance of thinking critically by engaging students in

> [r]esearch-led teaching, which encourages students to develop an ability *to use their knowledge critically* by involving them actively in research.[15]

As a result, the ability to think critically is required to attain a first-class degree; but what is a 'first-class' answer? What do you need to demonstrate to achieve such a result?

First-class grade (70+%)[16]

A first-class answer has a thoughtful structure, a clear message displaying personal reflection informed by wider reading of articles and/or other commentaries and a good grasp of detail (as evidenced by the choice of relevant examples which are well integrated into the answer's structure). The answer is complete with no errors or omissions.

First-class answers are ones that are exceptionally good for an undergraduate and which excel in at least one and probably several of the following criteria:

- comprehensiveness and accuracy;
- clarity of argument and expression;
- integration of a range of materials;
- evidence of wider reading;
- insight into theoretical issues.

Although there is no expectation of originality of exposition or treatment, a first-class answer is generally expected to spot points rarely seen. A high first-class answer

15 University of Reading (2013–2018) 'Learning and Teaching Strategy.' Available at www.reading. ac.uk/web/FILES/cdotl/University-of-Reading-Learning-and-Teaching-Strategy-2013-18.pdf.
16 Webley, *supra* note 4, pp. 10–11. Emphasis added.

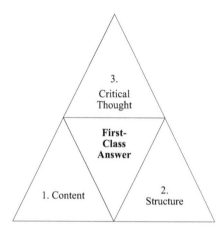

Figure 1.2 First-class triangle

(75+%) is expected to display originality and excel in most if not all the aforementioned criteria.

As shown in the 'first-class triangle' in Figure 1.2, there are three key elements to achieving a first-class answer. These are:

1   First, an answer must contain *content* with 'a clear message' or argument, evidenced by 'wider reading' (from a variety of sources including books and journal articles) and engagement with 'theoretical issues', where appropriate;

2   Second, it must have a 'thoughtful *structure*' with the discussion being set out logically and coherently, sub-headings used where appropriate; and

3   Finally, a first-class answer must demonstrate *critical thought* by displaying self-reflection as well as 'originality' and creative thinking.[17]

Structure of the book

As stated at the outset, the aim of TCAL is to consider what it is that makes thinking about law 'critical'. In other words, how do *you* think critically about law? And how can *you* demonstrate that you have been thinking critically in your assessments? To investigate these questions, both the theoretical aspects and practical steps for demonstrating your critical thinking are discussed. The following seven chapters are divided into two parts. The first part of TCAL considers the theoretical aspects of thinking critically. The next chapter, Chapter 2, crucially explores the questions: *what* is it and *why* is it important to think critically? In relation to these questions, first, the importance of developing critical thought while studying at university and, second, to a legal career and, finally, to a democratic society in general are discussed. The difficulty in defining the term is illustrated, with findings from the studies and criticisms

---

17 *Ibid.*, pp. 10–11.

of thinking critically also being considered. To think critically about it, you need to gain an understanding and appreciation of the nature of law. Chapter 3 importantly explores the theoretical question: what is 'law'? There are two aims for the third chapter. These are, first, to briefly outline the important role of legal theories and, second, to provide a brief introduction to seven legal perspectives, namely: natural law theory, legal positivism, Marxism, critical legal studies (CLS), feminism(s), critical race theories (CRTs) and legal pluralism(s).

The chapters in the second part of the book provide practical guidance for thinking critically while studying law at an undergraduate level and beyond. The fourth chapter focuses on the transition from studying law at school or college to the different expectations at university. Examples include putting your critical thinking into practice by asking questions during lectures and through adequate preparation for tutorial and seminar sessions. The fifth chapter discusses how to think critically about your assessments. As well as the traditional essay and examination process, alternative forms of assessment (such as group presentations and posters) are also discussed. Several ways of constructively using feedback from non-assessed and assessed work are outlined, and the importance of self-reflection for thinking critically is emphasised. The sixth chapter contains the findings from a survey conducted with law graduates to consider their engagement with critical thinking. Other career opportunities are also discussed in the penultimate chapter. The concluding chapter, finally, highlights the key points that are discussed throughout the book. TCAL is a book that can be read holistically or dipped in and out of as the tasks and assessments of your course require.

Tasks

In what ways could your understanding of critical thinking be improved?

Mainly through practice, it's an acquired skill which takes time to accomplish.[18]

The opportunity to practice critical thinking skills is important because it is an 'active' thinking process.[19] Active learning is required for you to develop your abilities. For this reason, TCAL contains more than thirty-five practical tasks for you to undertake. Each chapter includes at least one task for you to practice and refine your skills of thinking critically about law. Your first tasks to complete are as follows:

 TASK ONE   *Thinking deeply about why you are at university*[20]

What are you trying to accomplish at university? Are you committed to developing your thinking in a deep way? Or are you going to university simply to get a job that requires a degree? Are you going to university just because your friends are going? Are you after the social life that university

18 First-year student, Cardiff.
19 Cohen, *supra* note 5, p. 1.
20 Paul and Elder, *supra* note 5, p. 159.

offers? Or are you not sure what your real motivations are? If you had to complete the following statements, what would you say?

● **My fundamental purpose in going to university is. . .**

_____

_____

_____

● **I am committed to. . .**

_____

_____

_____

TASK TWO *Articulate your understanding of critical thinking*[21]

Before reading further, articulate your initial understanding of what critical thinking is. This task is repeated in the concluding chapter so that you can look back and see how your thinking has developed. Complete the following statements:

1 **To me, critical thinking means:**

_____

_____

_____

2 **In other words (this should be at least four to five sentences):**

_____

_____

_____

3 **I can apply critical thinking to my life in the following ways:**

_____

_____

_____

21 Ibid., p. 14.

Tips

A variety of tips are also included in the chapters in the second part of TCAL. These provide useful suggestions of how to use a particular critical thinking or study tool.

Suggested reading

TCAL is a 'complementary' textbook. It complements other core law textbooks and resources on legal and critical thinking skills. For this reason, a traffic light system is used to indicate other relevant texts and materials for you to research on a particular topic. The traffic light system works as follows:

Traffic light system

○   Easy introductory guide to subject matter.
◍   Moderate introduction to subject matter.
●   Advanced reading on subject matter.

II. Why is it important to have an inquisitive mind when studying law?

Building upon Sagan's premise stated at the outset, that there is no such thing as a dumb question, we gain an appreciation of the importance of having an inquisitive mind when studying law. An inquisitive mind is one that basically asks lots of questions: a mind that is eager for knowledge and filled with curiosity.[22] The good news is that every person has an inquisitive mind – even you. Can you remember when you were a small child and you constantly asked 'why this and why that?' For example, a small child may ask his or her parents the question 'why am I not allowed to cross the road without holding your hand?' To this question about the rule that has been set out (that for the child to cross the road, they must hold the hand of a parent), one of the parents may respond something to the effect that 'it is safer for you to cross the road while holding my hand'. Here the parent explains to the child the *reason* behind the rule. The child may respond to this explanation by asking: 'but *why* is it safer for me to hold your hand?' The child is essentially asking for a further explanation as to the reason behind the rule. The parent may then respond that this is because 'it is safer for you to hold my hand when you cross the road in case you trip over or a car comes along really fast'. Following this reasonable explanation, however, the child may then ask again 'but *why*?' By this point the poor, exasperated parent may well respond by shouting 'BECAUSE I SAY SO!' Thus, the parent is using his or her position of authority over the child to assert power and control, in addition to the health and safety concerns, for holding the child's hand while crossing the road. If you can remember asking your

---

22 John Dewey (1933/1991) *How We Think: A Restatement of the Relation of Reflective Thinking to the Educative Process.* New York: Prometheus Books.

parents a similar line of questions, then you have evidence of your own inquiring mind from your infancy.

> It is not possible to become a good thinker and be a poor questioner. Thinking is not driven by answers, but rather, by questions . . . To learn a subject is to learn to ask the questions the best thinkers in the field routinely ask.[23]

The unfortunate news is that for some reason, we stop constantly asking 'why'? Why is that? I do not know for sure. Perhaps it is because, as we get older and more of the world gets explained to us, we think that we understand it and start to *assume* the answers to the questions we have rather than asking other people or reading books that may help explain the answers to us. Alternatively, it could be that we feel that it undermines our intelligence to ask a lot of questions. After a while, people who we question seem to grow tired and exasperated with providing explanations and may even tease us for our questioning by saying something like, '*I can't believe you asked that! You're so dumb not to know the answer to that already!*' I am not exactly sure why it is that we stop constantly asking 'why', and it is too large a psychological question to explore here. For now, perhaps it is best simply to contemplate the question: *why do you think that we stop asking why?* Remember the daily questioning process that you went through as a child and apply that same process to your legal studies: after all, in academia *there is no such thing as a dumb question.*

The philosophical background of critical thinking: 'philosophy', 'intellectualism' and 'academia'

> The need for a questioning or inquisitive mind and critical thinking can be traced to Ancient Greek philosophy. 'Philosophy' is basically the critical study of the basic principles and concepts of a particular branch of knowledge (for example, law), particularly with the view of improving or reforming them. The word 'philosophy' is derived from two Greek words, philos ('lover') and sophia ('wisdom').[24]

Critical thinking is traditionally a branch of philosophy.[25] As stated, the notion of critical thinking can be traced back to Ancient Greek philosophy. 'Ancient Greek' philosophy was established in Greece from the sixth century and was a new way of thinking which provided the foundation of Western intellectualism. The term 'intellectualism' refers to the idea that knowledge is chiefly derived from reason. For example, a person who is an 'intellectual' is someone who engages in critical study, thought and reflection and usually produces or defends a particular system of values (such as utilitarian, liberal or Marxist, *etc.*).

> The Intellectual is someone who meddles in what does not concern him.[26]

The word 'academia' also comes from Ancient Greek, deriving from the mythical hero Akademos. The story goes that the Athenian King Theseus (slayer of the Minotaur), after being widowed and reaching the age of fifty, abducted the beautiful twelve-year-old

---

23 Paul and Elder, *supra* note 5, p. 138.
24 Anthony Harrison-Barbet (2001) *Mastering Philosophy.* Basingstoke: Palgrave Macmillan, p. 1.
25 Cohen, *supra* note 5, p. 2.
26 Jean-Paul Sartre as cited in Annie Cohen-Solal (1989) *Jean-Paul Sartre.* Paris: Gallimard, pp. 588–589.

Helena (before she was the cause of the Trojan War).[27] Due to this outrage, her twin brothers Castor and Pollux invaded Attica to liberate their sister and threatened to destroy Athens. Akademos told them where she was hidden and was held to be the saviour of the city. Consequently, whenever the Lacedaemonians invaded Attica they always spared Akademos' land. This piece of land was adorned with olive groves and called 'Academia' after its owner. Within these groves the philosopher **Plato** gave his lectures, and thus Akademos' name was linked to the site for Plato's Academy. One of the most famous pupils of Plato's Academy, **Aristotle** (eventual tutor to Alexander the Great), created the powerful logical system based on what 'is' and what 'is not': in other words, using boxes to categorise our knowledge.

The Socratic method of thinking

Socrates used a questioning form of argument where he asked people to state, in a short sentence, what they thought they knew.[28]

Building upon the ideas of sophists (basically thinking-skills experts who offered their services for a fee), the Socratic method of thinking is essentially a technique to engage people in debate. Developed by the famous Greek philosopher **Socrates**, the basic idea is that a person learns how best to win arguments with a philosopher. Plato describes the Socratic method in Meno (a dialogue between Socrates and Meno – a political figure in Ancient Greece).[29] The story here goes that a slave boy (who had no formal education) was asked certain, simple questions by Socrates to clarify his thoughts and ideas and as a result was able to answer a geometric question – Pythagoras' theorem. The story of the slave boy illustrates how the process of using reasoning in response to questions can establish and solidify our ideas and develop knowledge. As stated at the outset, there is no such thing as a 'dumb' question. However, for your questioning to exhibit the 'Socratic method' you need to approach problems in a disciplined, orderly and systematic way. Following are several examples of how to demonstrate this ability.

EXAMPLES

- Seek to understand – when possible – the ultimate foundations for what is said or believed and follow the implications of those foundations through further questions.
- (You might ask, for example, 'On what do you base your beliefs? Could you explain your reasoning to me in more detail so I can more fully understand your position?')
- Recognise that any thought can exist fully only in a network of connected thoughts. Therefore, treat all assertions as connecting points to further thoughts. Pursue those connections.
- (You might ask, for example, 'If what you say is true, wouldn't X or Y be so?')[30]

---

27 Recently depicted in the movie Troy (2004) Warner Bros.
28 Mike Metcalfe (2006) Reading Critically at University. London: Sage Publications, p. 14.
29 Plato (2012) Meno. York: Empire Books.
30 Paul and Elder, supra note 5, pp. 144–145.

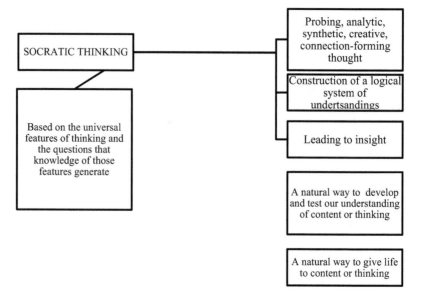

Figure 1.3 Socratic thinking diagram[31]

Socratic thinking is an integrated, disciplined approach to thinking, as illustrated in Figure 1.3 above.

The big three[32]

In summary, from the Gang of Three (in Ancient Greek philosophy, namely Socrates, Plato and Aristotle) came a thinking system which was based on:

- analysis
- judgment (and boxes)
- argument; and
- criticism.

Criticisms of the Socratic method

One criticism of the Socratic method is that sometimes the questions posed can be leading ones. Leading questions can be equated to 'learning by rote', which is basically when students learn to repeat and memorise what is told to them by their teachers. Rote learning is commonly how one learns his or her times tables at school: do you remember learning 'one times one is one; two times two is four; three times three is nine, and so on'? Arguably, memory tests are important ways of learning

---

31 Ibid., p. 145.
32 Edward de Bono (1996) *Teach Yourself to Think*. London; Penguin Books, p. 11.

information; however, they do not develop or assess a person's ability to think critically. To develop this ability we first need to know (or remember) what a thing is itself – for example, that theft is defined as the dishonest appropriation of property belonging to another with the intention to permanently deprive the other of it (section 1(1) of the Theft Act 1968). This is very different from providing a critical assessment as to whether the 1968 Act adequately defines the term 'property' (see *Oxford v Moss*).[33]

Another criticism of the Socratic method is that a person who uses the inquisitive part of their mind to the extreme is labelled a 'sceptic'. Scepticism basically involves 'bringing an element of polite doubt'.[34] Sixteenth-century French philosopher **René Descartes** famously coined the phrase '*dubito ergo cogito; cogito ergo sum*' ('I doubt, therefore I think; I think, therefore I am').[35] Descartes went through a mental process of doubting the existence of *all things* to prove the existence of them. Through his process of doubt, Descartes proved his own existence in the world. To doubt something is therefore an incredibly powerful mental ability, because we can doubt – we exist! When used to the extreme, however, scepticism is unproductive and produces uncritical thought(s).

Historical background of university education

The Academic approach is named after the first university founded by Plato . . . The primary means of instruction was the lecture, a one-sided affair in which professors verbally delivered elements of their expert knowledge to an entirely passive audience.[36]

University is a crucial place to exercise and develop (perhaps recapture from your youth) an inquisitive mind. A university is a higher educational learning institution that is granted degree-giving powers by the government. The word 'university' is derived from the Latin phrase *universitas magistorum et scholarium* (which means a 'community of teachers and scholars'). In Europe, HE was established in the sixth century in Christian cathedral schools, where monks and nuns taught classes. The first universities in Europe were the University of Bologna (Italy, 1088), University of Paris (France, 1150) and University of Oxford (England, 1167). In England, after disputes between students and residents of Oxford in 1209, some academics fled from the violence to Cambridge and later founded the University of Cambridge (1209); thus, Oxbridge was established.

Today, there are three main types of universities in England. These are: first, 'modern red-brick universities' (referring to the nine universities founded in the major industrial cities in the nineteenth and twentieth centuries); second, 'ex-poly-technics' (thirty-five 'new' universities since the enactment of the Further and Higher Education Act 1992) and finally, 'Russell Group' institutions (formed in 1994 and now with twenty-four members). There are several ways in which to find

33 (1979) 68 Cr App Rep 183.
34 Cottrell, *supra* note 5, p. 2.
35 René Descartes (1644/2016) *The Principles of Philosophy*. London: CreateSpace Independent Publishing Platform.
36 Cohen, *supra* note 5, p. 226.

out information about a university that you are interested to attend. These include looking at newspapers, such as *The Times* 'Good University Guide'[37] or *The Guardian* 'Guardian University Guide'[38] or the responses of current students to the National Student Survey[39] as well as visiting an institution's website.

III. Why study law at university?

> Law is the cement of society . . . Its study at university enables you to explore how and why this is so. A common misunderstanding is that the study of law involves little more than the rote learning of legal rules. Closer acquaintance will show that it is far more complex and challenging than that.[40]

Law is a popular profession and subject to study at university. It is a subject which both shapes and reflects societal rules, norms and values. Lawyers are said to be the 'gatekeeper[s] to legal institutions'[41] and are required to have an ability to explain complex issues to clients succinctly (in both written and oral form), to problem solve and work well as a team. A law degree is a great asset to have for any profession and a varied and interesting topic to study at university (its subjects ranging from legal history to criminal law or space law).

Current aims of legal education

> Law is rarely out of the news and frequently stimulates controversy.[42]

Due to today's economic climate[43] and changes made to tuition fees,[44] wanting to gain a university degree requires solid justifications. So why is it beneficial to attain a law degree? The first reason is that it is important to obtain a law degree if you want to be a lawyer. Law is seen as a decent profession, and lawyers are among the highest paid professionals. More than eighty per cent of law graduates are employed three

---

37 Available at www.thetimes.co.uk.
38 Available at www.theguardian.com/education/universityguide.
39 Available at www.thestudentsurvey.com.
40 Glanville Williams (2016) *Learning the Law*. London: Sweet & Maxwell, p. 2.
41 William L. F. Felstiner, Richard L. Abel and Austin Sarat (1981) 'The Emergence and Transformation of Disputes: Naming, Blaming, Claiming'. 15 *Law and Society Review*, 631–654, p. 645.
42 Raymond Wacks (2009) *Understanding Jurisprudence: An Introduction to Legal Theory*. Oxford: Oxford University Press, p. xii.
43 See the study conducted by the Office for National Statics in 2014 that concluded that having a degree has 'little impact' on a person's ability to gain employment: Office for National Statistics. '2011 Census, Qualifications and Labour Market Participation in England and Wales'. 18th June 2014. Available at www.ons.gov.uk/ons/dcp171776_367378.pdf.
44 See the Browne Review: Independent Report. 'The Browne Report: Higher Education Funding and Student Finance'. Department for Business, Innovation and Skills. 12th October 2010. www.gov.uk/government/uploads/system/uploads/attachment_data/file/422565/bis-10-1208-securing-sustainable-higher-education-browne-report.pdf.

years after leaving HE.[45] According to *Black's Law Dictionary*, a lawyer is 'a person learned in the law; as an attorney, counsel or solicitor; a person who is practicing law':[46] if you are a law student, you are already a lawyer. Although obtaining a law degree is not the only route into the profession (for example, you could obtain a degree in another subject and then undertake a Common Professional Exam [CPE] or Graduate Diploma in Law [GDL] or be trained by a firm 'in house'): law is a vocation. A vocational subject is one that links to a trade or profession, such as the legal profession. Currently there are three stages to qualifying as a practicing lawyer. These are:

Three stages of qualifying as a lawyer

1   The first stage is *academic* (obtaining a law degree);
2   The second is attaining a *postgraduate diploma* (either on the Legal Practice Course [LPC] or on the Bar Professional Training Course [BPTC]); and
3   The final stage is *practical* (gained during a vacation contract or pupillage).

To enable students to have a Qualifying Law Degree (QLD) to undertake the second vocational element (the LPC or BPTC course), a degree programme must meet requirements specified by professional bodies such as the Solicitors Regulation Authority (SRA) and Bar Standards Board (BSB). There are certain 'core modules' (or foundation subjects) that a student must pass to gain a QLD. These subjects are set out as follows.

Core law modules
To obtain a QLD, the core modules you must pass are:

● Contract
● Criminal Law
● Equity and Trusts
● European Union Law
● Land Law
● Public Law
● Tort

To pass these modules, you must achieve a mark of at least forty per cent.

The second reason it is important to obtain a law degree, even if you do not wish to practice as a lawyer, is that law is an academic discipline in its own right. While some students studying law become solicitors or barristers and practice law in an array of different areas, others use the transferable skills that they attain on the

---

45 See the Higher Education Statistics Authority. 'Destinations of Leavers from Higher Education Longitudinal Survey 2016/17'. Available at www.hesa.ac.uk/data-and-analysis/publications/long-destinations-2012-13.
46 Henry Campbell Black (1979) *Black's Law Dictionary*. St Paul, MN: West Publishing Co.

programme (in critical thinking, argument formulation, public speaking, etc.) in various other careers. Due to these reasons, law is a highly regarded degree to obtain.

Essentially, legal education instils the ability for you to 'think like a lawyer'.[47] Thinking critically about law essentially aids you with 'what to do when no obvious answers or set of methods are available'.[48] In law, as with other subjects, there are no 'yes' or 'no', 'right' or 'wrong or 'black' or 'white' answers to questions. Instead, there are shades of grey in between (about fifty of them, apparently!) One classic example of a controversial case is Re A (Children) (Conjoined Twins: Surgical Separation).[49] The case was concerned with several legal, ethical and religious dilemmas surrounding the surgical separation of conjoined twins named Jodie and Mary. It involved the interaction of the principles of medical law, family law, criminal law and human rights. The essential question put to the court was: is it permissible to kill one twin to save the other? During the Court of Appeal's decision of the case, Ward LJ stated that

> [i]n this case the right answer is not at all easy to find . . . difficult for the seemingly irreconcilable conflicts of moral and ethical values and difficult because the search for settled legal principle has been especially arduous and conducted under real pressure of time.[50]

As stated, at school you tend to learn by rote ('one times one is one', etc.), whereas at university you are encouraged to ask deeper questions, such as why does one times one equal one? and metaphysical (theoretical or hypothetical) questions, such as what is 'one'? Who decides what these numbers mean? Should they be called something else?

Sources of law

As stated, a sceptical approach to learning can be useful because it requires information to be supported by evidence. A sceptical approach (when not taken to the extreme) is a useful approach to adopt when thinking critically about law. This is because every statement that you make should be supported by reference to a relevant source of law. The English common law system has a clearly defined hierarchy of legal authorities. These are as follows:

Hierarchy of legal authorities

1   **Legislation:** The words written in, for example, international treaties, European conventions and domestic statutes.

---

47 Mary Kate Kearney and Beth Beazley (1991) 'Teaching Students How to "Think Like Lawyers"': Integrating the Socratic Method with the Writing Process'. 64(4) Temple Law Review, 885–908; David ButleRitchie (2002) 'Situating "Thinking Like a Lawyer" Within Legal Pedagogy'. 1(1) Cleveland State Law Review, 29–56 and P. Knott (2009) 'Thinking Like a Lawyer: An English Interpretation'. 10(3) Transactions: Tennessee Journal of Business Law, 179–188.

48 Cohen, supra note 5, p. 20.

49 [2000] 4 All ER 961; [2001] 2 WLR 480; [2001] Fam 147.

50 Ibid., at p. 155.

2   **Cases:** How the words in legislation have been interpreted (either literally or purposely, *etc.*) by the courts, such as the European Court of Human Rights (ECtHR) or Supreme Court.

3   **Academic opinions:** How the words written by Parliament, interpreted by the courts have been upheld or critiqued by academic's in journal articles. This also includes how academics or bodies such as the Law Commission suggest that the words written in legislation or the decisions of judges could be amended or reformed.

The offence of theft provides a clear example of how the hierarchy of sources of law operates. Theft is a statutory offence, the first source of law listed. As provided under section 1(1) of the Theft Act 1968: if 'property' (defined in section 4(1)), 'belonging to another' (section 5(1)) is 'appropriated' (section 3(1)) 'dishonestly' (section 2(1)), then (under section 6(1)) a person is treated as having the necessary intention to permanently deprive the owner of it.

Where the wording of a statute is ambiguous or vague or becomes outdated, judges interpret or update the meaning of legislation in case law, the second source of law listed. For example, section 2(1) of the Theft Act 1968 does not provide a statutory definition of 'dishonesty'. Therefore, Lord Lane CJ established the *Ghosh* test[51] (that the jury must decide whether what was done was dishonest by the standards of reasonable and honest people) to cover cases in which a defendant claims that he or she was not acting dishonestly under section 2(1).

One criticism raised by academics, the final source of law listed, of *Ghosh* is that it creates a 'Robin Hood' defence (that we are justified in robbing from the rich to give to the poor). This is because the meaning of dishonesty, defined by the jury, will fall within the social context of the time.[52] In summary, statutes and cases (sources one and two) are generally facts that need to be known (or remembered), whereas the third source of law are opinions that help us evaluate the usefulness and effectiveness of the current law.

Murder, the most horrendous crime in English law, is a 'common law' offence because it is not defined by statute (avoid the frequent mistake made by students that a definition is provided under section 1 of the Homicide Act 1957!). Although there is no statutory definition of murder, Elizabethan lawyer **Sir Edward Coke** famously asserted that

> [m]urder is when a man of sound memory, and of the age of discretion, unlaw-fully killeth within any country of the realm any reasonable creature *in reum natura* under the King's peace, with malice aforethought . . . so as the party wounded, or hurt, *etc*, die of the wound or hurt, *etc*, within a year and a day after the same.[53]

Coke's academic definition of what murder is has been accepted by the courts in a string of cases. For example, there must be an unlawful killing, in comparison to one

51 R v *Ghosh* [1982] 3 WLR 110, at p. 1064.
52 See Edward Griew (1985) 'The Objections to Feely and Ghosh'. *Criminal Law Review*, 341–354.
53 Edward Coke (1797) *Institutes of the Lawes of England*. London: E & Brooke, p. 47.

that is lawful, such as withdrawing life support treatment via a court declaration;[54] of a creature *in reum natura*, which means that a foetus is not classed as a human being.[55] There has even been statutory acceptance, in the form of the Law Reform (Year and a Day Rule) Act 1996, that abolishes the Year and a Day Rule.

Due to the many pressures on students studying at university, it is unsurprising that many are strategic learners. A strategic approach to learning is similar to rote learning: learning on a 'need to know' basis what information is essential for an exam. By adopting a strategic approach, however, students develop a limited and uncritical perspective. Law students who are strategic in their learning tend to answer problem rather than essay-style questions. These students focus their efforts of learning the first and second sources of law (listed earlier) rather than grappling with the more conceptual and theoretical issues discussed by the final source. One of the aims of TCAL is to provide practical guidance on how to engage critically with the legal topics by thinking philosophically, theoretically and creatively about law.

Future prospects

If you wish to practice law, you need to keep up to date with potential changes suggested by professional bodies. The BSB recently decided that it will authorise a limited number of future training routes for prospective students to qualify as barristers, and changes are planned at the vocational stage from autumn 2018.[56] The SRA is also developing a new admission framework that means that the regulations that specify how to qualify as a solicitor will change.[57] It may mean that the current way to qualify (LLB or QLD + LPC + recognised training period) changes and/or that it becomes just one way to qualify among others. A law degree would therefore become an optional component to becoming a lawyer rather than a requirement. In addition to these developments, there are expected to be many changes in the law resulting from Brexit, particularly the relationship between English and European law, as well as the threatened repeal of the Human Rights Act (HRA) 1998 and the relationship with the Strasburg Court under the European Convention of Human Rights 1950. These changes aside, law is an important and worthwhile academic pursuit in its own right that is always subject to change and development.

Chapter aims and key points

Each chapter contains a 'chapter aims' and a 'key points' section at the beginning and end to clarify and summarise the points under discussion. Three key points were discussed in this introductory chapter about thinking critically about law. These were:

1   In academia there is no such thing as a dumb question.

---

54 *Airedale Hospital Trustees v Bland* [1993] 2 WLR 316.
55 *Attorney-General's Reference (No 3 of 1994)* [1998] AC 245.
56 Outlined at www.barstandardsboard.org.uk/qualifying-as-a-barrister/future-bar-training/future-ways-to-qualify-as-a-barrister.
57 SRA (2013) 'Training for Tomorrow'. Available at www.sra.org.uk/sra/policy/training-for-tomorrow/resources/policy-statement.page.

2   The hierarchy of legal authorities works as follows:

- First, how wording is written in legislation;
- Second, how legislation is interpreted by judges in their decisions on cases; and
- Finally, how case law and legislation is scrutinised by academic opinions found in books and journal articles.

3   The aim of TCAL is to encourage you to ask yourself the question:

What does the phrase 'critical thinking' mean to you?

Part I

Thinking critically about law in theory

Chapter 2

What *is* 'critical thinking'?

Chapter contents

Chapter aims

This chapter investigates the question: what is 'critical thinking'? The two key aims of the present chapter are to:

1   Gain a theoretical and philosophical appreciation of what 'critical thinking' is; and
2   Provide an opportunity for you to develop, practice and hone your thinking skills.

To demonstrate critical thought in your assessments, it is important to have an idea about what thinking critically actually 'is', a working definition if you will. So what is it that makes our thinking 'critical'? How do we move from 'thinking' and demonstrating 'critical' thoughts about law? These questions are discussed in the first part of the present chapter. Once a clearer idea about what thinking critically about law is emerges, the second part of the chapter provides reasons as to why it is important to think critically in the legal context. The types of questions considered in this part are: why is it such a problem for students to think critically? Why is it important to think critically at university? For a legal career? For citizens of a democratic society? The final part of the chapter thinks critically about critical thinking. Key questions commonly asked by students in relation to critical thinking are discussed to provide a clearer picture of what critical thought is and is not. The main aim of this chapter is to encourage you to contemplate theoretically and philosophically about critical thinking as well as providing an opportunity for you to develop, practice and hone these important skills.

I. What *is* 'thinking'?

What is a 'thought'? As stated in the previous chapter, according to Descartes' Cartesian philosophy: '*dubito ergo cogito; cogito ergo sum*' ('I doubt, therefore I think; I think, therefore I am'); we exist *because* we can think.[1] A thought is '[e]verything that comes to mind, that "goes through our heads"'.[2] At a basic level, we arrange or order our thoughts to protect us from danger (for example, knowing that fire is hot and will burn us) or to get what we need to survive (such as finding food and water). The following task will help you to experience thinking for yourself.

> **TASK THREE**   *Experience thinking itself*[3]
>
> Just with sounds, *notice* your thoughts as events in the mind simply as noise rather than trying to follow the meaning. Some people imagine their thoughts are like clouds in the sky; some are heavy, some are light, some

---

1 However, philosopher A. J. Ayers contends that all we can know is that there are thoughts: see A. J. Ayers (1936) *Language, Truth and Logic*. New York: Dover Publications.
2 John Dewey (1933/1991) *How We Think: A Restatement of the Relation of Reflective Thinking to the Educative Process*. New York: Prometheus Books, p. 1.
3 Ruby Wax (2014) *Sane New World*. London: Hodder, p. 175.

are threatening but they all keep moving and changing. You can choose whether to jump on one of them but it would be like jumping on a cloud, they aren't solid structures so you'll fall through.

Sometimes we bring our attention to our thoughts to quieten them (through the practices of mindfulness or meditation, for example). Other times, we want to use our thoughts to 'figure out some situation, solve some problem, answer some questions, resolve some issue'.[4] To use our thinking to achieve this goal, we need to be in control of our thoughts. Consider the following figure:

Figure 2.1 Controlling your thinking[5]

Your thinking controls every part of your life, but do you control your thinking?

Assessing your thinking skills

The following three tasks provide the opportunity for you to assess you thinking skills before your start taking control of your thinking and develop critical thinking skills.

TASK FOUR   *Beginning to think about your thinking*[6]

Consider your thinking in personal relationships, in dealing with friends, in relating to romantic partners, in sports, as a reader, as a writer, as a listener to lectures, as an employee, in planning your life, in dealing with your emotions and in figuring out complex situations.
Complete these statements:

1   Right now, I believe my thinking across all domains of my life is of _____ quality. I base my judgment on _____.

2   In the following areas, I think very well:

   a   _____

   b   _____

   c   _____

4 Richard Paul and Lisa Elder (2014) *Critical Thinking: Tools for Taking Charge of Your Learning and Your Life*. Essex: Pearson, p. 2.
5 Ibid., p. 67.
6 Ibid., p. 10.

3   In the following areas, my thinking is okay, not great, but not terrible either:

    a   _____

    b   _____

    c   _____

4   In the following areas, my thinking is probably poor:

    a   _____

    b   _____

    c   _____

TASK FIVE *Brain teaser*[7]

A famous architect builds a hexagonal holiday house in such a way that windows on each side point to catch the sun. The first day that the new owners are in the house, they're amazed to see through the windows a large, furry animal slowly walk right round the house!

Two skill-stretching exercises are:

1   What colour is the beast?

_____

_____

_____

2   How do you know?

_____

_____

_____

Is the beast:

a)   Brown, because most large furry animals are brown.

b)   Black, because bears are black.

c)   White, because of the specifications for the windows of the house.

d)   There's no possible way to answer this question, and if this is thinking critically, it is stupid.

•   See 'Task answers' section for outcome.

---

7 Martin Cohen (2015) *Critical Thinking Skills for Dummies*. Chichester: John Wiley & Sons Ltd, p. 69.

TASK SIX　　*Schrödinger's cat*[8]

Professor Schrödinger came up with the following 'what if?' challenge:

Imagine there is a cat locked in a box with a radioactive atom and a Geiger counter. If the atom decays, then a particle is released but no one would know. Now – fiendish touch – suppose that the Geiger counter is set up so that if it registers a particle, poison gas is released and the cat dies!

(If the atom doesn't decay, no particle, no triggering of the Geiger counter and the cat stays alive).

The point of the experiment is to illustrate the strange consequences of the theory in quantum (meaning very, very small) world, sub-atomic particles both exist and do not exist at the same time. Professor Schrodinger's imaginary experiment seems to put the cat in the same position, of existing and not existing – which is ridiculous, and that is his point. He thinks it is ridiculous to suppose that sub-atomic particles can both exist and not exist at the same time and are affected by whether anyone is watching them. His experiment links our furry friend's existence to the particle's state with a mechanism that is practically impossible if rather unlikely. He challenges anyone who says, 'why yes, sub-atomic particles can both exist and not exist – no problem' to also say the same thing about cats.

Does the thought experiment of Schrödinger's cat work – or mislead?

- See the 'Task answers' section for one objection.

Having the ability to control your thinking is important because

[w]hen we think, we bring together a variety of thoughts in some order. When the combined thoughts are mutually supporting and make sense in combination, the thinking is logical. When the combination is not mutually supporting, is contradictory in some sense, or does not make sense, the combination is not logical.[9]

Logic is therefore a central component of controlling your thoughts and developing the ability to think critically. Broadly speaking, logic can be described as a set of

---

8 Ibid., p. 106; see also the TV sitcom 'Big Bang Theory' (2007) season 1 episode 17, in which Sheldon explains Schrödinger's cat.
9 Paul and Elder, *supra* note 4, p. 113.

rational considerations that support a justification for any belief. Types of questions to ask that can help make your thinking more logical include:

- Does my thinking really make sense?
- Does it follow from what was previously said?
- How does my outcome follow from the evidence provided?

These questions are important because, as psychology and education professor Deanna Kuhn warns, '[t]o know and be in control of what [we] think may be the most important way in which people can hope to control their lives'.[10] Thinking critically is key because it is associated with *reasoning* or our capacity to rationalise our thoughts. Reasoning is basically mentally processing arguments, conclusions, judgments and the like, and the word 'rational' means 'using reasons to solve problems'.[11] The good news is that critical thinking skills can be developed, practiced and honed: you can learn how to think critically! To learn how to think critically, Paul and Elder state that there are three distinct levels of thinking: '[l]ower order thinking is often distinguished from higher order thinking'.[12] The traits associated with Paul and Elder's three levels of thinking are listed in what follows

Three levels of thinking

Level 1

Lower-order thinking

- Unreflective
- Low to mixed skill level
- Frequently relies on gut intuition
- Largely self-serving/self-deceived

Level 2

Higher-order thinking

- Selectively reflective
- High skill level
- Lacks critical thinking vocabulary
- Inconsistently fair, maybe skilled in sophistry

---

10 Matthew Wilks Kefer (1996) 'Distinguishing Practical and Theoretical Reasoning: A Critique of Deanna Kuhn's Theory of Informal Argument'. 18(1) *Informal Logic*, 35–55, p. 36, and see Deanna Kuhn (1991) *The Skills of Argument*. New York: Cambridge University Press.
11 Stella Cottrell (2011) *Critical Thinking Skills: Developing Effective Analysis and Argument*. Basingstoke: Palgrave Macmillan, p. 3.
12 Paul and Elder, *supra* note 4, p. 9.

Level 3

Highest-order thinking

- Explicitly reflective
- Highest skill level
- Routine use of critical thinking tools in analysing and accessing thinking
- Consistently fair

Paul and Elder assert that critical thinking tools are key to 'highest-order thinking', which requires 'explicitly reflective' thought that is 'consistently fair'. Highest-order thinking is also described as 'deep thinking'. Demonstrating our 'depth' of knowledge requires us not to take things at face value (or stereotypical thinking). The type of questions that focus on the depth of thought or knowledge include:

- How does your answer address the complexities of the question?
- How are you considering the problems in the question?
- How are you dealing with the most significant factors in the problem?

We think deeply when we get beneath the surface of an issue or problem, identify its complexities and contemplate them intellectually. Considering the 'breadth' of thought, compared with demonstrating its 'depth', is also an important consideration because a line of reasoning may be 'deep' (clear, accurate and precise) but lack breadth. The types of questions that focus on making thinking broader include:

- Do you need to consider another point of view?
- Is there another way to look at this question?
- What would it look like from the point of view of. . .?

When we consider the issue from every relevant viewpoint, we are thinking broadly. Otherwise, when we fail to give due consideration to multiple points of view on an issue, we are narrow-minded because we are not addressing alternative, or opposing, viewpoints.

This section has discussed thinking as all those things going through our minds: thoughts. We can learn how to control our thoughts, either to quieten them (through practicing mindfulness or meditation) or to use them for a particular purpose (to avoid danger or solve a difficult analytical problem). If we do not develop, practice and hone our thinking skills we suffer from illogical thoughts (thinking based upon assumptions and stereotypes). However, if we use logic and reason to control our thought processes we can solve complex problems. Thinking critically relates to highest-order thinking and requires us to be reflective in our thought processes and consistently fair; but what is meant by the phrase '*critical thinking*'?

What is 'critical' thinking?

The word critical derives etymologically from two Greek roots: kriticos (meaning 'discerning judgment') and krierion (meaning 'standards'). Etymologically, then, the word implies the development of 'discerning judgment based on standards'.[13]

This section builds upon the previous to consider the question: what is 'critical' thinking? Dictionary definitions of the word 'critical' show that in medicine it means 'nearly dead', in mathematics it means 'a value being absolutely necessary to a problem' and in nuclear physics it means 'about to explode'.[14] When the word 'critical' used in everyday language it is linked to providing a 'critique' of something. This is where I think students become confused and view critical thinking as a negative exercise; but the Oxford English Dictionary states that a critique is: '[a] detailed analysis and assessment of something, especially a literary, philosophical, or political theory'. This definition of 'critique' requires a detailed analysis of an issue to form a judgment, weighing up the pros and cons of a situation, rather than simply illustrating its faults or negative attributes. Putting the words 'thinking' and 'critically' together into dictionary.com provides the following result:

Dictionary definition of 'critical thinking'

'Thinking' =
1. Rational; reasoning: *People are thinking animals.*
2. Thoughtful; reflective: *Any thinking person would reject that plan.*

'Critical' (or 'critically') =
[several options to choose from – the one most relevant to TCAL is:]
3. involving skilful judgment as to truth, merit, *etc.* judicial: *a critical analysis.*

The 'critical' aspect of thinking appears to refer to making a judgment or critical analysis of information. However, we still need a definition of what a 'skilful judgment' might be and/or what 'critical analysis' is. Perhaps academics who have thought about and studied the topic agree on a definition and what it entails.

Academic definitions of critical thinking: critical thinking is

'Critical thinking is the art of thinking about your thinking while you're thinking in order to make your thinking better'.[15]

'. . . a cognitive activity, associated with using the mind'.[16]

---

13 *Ibid.*, p. 7.
14 Mike Metcalfe (2006) *Reading Critically at University*. London: Sage Publications, p. 3.
15 Paul and Elder, *supra* note 4, p. 1.
16 Cottrell, *supra* note 11, p. 1.

'The aim of critical thinking is to maintain an "objective" position'.[17]

'. . . the ability to consider a range of information derived from many different sources, to process this information in a creative and logical manner, challenging it, analysing it and arriving at considered conclusions which can be defended and justified'.[18]

Richard Paul (founder of the Foundation for Critical Thinking)[19] and Lisa Elder affirm, in the first statement, that critical thinking is thinking about your thinking to make it better. Other academics define critical thinking as a 'cognitive ability', maintaining an 'objective position' or the consideration of a 'range of information'. The various definitions of critical thinking provided by academics show that there is no agreement regarding the meaning of the phrase. Over the years, educationalists have been one branch of academics attracted to undertaking research on critical thinking. How to teach critical thinking skills at primary and secondary schools has been a key focus. John Dewey, professor of education in the United States (US), for example, examined what separates thinking from thinking well (or critical thinking). Dewey recognised that we are all born with the ability to think, and it is the educator's role to teach us how to think well. He provides an example of a man entering a shop full of different chairs and asserts that the man's past experiences will help him choose the chair that suits him best.[20] For this reason, Dewey defined critical thinking as 'reflective thought'. Reflection requires us to suspend our judgments and maintain a healthy level of scepticism as well as keep an open mind. For Dewey, critical thinking requires us to 'do things' (such as ask probing questions) and to 'think about what we are doing' (for example, reflecting on the feedback you receive from tutors). Although Dewey asserted a clear description of critical thinking, he does not provide a breakdown of the key elements involved in critical thinking. Benjamin Bloom's learning pyramid delivered the categorisation of thinking critically that Dewey's definition lacked. Bloom's pyramid identified a hierarchy of study and thinking skills. He made a pyramid that rises upwards through six levels to show the highest form of learning, which for him was evaluating information. The levels of Bloom's pyramid are as follows:

1   Knowledge
2   Comprehension
3   Application
4   Analysis
5   Synthesis
6   Evaluation[21]

Bloom wanted to promote critical thinking in education through the use of analysis and evaluation of material 'away from teachers just drilling people into remembering

17 Open University (2008) *Thinking Critically*. Milton Keynes: Open University, p. 7.
18 Jennifer Moon (2008). *Critical Thinking: An Exploration of Theory and Practice*. London: Routledge, p. 30.
19 The Foundation for Critical Thinking website it available at www.criticalthinking.org.
20 John Dewey (1966) *Democracy and Education: An Introduction to the Philosophy of Education*. London: Collier-Macmillan.
21 Benjamin Bloom (1956) *Taxonomy of Educational Objectives* 1 & 2. London: Longman.

facts and rote learning'.[22] According to Bloom, critical thinkers apply, analyse, synthesise and evaluate information from a variety of sources to present their justified interpretation of an argument or issue. This is known as employing 'highest-order thinking' skills, as discussed by Paul and Elder, used 'to analyse and manipulate information (rather than just memorise it)'.[23] Lorin Anderson (one of Bloom's former students) and David Krathwohl updated Bloom's pyramid to reflect new twenty-first-century insights into how people think.[24] The key changes made were:

✓   Changing the names of the six categories from plain-speaking nouns to gerunds at each level. (*Gerunds* are verbs turned into active nouns by adding the 'ing' ending).
✓   Rearranging the hierarchy. The biggest change is that 'creating' is now at the top of the pyramid – a skill that Bloom did not even mention. The other changes seem to be changing the style more than the substance.[25]

A term difficult to define

As academics and educationalists provide a range of different descriptions of the phrase 'critical thinking' the meaning of the term appears to vary. Thinking critically is consequently a term difficult to define for several reasons. One reason is because critical thinking relates to highest-order thinking, to subjects that commonly do not have a simple 'yes' or 'no' answer. Another reason is that it relates to cognition (or thoughts), and we are unable to know exactly what is going on inside another person's head. Perhaps it is a term difficult to define because it is not an experience we all share. Thinking critically appears to be an important aspect in the formation of formulation of our beliefs, judgments and interpretations, all of which are dependent on the context that they are created in. If critical thinking is context specific, then what do *law* students think that thinking critically *is*? What do law teachers think? To provide an answer to these questions, I captured the following responses when I asked law students and teachers the question: what does 'critical thinking' mean to *you*?

Law students' definitions of critical thinking: critical thinking is

'I personally think that critical thinking is like a domino effect: from critical thinking you get confidence which leads to good presentation skills, to good communication skills, to good leadership skills, etc.'.[26]

'. . . [a]nalysing and picking apart cases'.[27]

22 Cohen, *supra* note 7, p. 165.
23 Open University, *supra* note 17, p. 9.
24 Lorin W. Anderson and David R. Krathwohl (eds) (2001). *A Taxonomy for Learning, Teaching and Assessing: A Revision of Bloom's Taxonomy of Educational Objectives*. New York: Longman.
25 Cohen, *supra* note 7, p. 168.
26 First-year student, Reading.
27 First-year student, Cardiff.

'. . . consider[ing] information holistically, weighing opposing views against a notion presented and questioning whether there is evidence of the information's truthfulness'.[28]

'. . . a way of thinking about things'.[29]

'. . . dissecting and analysing a particular issue or topic'.[30]

'. . . looking at something rather than just accepting it at face-value or taking in what you read, it's actually "do you agree with it? What could be improved?" that sort of thing'.[31]

Law teachers' definitions of critical thinking: critical thinking is

'. . . it's a process, a way of thinking a little bit more deeply about issues'.[32]

'. . . demonstrated implicitly by the way in which the student deals with the material. It is clear when a student has done more than digest the material but has also played with it'.[33]

'. . . [t]o approach the analysis of legal rules and phenomena in a way that takes account of influences from social structures, processes and dynamics'.[34]

'. . . [t]aking an informed position on a particular area of study or discussion . . . Perhaps I should add the gloss . . . that thinking critically is about making an argument'.[35]

'. . . means a lot of things, obviously, I think that it means that you don't take anything necessarily at face-value, that you're aware of where it's coming from, the source, the time, the context, the audience and that, eventually, you learn that you have a view of your own'.[36]

As shown from the statements quoted, the term 'critical thinking' resonates differently for people at various levels of academia. For example, responses ranged from

---

28 First-year student, Leeds.
29 Second-year student, Reading.
30 Second-year student, Cardiff.
31 Final-year student, Reading.
32 Teaching fellow, Reading.
33 Lecturer, Cardiff.
34 Lecturer, Leeds.
35 Lecturer, Reading.
36 Law professor, Reading.

not taking information at face value to what is described as a 'process' involving the thinker in developing an 'informed position' or 'argument'. Such a wide range of answers illustrates the difficulty in defining the concept of critical thinking. For example, is critical thinking a 'type' of thinking or 'cognition'? Is it a 'skill'? Or is it a 'process of thought'? As thinking critically is consequently context specific and varies from person to person, what are its key elements?

Key elements of thinking critically

Putting the 'new' Bloom learning pyramid into the legal context, TCAL's learning pyramid is set out in Figure 2.2, followed by a full description of each of the six key elements for thinking critically about law.

• **Level One – Knowledge:** Knowledge comes from remembering previously learned material. An example is recalling data or information, such as knowing that wounding or inflicting grievous bodily harm (GBH) are provided in sections 18 and 20 of the Offences Against the Person Act (OAPA) 1861.

• **Level Two – Understanding:** The next level up from knowledge is 'understanding' (the ability to grasp the meaning of material). An example of understanding a text is being able to restate something in your own words, like paraphrasing the wording of a statute: for example, that section 18 OAPA 1861 provides for the offence of inflicting GBH with intent which results in life imprisonment.

• **Level Three – Application:** A stage up in the hierarchy is application because it requires the ability to apply or to use learned material in new situations. An example would be applying section 20 OAPA 1861 to a problem scenario.

• **Level Four – Critical Analysis:** Analysis (meaning 'taking things apart') requires splitting up an argument into its component parts to better understand its structure – perhaps to spot illogical aspects of someone's reasoning. An example of critical analysis is providing an assessment as to whether the requirement to 'maliciously' wound or inflict GBH, dating from the 1861 Act, is relevant today (see R v Barnes).[37]

• **Level Five – Reflection:** Follows analysis because it refers to the ability to assess and evaluate the value (or perhaps the 'usefulness') of the knowledge comprehended, applied, analysed and synthesised at the earlier levels: or considering whether an answer or argument works. For an example of this, see Mark James's evaluation of the Barnes appeal.[38]

• **Level Six – Creative Thinking:** Creativity is key to putting information and ideas in a new or original way. Synthesis is needed to create a new meaning or interpretation. Putting forward an original suggestion for reform of section 20 of the 1861 Act would be an example of creative thinking.

Whether adopting Bloom's original or new or TCAL's learning pyramid, the resulting key elements of knowledge, comprehension, application, critical analysis, reflection

---

37 [2005] EWCA Crim 3246.
38 Mark James (2013) 'Player Violence and Compensation for Injury: R v Barnes [2005] 1 Cr App Rep 507' in J Anderson (ed.) Leading Cases in Sports Law. The Hague: TMC Asser Press.

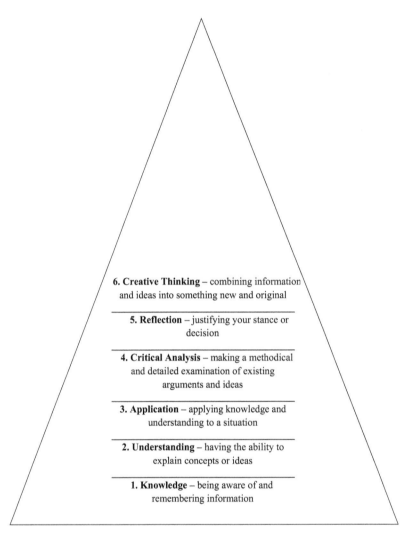

Figure 2.2 TCAL's learning pyramid

and creative thinking denote that thinking critically is a 'toolbox': not one tool but lots.[39] Another useful perspective provided by Stella Cottrell is that critical thinking is a 'process of thought':[40] it is an 'intellectually disciplined process'.[41] It is therefore an important skill to learn at university, where the exploration of intellectual endeavours

39 Cohen, *supra* note 7, p. 14.
40 Cottrell, *supra* note 11.
41 Michael Scriven and Richard Paul (2008) 'Defining Critical Thinking'. *Foundation for Critical Thinking.* Available at www.criticalthinking.org/aboutCT/definingCT.cfm.

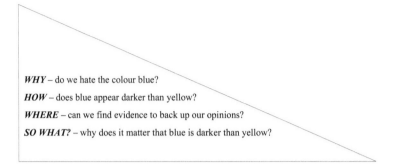

WHY – do we hate the colour blue?

HOW – does blue appear darker than yellow?

WHERE – can we find evidence to back up our opinions?

SO WHAT? – why does it matter that blue is darker than yellow?

Figure 2.3 Critical thinking as a process of thought

is encouraged. To achieve a critical thought process, certain questions have to be posed, such as:

- *Why* – 'why' is something the way that it is? What are the reasons for it to be the case?
- *How* – 'how' did something come to be the way that it is, perhaps in comparison to something else?
- *Where* – 'where' can we find evidence to back up our opinions?
- *So what?* – 'so what' does it matter that we have found out what we have found?

Thinking critically about law is a two-stage process

It needs to be made clear that critical thinking is a key part of HE but something that can only be done once the learner has got to grips with the material.[42]

When asking the questions: *why, how, where* and *so what?* required in the critical thinking process, first, we need to understand the content of something and then we can think critically about it: in other words, have knowledge and understanding of the relevant information and apply it in a particular context (levels one, two and three of the learning pyramid). Then the second part of the process of critical thought is to critically analyse, evaluate and think creatively about the problem or issue posed (levels four to six of the pyramid).

The two-stage process

1   First, you need to understand some legal content (for example, a relevant statute or case);
     and then

42 Lecturer, Cardiff.

2   Second, you can demonstrate the ability to think critically by putting 'law'
     into context (be it political, social or economic), intellectualising it (philoso-
     phising or theorising about it) or critiquing it and suggesting how best it
     can be reformed (reflecting upon and thinking creatively about it).

To summarise, 'critical' thinking is 'highest-order thinking'. It is a difficult term to
define for a variety of reasons and is accordingly context specific. Thinking critically about law is a two-stage process that, first, requires us to have knowledge and
understanding of 'law'; then, second, we can apply it to critically analyse, reflect
upon and think creatively about a particular issue or problem posed. TCAL's aim
is to encourage you to develop your own definition and understanding of what
'critical thinking' is. Prior to you achieving this, it may be useful to assert a succinct, working (subject to change) definition of what thinking critically about law
is as follows:

TCAL's working definition of critical thinking

Thinking critically about law is an intellectually disciplined process of thought
whereby you develop your own informed legal opinions or argument(s) on a
particular issue.

II. *Why* is it important to think 'critically' about law?

As we now have a clearer understanding of what 'critical' thinking is, this part of the
chapter considers three environments in which thinking critically is important. These
are first, during your university studies, second, throughout your legal career and
finally, the importance of thinking critically for citizens living in a democratic society.

Importance for university studies

First, why is the ability to think critically an important skill to develop at university?
As stated in the introduction, today thinking critically is commonly asserted as a key
goal of university studies. Thinking critically is accordingly a key aspect of achieving a
first-class degree. Academic study, therefore, 'requires increasingly sophisticated levels
or critical analysis at every level of study'.[43] There is the increasing 'assumption that
"thinking" is the core competency of [a] graduate'.[44] The success of critical thinking
tests from the business sector is spilling over into education. There are reports that
in the future students will have to pass a test in critical thinking in order to graduate
from their degrees, and potentially such tests could be used as part of the application
process to secure a place on a course (see what follows for a further discussion about
critical thinking tests).

43   Cottrell, *supra* note 11, p. viii.
44   Metcalfe, *supra* note 14, p. 2.

TASK SEVEN *Checking your university marking criteria*

Have a look at your university's strategy to see how thinking critically is defined. If your university does not have such a strategy, does your school or department have a policy or guidance on thinking critically?
Ways to find out:

● Ask fellow students
● Ask your personal tutor or subject tutors

Importance for a legal career

The second reason it is important to develop the ability to think critically is that it is an important ability for a lawyer. Most of us require help from a legal professional at some point in our lives. Clients expect lawyers to be knowledgeable about the area of law they are experiencing an issue with. Lawyers are required to have an ability to take on a large amount of information and summarise what is relevant on an issue and to understand and appreciate the other side's perspective and potentially resolve a problem.[45] Recently there has been a growing use of critical thinking test as part of the entry-level application process of law firms. These psychometric (or psychological measurement) tests assess cognitive abilities of professionals. They measure critical thinking skills that are necessary for presenting a clear, structured, well-reasoned point of view and being able to convince others of your arguments. The most common critical thinking test was developed by Goodwin Watson and Edward Glaser and is called the Watson Glaser Critical Thinking Appraisal.[46] Another reason developing critical thinking skills is essential for future career prospects is because the majority of jobs students will work in have yet to be invented. Possible new legal positions may be created related to new legal arrangements for the country following Brexit, developments in medical law, space law, robot law and so on.

Importance to a democratic society

Finally, thinking critically is an important skill for citizens in a democratic society. This is because a democracy requires citizens of a society to have independent thought to exercise the freedom to elect rulers. To become responsible citizens, we need to have a command of a wide range of knowledge to understand the complexity of an ever-changing world.

---

45 See John O'Mudd (1983) 'Thinking Critically About "Thinking Like a Lawyer". 33 *Journal of Legal Education*, 704–711.
46 Additional information available at www.assessmentday.co.uk/watson-glaser-critical-thinking. htm. Free test available at www.jobtestprep.co.uk/watson-glaser-sample-questions.

Democracy can be an effective form of government only to the extent that the
public (that rules it in theory) is well-informed about national and international
events and think independently and critically about those events.[47]

One key reason for the importance of citizens to be able to think critically is to
overthrow the power of propaganda. 'Propaganda' originally meant 'planting ideas'.
Today, nearly all governments avoid propaganda due to the dealings of the National
Socialist German Workers Party (commonly referred to in English as the 'Nazi party').
This period of German history (1933–1945) is known as the Third Reich, when it
was governed by the dictatorship (governmental rule by one person) of Adolf Hitler.
In his autobiography, *Mein Kampf*,[48] Hitler (a rejected artist and disgruntled soldier)
based his political views on the popular opinions of the everyday man on the street.
In a few years under Hitler's marketing, the Nazis seized control of Germany. Some of
Hitler's all-too-influential ideas were that slogans are a much better way to influence
the mass opinion than arguments, and debate is always best avoided. Nazi prejudice
soon turned into the Holocaust (the mass killing of more than six million Jewish
people) and the forced imprisonment of an array of people in concentration camps
across Europe (such as Auschwitz).

Example of Nazi policy in everyday practice[49]

Liselotte Katscher was a nurse at the time of Nazi rule, and she writes about doctors –
I expect not very different and no better or worse than anyone else – who, pro-
pelled by the force of Hitler's argument, participated in the forced sterilisation of
a sixteen-year-old girl called Henny:

> Henny was examined by a doctor who diagnosed a slight feeble-mindedness –
> in my opinion it was only a slight feeble-mindedness, and they decided that she
> should be sterilized. I thought about it a great deal at the time, and felt sorry for
> the girl, **but it was the law**, and the doctors had decided. I personally took her to
> the maternity ward in the hospital where it took place. But I never got rid of the
> doubt in my mind that the decision was too harsh . . . The tragedy was that she
> was released very soon after this, then got a job and met a nice young man and
> was now not allowed to marry him because of her sterilisation.

Note the point in bold – how many people have the courage to oppose 'the law' and
expert opinion? Indeed, most of the time, they'd be wrong to do so!

---

47 Paul and Elder, *supra* note 4, p. 276.
48 Although cited here (and generally being an incredibly curious person), personally, I have chosen
    not to read the racist and fascist writings of Hitler; rather, I choose to contemplate the impact of
    the laws, rules and policies of the Nazi regime on the accounts of everyday people, such as Anne
    Frank (1947/2014), *The Diary of a Young Girl*. London: Prakash Book Depot.
49 Cohen, *supra* note 7, p. 58.

Another key reason citizens' ability to think critically is important is for the potential to overthrow 'groupthink'. Groupthink is a term coined by social psychologist Irving Janis.[50] Janis's notion of groupthink describes the tendency of people in groups to reach a consensus without properly considering their collective ideas, stifling creative and independent thought. Groupthink in action can be found in the Milgram experiment.[51] Following the Nuremberg Trials of Nazi party war criminals (such as lieutenant colonel Adolf Eichmann), psychologist Stanley Milgram created an experiment to investigate the question: could it be that Eichmann and his million accomplices in the Holocaust were just following orders? During the experiment Milgram's participants (ordinary people) were asked to inflict pain on another person because they were ordered to by a scientist. During the experiment, although most participants voiced their concern and desire to stop, many continued after being reassured that they would not be held responsible for any injury suffered by the other participant. Milgram explains,

> [o]rdinary people . . . without any particular hostility on their part, can become agents in a terrible destructive process. Moreover, even when . . . they are asked to carry out actions incompatible with fundamental standards of morality, relatively few people have the resources needed to resist authority.[52]

Thinking critically is an important resource to question the motivations of the collective (or groupthink). It is not that *every* point put forward by a person in authority should be doubted but rather that questions should be raised and their answers given serious consideration. A further benefit of citizens of a democratic society having the ability to think critically is to promote pluralism. People's thoughts, opinions and beliefs often differ greatly in our religious and ethical principles, political affiliations and so on. Arguably, these differences should not matter: it would be a dull world if we all agreed about everything. In itself, variety is a good thing; without it there could be no progress.

In short, this part of the chapter on thinking critically is an important skill developed at university that entails a life-long, professional commitment, providing learners with the ability to self-reflect and enhance their own self-development (discussed further in Chapter 6). Thinking critically is important for obtaining a first-class degree, for a professional legal career and the continuing self-development of a citizen in a democratic society.

III. Thinking critically about critical thinking

Following the discussion of what critical thinking is in the first part of the chapter and considering reasons why it is important to develop the skill in the second part, it is necessary to consider several critiques of thinking critically. Key questions about

---

50 Irving L. Janis (1971) 'Groupthink'. 5(6) *Psychology Today*, 43–76.
51 Stanley Milgram (1963) 'Behavioural Study of Obedience'. 67(4) *Journal of Abnormal and Social Psychology*, 371–378.
52 Stanley Milgram (1974) 'The Perils of Obedience'. *Harpers Magazine*.

critical thinking that were commonly raised by staff and students during the studies are listed in what follows.

Key questions and answers on critical thinking

- **What is 'critical' about critical thinking?**

  The 'critical' part of thinking signifies an 'evaluative component'.[53] 'Evaluation' requires 'an assessment of the validity of an argument'.[54] Following TCAL's two-stage process of critical thinking, which contains six levels (discussed in the previous part of the chapter) the critical aspect of thinking is found in the second stage that contains the final three levels (critical analysis, reflection and creative thinking).

- **Is critical thinking about providing a 'critique'?**

  For some, thinking critically has a negative connotation: it requires a critique to be provided. For example, during my discussions with a law professor at the University of Reading, they said they did not like the term 'critical thinking' because it implies a negative position or standpoint on a topic. However, thinking critically about law should be distinguished from providing a 'critique', which generally refers to disapproval. Rather, critical thought requires analysing positive and negative attributes (or weighing up the pros and cons) of something, and reasons as to why this is the case should also be provided.[55]

- **Is thinking critically about being 'sceptical'?**

  Some argue that thinking critically 'is about pressing points, sniffing a bit more sceptically at issues'.[56] As stated in the introductory chapter, 'scepticism' means doubting the truth of something. As critical thinking seems to require utilising an inquisitive mind through a process of questioning, it follows for some that thinking critically means being sceptical about everything. Cottrell states, however, '[c]ritical thinking gives you the tools to use scepticism and doubt constructively so that you can analyse what is before you'.[57] In other words, thinking critically is a constructive way to consider things at a deeper level by posing questions such as: Why? How? Where? And so what?[58]

- **Is critical thinking about thinking like a 'sophist'?**

  Also stated in the introductory chapter, 'sophistry' is the use of clever but false arguments with the intent of deception. Like a game, the objective of sophistic thinking is to win. Sophistic thinkers should be distinguished

---

53 Diane F. Halpern (2009) *Thought and Knowledge: An Introduction to Critical Thinking*. Mahwah, NJ: Lawrence Erlbaum Associates, p. 7.
54 Open University, *supra* note 17, p. 29.
55 Joel Rudinow and Vincent E. Barry (2008) *Invitation to Critical Thinking*. Belmont, CA: Thompson Wadsworth, p. 12.
56 Cohen, *supra* note 7, p. 9.
57 Cottrell, *supra* note 11, p. 2.
58 See Figure 2.1: 'Critical Thinking Process of Thought'.

from critical thinkers because the sophist uses low-level skills of rhetoric, or argumentation, by which they make unreasonable thinking look reasonable and reasonable thinking look unreasonable. This form of thinking is evident in the arguments of unethical lawyers and politicians who are more concerned with winning than with being fair and use emotionalism and trickery in an intellectually skilled way.[59]

- **Is thinking critically about 'independent' thought?**

Whether thinking critically is a process of developing independent thought is an interesting question to consider. On the one hand, as discussed in the previous part of the chapter, one of the key benefits of critical thinking is to overcome the pitfalls of 'groupthink'.[60] 'Groupthink' is a term that describes people's tendency to reach a collective agreement at the cost of individual thought. German nurse Liselotte Katscher's account of the sixteen-year-old girl Henny who was sterilised in the 'Example of a Nazi Party Policy in Everyday Life' illustrates the need for individual thought to challenge collective groupthink. On the other hand, critical thinking is not just about thinking for yourself 'but [it] also involves convincing and influencing others, hopefully as part of a process of improving the world'.[61] Critical thinking is also 'team thinking'.[62]

- **What is 'non-critical' thinking?**

TCAL's working definition of thinking critically, provided in the previous part of the chapter, is that it is 'an intellectually disciplined process of thought whereby you develop your own informed legal opinion or argument(s) on a particular issue'. In comparison, Karl Popper states that 'non-critical' thinking is problematic because

[i]f we are uncritical we shall always find what we want: we shall look from and find confirmations, and we shall look away from, and not see, whatever might be dangerous to our pet theories.[63]

Accordingly, non-critical thinking is daydreams, non-directed, automatic thinking, rote recall of information or the failure to consider evidence that might support a conclusion that you do not like.

- **What is the difference between 'critical thinking', 'critical analysis' and 'critical reflection'?**

Throughout my discussions, both students and staff struggled to make a clear distinction between the concepts of 'thinking critically', 'critical analysis' and 'critical reflection'. As a result, it appears that the terms critical 'thinking', 'analysis' and 'reflection' are used interchangeably, although they have

---

59 Paul and Elder, *supra* note 4, p. 16.
60 Janis, *supra* note 50.
61 Metcalfe, *supra* note 14, p. 1.
62 Cohen, *supra* note 7, p. 11.
63 Karl Popper (1957/2002) *The Poverty of Historicism*. London: Routledge Classics, p. 124.

different meanings. For example, one law lecturer reported that '[r]eally what we're saying is, the writing of an essay or giving a presentation or writing an exam answer requires the construction of an informed argument. So, the word 'critical' is only helpful insofar as distinguishes argument from description'. The key message here is the importance of the formulation of your argument. The different and nuanced meanings of critical 'thinking', 'analysis' and 'reflection' can be defined as follows:

- Critical *thinking* – an intellectually disciplined process of thought whereby you develop your own informed legal opinions or arguments on a particular issue.
- Critical *analysis* – emphasises that you should examine, scrutinise and question the validity of information and evaluate the strengths and weaknesses, pros and cons of an argument.
- Critical *reflection* – considering whether an answer or argument works as well as recognising one's own limitations and area's for improvement and further development (otherwise known as self-reflection).

- **Is the key to critical thinking self-reflection?**

  Paul and Elder state that the result of self-reflection on your own thinking is '[a] well-cultivated thinker'.[64] Someone who:

  - Raises vital questions and problems, formulating them clearly and precisely;
  - Comes to well-reasoned conclusions and solutions, testing them against relevant criteria and standards; and
  - Thinks open-mindedly within alternative systems of thought, recognizing and assessing, as need be, their assumptions, implications and practical consequences.

- **What is the difference between 'weak' and 'strong' critical thinking?**

  According to Paul and Elder, critical thinking can serve two incompatible ends: self-centredness or fair-mindedness. We can use our critical thinking in either a selfish or a fair-minded way. This is the difference between 'weak' and 'strong' critical thinking.

  - *Weak critical thinking*: misses certain important, higher and highest-order thinking skills (see the 'Three Levels of Thinking'). According to Paul and Elder '[m]ost significantly, it fails to consider, in good faith, viewpoints that contradict its own viewpoint. It lacks fair-mindedness'.[65]
  - *Strong critical thinking*: the striking characteristic of thinking critically in the strong sense is the consistent pursuit of the fair and just arguments. Paul and Elder assert that

64 Paul and Elder, *supra* note 4, p. 7.
65 Ibid., p. 16.

[t]hese thinkers strive always to be ethical – to behave in ways that do not exploit or otherwise harm others. They work to empathize with the viewpoints of others. They are willing to listen to arguments they do not necessarily hold. They change their views when faced with better reasoning.[66]

See Chapter 6 for a further discussion on thinking ethically about law.

Key points

Thinking critically about law is a two-stage process that involves six steps:

Stage 1:

1   Knowing the information: such as the relevant statutes, cases and academic opinions on a legal topic;
2   Understanding information: for example, what does the wording of a statute mean? How has it been interpreted by the courts?
3   Application: applying the relevant statute, case or academic opinion to the question posed;

Stage 2:

4   Critical analysis: split up an argument into its component parts and weigh up the pros and cons;
5   Reflection: reflect upon whether an argument works; and
6   Creative thinking: produce a new and original argument or solution.

TCAL's working definition of critical thinking

Thinking critically about law is an intellectually disciplined process of thought whereby you develop your own informed legal opinions or argument(s) on a particular issue.

Suggested reading

○   Paul, Richard and Lisa Elder (2014) *Critical Thinking: Tools for Taking Charge of Your Professional and Personal Life.* London: Pearson.
○   Cottrell, Stella (2011) *Critical Thinking Skills: Developing Effective Analysis and Argument.* Basingstoke, Palgrave Macmillan.
●   Davis, Margaret (2008) *Asking the Law Question.* Sydney: Thompson Law Book Co. Chapter 1: Asking the Law Question (What is it?).

66 Ibid., pp. 16–17.

Useful resources

Website
Foundation for Critical Thinking (www.criticalthinking.org)

Online tutorial
Learn Higher, 'Critical Thinking and Reflection Tutorial'. 26th January 2012. Available at: www.learnhigher.ac.uk/learning-at-university/critical-thinking-and-reflection/critical-thinking-and-reflection-tutorial/.

Video
Meegan, Gary (2012). 'What Is Critical Thinking? A Definition'. YouTube. Available to watch at: www.youtube.com/watch?v=ZLyUHbexz04.

Chapter 3

What *is* 'law'?

Thinking critically about legal perspectives

Chapter aims

This chapter will help you develop thinking critically about law in relation to:

- Having an appreciation of the philosophies of law and jurisprudence;
- Thinking critically about different legal perspectives; and
- Gaining an understanding for theoretical and methodology sections for analytical essays and dissertations.

The previous chapter considered the question: what is 'critical thinking'? A wide range of sources (from academic opinions to discussions with law students and teachers) were considered to provide an answer to that question. Succinctly, it was concluded that over the duration of your course, you should be developing your own definition and understanding of what thinking critically about law is. In the meantime, the previous chapter concluded that thinking critically about law involves a two-stage process (which requires understanding and application of knowledge for the first stage, which can be critically analysed, reflected upon and thought creatively about, in the second). As thinking critically about law is an 'intellectually disciplined process of thought', part of the process of thinking critically is to consider, appraise or evaluate other people's ideas. The present chapter moves on to consider how scholars have answered the essential question: what is 'law'? This involves another important sub-question: what is 'jurisprudence'?

What is 'law'?

Much like the discussions surrounding critical thinking considered in the previous chapter, the question: what is 'law'? has been contemplated by scholars and philosophers for centuries. It is described as a 'big' (fundamental or essential) question because it is about defining the nature of law or a legal system. The 'laws' of physics and mathematics and so forth differ distinctly from those governing the 'law of nature' (or natural law) or 'social ordering' (the societal system of institutions that regulate human behaviour). In relation to 'asking the law question', Margaret Davies provides the following definition:

> [l]aw regulates human behaviour, and the relationships between members of society. Beyond this, of course, it may attempt to enshrine certain ideals, such as equality, freedom, and justice.[1]

In terms of enshrining the ideals of equality, freedom and justice over the centuries, scholars have provided a range of legal perspectives. For example, for Greek and Roman philosophers Plato and Saint Thomas Aquinas, law consists of a set of universal moral principles in accordance with nature. On the other hand, for nineteenth-century thinkers such as Jeremy Bentham and John Austin law is basically a collection

---

1 Margaret Davies (2008) *Asking the Law Question*. Sydney: Thompson Law Book Co, p. 6.

of 'positive' (deriving from the verb 'to posit') man-made 'commands' or 'norms' (as Hans Kelsen states, the term 'norm' refers to principles related to the word 'normal').

Critically, the Communist Karl Marx held that behind the laws of the 'proletariat' (or working classes) lie 'bourgeois' (middle-class) interests and prejudices. Feminist scholars such as Catharine MacKinnon believe that law is fundamental in the subordination (or oppression) of women, whereas critical race theorists, such as Patricia Williams, claim that laws' objectivity masks the reality of white supremacy and racial power. In the alternative, Jürgen Habermas emphasises the need for 'communicative action' (the cooperation based upon mutual deliberation), and legal pluralists, such as John Griffiths, study law as a multi-sited social phenomenon. Although all these scholars provide distinct responses to the 'law question', what they have in common is that they generate their own unique legal perspective.

What is 'jurisprudence'?

As a lawyer, you should study jurisprudence as a simple matter of intellectual self-respect.[2]

Jurisprudence is basically 'the theoretical or philosophical study of law'.[3] The phrase is used interchangeably with other terms such as 'legal philosophy' and 'legal theory'.[4] However, 'jurisprudence' focuses on theoretical analyses of law, whereas 'legal philosophy' is concerned with providing a philosophical argument, and 'legal theory' is often used to denote theoretical enquiries about law (for example, Marxist approaches to legal domination). As Mike Metcalfe explains,

[h]uman activity can be studied from a range of different views, viewpoints, worldviews, perspectives . . . paradigms, angles, approaches and stances.[5]

In this chapter I call these different philosophical approaches, schools or stances 'legal perspectives' because each scholar generates a unique perspective on law. Appreciation of different legal perspectives is an essential component to your studies, as it will empower you, theoretically, to think critically about law. It is not always necessary to think philosophically about law. You could go through your entire journey at university and never explicitly tackle these big questions. For example, answers to some problem questions and tasks in conveyancing (preparing documents for the sale of a property) do not require you to have a philosophical understanding of law: you simply need to answer the problem question or produce an outcome for your client referring to the current law or legal precedent (the law as it is). For you to have thought about the Marxist or Habermasian perspectives of law, however, and have your own idea is an important part of your own self-reflection process. It can make

2 James E. Penner and Emmanuel Melissaris (2012) *McCoubrey and White's Textbook on Jurisprudence*. Oxford: Oxford University Press, preface.

3 Ibid., p. 1.

4 Raymond Wacks (2009) *Understanding Jurisprudence: An Introduction to Legal Theory*. Oxford: Oxford University Press, p. xiii.

5 Mike Metcalfe (2006) *Reading Critically at University*. London: Sage Publications, pp. 2–3.

you a 'better' lawyer: for you to have your own answer to the 'law question' is part of thinking critically about law. A law degree provides you with time and space to consider these big questions. Indeed, you are encouraged to (and rewarded for) do so. You may be grappling with some of these questions during your degree implicitly, or you might be someone who really enjoys thinking this way about law. Sometimes you are explicitly required to think jurisprudentially. For example, while studying modules like jurisprudence and criminal law (when theorising about the principles of criminalisation)[6] or demonstrating that you have thought about a question theoretically or philosophically in a dissertation (more about legal methodologies in Chapter 5). Knowing where and when (in what forum and setting) it is appropriate to discuss your answer to the 'law question' is another aspect of thinking critically. So, although you are not always required to think jurisprudentially, philosophically or theoretically, if you do not shy away from considering the big questions you will become a better lawyer, have intellectual self-respect and think critically about law.

The aim of the present chapter is to provide a succinct introduction to jurisprudence. It is structured in two parts. The first part provides an overview of the importance of legal perspectives to the study of law, and the second offers an introduction, as well as examples of established legal perspectives adopted by some scholars who have tackled the 'law question' (such as Plato, Aquinas, Bentham and Austin, *etc.*). Some scholars have been critical of these perspectives (Marx, MacKinnon and Williams, for example), while others have provided alternative approaches (Habermas and Griffiths). The seven key legal perspectives discussed in this chapter are namely:

1   Natural law theory
2   Legal positivism
3   Marxism
4   Critical legal studies (CLS)
5   Feminism(s)
6   Critical race theories (CRTs)
7   Legal pluralism(s)

It should be noted that this is not an exhaustive list of possible legal perspectives. Other perspectives could have been included (such as an economic perspective of law), and others are discussed to a limited extent (for example, postmodernism and queer theory). Seven have been selected because, as George Miller states, it is a 'magic number'.[7] These perspectives are simply a 'collection of examples, a few starting point suggestions'.[8] Therefore, my intention is merely to provide you with a starting point from which you can develop your own legal perspective from which to think critically about law.

---

6 See Jeremy Horder (2016) *Ashworth's Principles of Criminal Law*. Oxford: Oxford University Press.
7 George A. Miller (1956) 'The Magic Number 7, Plus or Minus Two: Some Limits on Our Capacity for Processing Information'. 63 *The Psychological Review* 81–97.
8 Metcalfe, *supra* note 5, p. 4.

I. Legal perspectives and the study of law

The seven selected legal perspectives discussed in the present chapter are all theories of law. In basic terms, a theory is

> a set of ideas that helps explain why something happens . . . Theories are based on evidence and reasoning, but have not been proved conclusively.[9]

The legal perspectives discussed here are theoretical in nature because they cannot be conclusively (or scientifically) proven. For example, how could proletariat, female or African-American experiences of oppression be assessed and measured to prove that the legal perspectives of Marxism, feminism(s) and CRTs are 'true' as a verified fact of reality? These perspectives are simply not verifiable in that same way as quantifiable mathematical laws. However, qualitative research (or 'empirical studies' – explanation provided in the next chapter) have been conducted and found colloquial evidence to conclude that people feel and experience oppression in a variety of ways and social contexts. Consequently, the legal perspectives of Marxism, feminism(s) and CRTs have 'a crucial role to play in defining, shaping and safeguarding the values that underpin our society'.[10]

While studying for a law degree, you are encouraged to take a critical approach to academic ideas and theories. Your lecturers expect you to question and challenge published material. Many students find it difficult to provide a critique of academic ideas and theories as well as challenge the ideas of others. Perhaps this is because they feel they will have their own assumptions challenged in return, and it can be hard to have our deeply held religious, political and ideological beliefs challenged. Thinking critically about our assumptions provides more consideration to be given to the evidence that supports the arguments on which those ideas or theories are based. The social, moral and cultural foundations of the law and the theories that both inform and account for them are no less important than the law's 'black letter'. Legal perspectives therefore have a decisive role to play in defining and defending the values and ideals that shape our way of life.

Suggested reading

○ Wacks, Raymond (2006) *Philosophy of Law: A Very Short Introduction*. Oxford: Oxford University Press.
● Penner, James E. and Emmanuel Melissaris (2012) *McCoubrey and White's Textbook on Jurisprudence*. Oxford: Oxford University Press.

---

9 Stella Cottrell (2011) *Critical Thinking Skills: Developing Effective Analysis and Argument*. Basingstoke: Palgrave Macmillan, p. 149.
10 Wacks, *supra* note 4, p. 11.

II. Seven key legal perspectives

> In what ways could your understanding of critical thinking be improved?
>
> By encouraging the need to critically analyse a topic to understand the different views on it.[11]

The seven key legal perspectives discussed in this chapter can be divided into two categories. In the first category are theories on 'the nature of law', such as natural law theory and legal positivism, because these perspectives seek to provide a definition and explanation of the legal system. These are 'doctrinal' perspectives of law because they set forth a theory to elucidate a particular legal doctrine. The second category comprises critical legal perspectives, such as Marxism, CLS, feminism(s), CRTs and legal pluralism(s). These are called 'critical legal perspectives' because they contain some critique or criticism of doctrinal law.

Function machine

The image of a mathematical 'function machine' is a useful way to visually and comparatively explain the nuances of each of the seven legal perspectives. A function machine takes in a number as an input and gives another number as an output. For example see the mathematical function machine in Figure 3.1 in what follows.

However, instead of numbers, I will input a legal provision. The legal provision selected is Article 9 of the European Convention on Human Rights and Fundamental Freedoms 1950 (ECHR), which provides a right to freedom of thought, conscience and religion. Article 9 reads:

Article 9 ECHR

1   Everyone has the right to freedom of thought, conscience and religion; this right includes freedom to change his religion or belief and freedom, either alone or in community with others and in public or private, to manifest his religion or belief, in worship, teaching, practice and observance.

2   Freedom to manifest one's religion or beliefs shall be subject only to such limitations as are prescribed by law and are necessary in a democratic society in the interests of public safety, for the protection of public order, health or morals, or for the protection of the rights and freedoms of others.

To Article 9, I will add each of the seven legal perspectives in order to demonstrate the likely output (or, in other words, likely critical analysis of the law). For example see the legal perspectives function machines in Figure 3.2 in what follows.

In order to illustrate how to use these different legal perspectives and demonstrate the key similarities and differences between them, an English case has been

---

11 Second-year student, Cardiff.

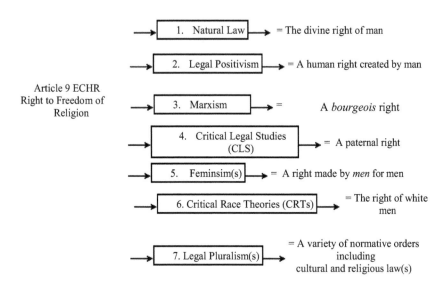

INPUT ⟶ FUNCTION MACHINE ⟶ OUTPUT

In other words, if you input a score of 1 and increase it by 2, it equals an output of 3:

$$1 \longrightarrow \boxed{+2} \longrightarrow = 3$$

Figure 3.1 Mathematical function machine

Article 9 ECHR
Right to Freedom of
Religion

⟶ 1. Natural Law ⟶ = The divine right of man

⟶ 2. Legal Positivism ⟶ = A human right created by man

⟶ 3. Marxism ⟶ = A *bourgeois* right

⟶ 4. Critical Legal Studies (CLS) ⟶ = A paternal right

⟶ 5. Feminsim(s) ⟶ = A right made by *men* for men

⟶ 6. Critical Race Theories (CRTs) ⟶ = The right of white men

⟶ 7. Legal Pluralism(s) ⟶ = A variety of normative orders including cultural and religious law(s)

Figure 3.2 Legal perspectives function machines

selected for critical analysis. The selected case is: R (*on the application of Begum*) v *Headteacher and Governors of Denbigh High School* (hereinafter *Begum*).[12]

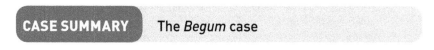

CASE SUMMARY — The *Begum* case

Brief facts of the case

The case was concerned with whether a student's (Shabina Begum's)[13] alleged exclusion from a state school (Denbigh High School, Luton) for wearing a *jilbab* (a long coat-like garment which covers the whole body except the hands and face)

---

12 [2007] 1 AC 100; [2006] UKHL 15; [2006] 2 WLR. 719; [2006] HRLR 21.
13 Hereinafter called 'Shabina' to illustrate the unequal power relationship between the appellant/respondent and various Lords and Lady Justices as well as academic scholars commenting on the case (denoted by their surnames).

Table 3.1 The various court decisions of *Begum*

Questions of law:	High Court	Court of Appeal	House of Lords	Minority Opinion
1 Was Shabina unlawfully excluded from attending school?	X	✓	X	•
2 If so, was the unlawful exclusion due to an infringement of her right under Article 9(1) ECHR to manifest her religion?	X	✓	X	✓
3 If Shabina was unlawfully excluded and her Article 9(1) right was infringed, was the school justified in limiting her right to manifest her religion under Article 9(2)?	✓	Maybe. Guidelines on the procedure under the HRA.	✓	✓
4 Also, was Shabina's right to an education, under Article 2 of the First Protocol, infringed?	X	X	X	X

Key:
X No
✓ Yes
• Not mentioned in the judgment
Note that a table of the various decisions of a case is a useful addition to your notes to work out complicated cases such as *Begum*.

infringed her right to manifest her religion under Article 9 and right to an education under Article 2 of the First Protocol ECHR.

Ratio decidendi
The House of Lords[14] held that there had been no infringement of the student's right protected under Article 9(1) ECHR and, if there had been such an infringement, this was justified under Article 9(2), as the Headteacher and Governors had developed a uniform policy with the legitimate aim of enabling social cohesion in a multi-cultural and multi-faith school. *Begum* is important and interesting to critically analyse because it remains the leading case on religious dress in Britain.

14 Note that the case was decided before the Constitutional Reform Act 2005 came into effect in October 2009, which established the Supreme Court in the UK.

> **TASK EIGHT** *Reading* Begum
>
> Before continuing to read the present chapter, find and read the House of Lords' decision of *Begum* (see Chapter 4 for more information on how to read cases critically).

Further reading

- Codling, Amy R. (2012) 'A Critical Legal Pluralist Analysis of: R (*on the application of Begum*) v *Headteacher and Governors of Denbigh High School*'. 169 *Law & Justice* 224–225.

A. Perspectives on the nature of law

This section discusses natural law theory and legal positivism. These are theories on the nature of law as they attempt to define and explain law and the legal system. These are called 'doctrinal' or 'black-letter law' approaches because they focus on law 'as an internal self-sustaining set of principles which can be accessed through reading court judgments and statutes with little or no reference to the world outside the law'.[15]

1 Natural law theory

> The best description of natural law is that it provides an intersection between law and morals.[16]

In law, there is a philosophical tension between what law 'is' (positive or descriptive statements) and what it 'ought' to be (normative statements). Natural law theorists attempt to resolve this tension. Naturalists assert that there is a universal set of moral principles that are in accordance with nature. Just as ideas and theories about critical thinking can be traced back to Ancient Greek philosophers, so can perspectives about law. **Plato** (428–348 BC), for example, considered the nature of law in his notion of the forms, such as the form of the 'good'. The **Greek Stoics** first accorded natural law with reason. The Stoic view informed the approach adopted by the Romans, who recognised that laws which did not conform to reason were invalid. Roman lawyer **Marcus Tullius Cicero** (106–143 BC) famously drew upon **Socrates'** philosophies to identify three main components of natural law theory. These were:

1. First, law can be discovered in the application of human reason;
2. Second, law is unalterable; and
3. Finally, law is legislated and enforced by a supreme being.[17]

The three components identified by Cicero emphasise the universal and unchanging nature of law, deemed as 'higher' or 'natural law'.

---

15 Mike McConville and Wing Hong Chui (2007) *Research Methods*. Edinburgh: Edinburgh University Press, p. 1.
16 Alexander Passerin D'Entrèves, (1970) *Natural Law*. London: Hutchinson University Library, p. 116.
17 Marcus Tullius Cicero (1928) *On the Republic: On the Laws*. Harvard: Loeb Classical Library, p. 210.

Classical naturalism: from Aquinas to Hobbes and Locke

During the sixth century, the Greek description justified unjust laws. By the fifth century, therefore, it was acknowledged by the Roman Catholic Church that there might be conflict between the law of nature and the law of man. In his work the Summa Theologiae[18], **Saint Thomas Aquinas** (1225–1274) expressed a comprehensive statement of Christian doctrine. Aquinas distinguished between four categorises of law. These were:

1   Eternal law (divine reason only known by God);
2   Natural law (the participation of the eternal law in rational creatures, discoverable by reason);
3   Divine law (revealed in scriptures); and
4   Human law (supported by reason and enacted for the common good).

The aspect of Aquinas's theory that attracted particular attention and controversy was that laws that conflict with the requirements of natural law lose their power to bind us morally. A government that abuses its authority by enacting laws that are unjust loses its right to be obeyed because it lacks moral authority. Aquinas, however, did not assert that one is always justified in disobeying a corrupt law.

By the seventh century in Europe, the expanding area of public international law purported to be founded upon a natural law grounds. **Hugo de Groot (Grotius)** (1543–1645), for example, based his philosophy of international law on natural law ideals (see the renaissance of natural law theory section in what follows). In his influential work, *De Jure Belli ac Pacis*, Grotius asserted that even if God did not exist, natural law would have the same content: certain things are morally and intrinsically wrong.[19] Scholars writing in the eighteenth century approved natural law theory in England. In **Sir William Blackstone's** (1723–1780) leading work, the *Commentaries on the Laws of England*, for example, it was declared that English law derives its authority from natural law.[20] Similarly, **Sir Edward Coke** (1552–1634), known for his definition of murder (discussed earlier), stated that human nature determined the purpose of law, and law was superior to any one man's direction.[21]

In his famous work *Leviathan*, **Thomas Hobbes** (1588–1679) contended that by establishing a 'social contract' we surrender our natural freedom to form an orderly society.[22] Hobbes argued that we are all (mentally and physically) equal. Pessimistically, however, he contended that every act we perform is self-serving (as, for example, donating to charity is viewed as the enjoyment of power). Hobbes's theory is a rather different interpretation of natural rights supported by classical natural law theorists such as Aquinas. Instead, Hobbes's account is a modern view of natural rights, one premised on the basic right of every person to preserve his or her own life.

18 Thomas Aquinas (1969) 'Summa Theologica Part II' in Dino Bigongiari (ed.) *The Political Ideas of St Thomas Aquinas: Representative Selections*. New York: Hafner.
19 Hugo de Groot (1625/2010) *De Jure Belli ac Pacis*. London: Nabu Press.
20 William Blackstone (1825/2013) *Commentaries on the Laws of England*. London: Waxkeep Publishing.
21 Edward Coke (1797) *Institutes of the Lawes of England*. London: E & Brooke.
22 Thomas Hobbes (1651/2017) *Leviathan*. London CreateSpace Independent Publishing Platform.

Building upon Hobbesian theory, the seventeenth-century philosopher **John Locke** (1623–1704) argued that each man has a natural right to 'life, liberty and property'.[23] Similar to Hobbes, Locke claimed that before the establishment of the social contract, life was a paradise apart from one shortcoming – in our natural state property was inadequately protected. Drawing influence from Aquinas, Locke's 'liberal' theory (see what follows) rests on an account of human rights and obligations to God. His theory was revolutionary, as it accepted the right of people to overthrow tyranny and emphasised the right to own property.

French philosopher **Jean-Jacques Rousseau's** (1712–1778) conception of the social contract inspired the ideologies that led to the French Revolution.[24] His idea was that the social contract represents agreement between the individual and the community. For this reason, Rousseau contended that individuals may be selfish and decide that their personal interest should override the collective interest. However, as part of a community, the individual disregards their own egotism and creates their own 'general will' – which determines the good for society.

Liberalism

Life, liberty and the pursuit of happiness.[25]

Liberalism is a political philosophy and ideology founded on the key principles of 'liberty' (securing individual freedom from control) and 'equality' (all people being treated equally). Other key ideals of liberalism include individual autonomy, freedom of religion, democracy and human rights. Liberalism became a political movement during the 'Age of Enlightenment' (discussed in what follows). Locke is credited with founding liberalism as a distinct philosophical tradition, and liberal ideals were prominent in the ideas underpinning the American (1765–1783) and French Revolutions (1789–1799). There are several liberal perspectives, such as: classical, social and neo-liberalism.

Classical liberalism emphasises the role of liberty and the 'rule of law'. It is a response to the mass urbanisation due to the Industrial Revolution in eighteenth-century Europe (the transition to new manufacturing processes from the feudalist-landowning system between 1760 to 1840). English law professor Albert Venn Dicey developed the concept of the rule of law in his book *The Law of the Constitution* from three principles:

1   No man should be lawfully punished by the authorities except for breaches of law, established before the courts of the land.
2   No man is above the law and everyone, whatever his condition or rank, is subject to the laws of the land.
3   The result of the ordinary law of the land is the constitution.[26]

23 John Locke (1689/2017) *Second Treatise of Government*. London: CreateSpace Independent Publishing Platform, p. 4.
24 Jean-Jacques Rousseau (1762/2017) *Social Contract, Or Principles of Political Right*. London: Independently Published.
25 Thomas Jefferson, United States of America Declaration of Independence, 4th July 1776.
26 Albert Venn Dicey (1885/1982) *Introduction to the Study of the Law of the Constitution*. London: Elibron Classics Series.

Social liberalism emerged at the end of the nineteenth century and gained popularity as an ideology following the Second World War (1939–1946). Social justice requires a government to address economic and social issues such as poverty, health care and education. Notable social liberal thinkers include Winston Churchill and John Rawls (see what follows).

Neo-liberalism is a reaction to social liberalism that emerged in the late twentieth century. Neo-liberalists called for privatisation of social services, such as the National Health Service (NHS). The thinking of neo-liberals influenced the politics of Margaret Thatcher (prime minster of the United Kingdom 1979–1990) and Ronald Reagan (president of the United States of America 1981–1989).

Suggested reading

* Freeman, Michael (2015) *Liberalism: A Very Short Introduction*. Oxford: Oxford University Press.

Communitarianism

[D]iscovering one's identity is not achieved in isolation, but negotiated through dialogue, partly overt, partly internal, with others.[27]

In comparison to liberalism (focused on the individual), communitarianism is a community-centred approach. Communitarianism gained momentum amongst legal and political theorists in response to John Rawls's writings in *A Theory of Justice* (see what follows).[28] Communitarians reject the liberal conception of the individual, conceiving of persons instead, as Michael Sandel put it, as 'situated selves rather than unencumbered selves'.[29] The communitarian response, articulated by the Canadian philosopher Charles Taylor, is that the identities of individuals are partly defined by their communities.[30] Taylor, for example, follows the Hegelian dialectic (see further what follows) of the master and the slave: the slave would not be so called without the master and *vice versa*. The identity of one rests on the existence of the other, as one becomes a subject by the recognition of another subject. The liberal individual is therefore inaccurately viewed as a detached, independent and autonomous agent: he or she is 'stripped of all possible constitutive attachments, is less liberated than disempowered'.[31] We cannot, in the view of communitarians, be understood as persons without reference to our social roles in the community: as citizens or members

---

27 Charles Taylor (1994) 'The Politics of Recognition' in Amy Gutmann (ed.) *Multiculturalism: Examining the Politics of Recognition*. Princeton, Princeton University Press, 25–74, p. 25.
28 John Rawls (1971/1999) *A Theory of Justice*. Oxford: Oxford University Press.
29 Michael Sandel (1982) *Liberalism and the Limits of Justice*. Cambridge: Cambridge University Press, pp. 11–13.
30 See Charles Taylor (1989) *Sources of the Self: The Making of the Modern Identity*. Cambridge: Cambridge University Press.
31 Sandel, *supra* note 29, p. 178.

of a family. This powerful idea has exerted considerable influence in moral, political and legal theory and appears to injure the concept of human rights.

Suggested reading

- Sandel, Michael (1982) *Liberalism and the Limits of Justice*. Cambridge: Cambridge University Press.

The decline of naturalism

The declining influence of natural law theory, especially in the nineteenth century, resulted in the emergence of another legal perspective, namely, legal positivism. **David Hume** (1711–1776) was the first to remark that naturalists seek to derive an *ought* from *is*: we cannot conclude that the law should assume a particular form merely because a certain state of affairs exists in nature.[32] Hume sought to show that facts about the world or human nature cannot be used to determine what *ought* to be done or not done. Therefore, legal positivists (who deny that the legal validity of a norm depends on its moral qualities) rejected the central claims of natural law theory. The perspective of legal positivism is considered in the next section.

Suggested reading

- Wacks, Raymond (2009) *Understanding Jurisprudence: An Introduction to Legal Theory*. Oxford: Oxford University Press. chapter 2: Law and Morals.

2 Legal positivism

In any legal system, whether a given norm is legally valid, and hence whether it forms part of the law of that system, depends on its sources, not its merits.[33]

Legal positivism is a legal perspective largely developed in the eighteenth and nineteenth centuries by Jeremy Bentham and John Austin. The most prominent modern figure in the field is H.L.A. Hart, who adopted a considerably more sophisticated approach to the concept of law, which denies a link between law and morality purposed by natural law theorists. More recently, Ronald Dworkin attacked some of the central claims of legal positivism. The term 'positivism' derives from the Latin word *positum*, which refers to the law as it is 'posited' or laid down. The core of legal positivist thought is the rejection of the view, held by natural lawyers such as Aquinas, that law exists independently from human enactment. For positivists, a clear distinction

---

32 David Hume (1738/2017) *Treatise of Human Nature*. London: CreateSpace Independent Publishing Platform.
33 John Gardner (2001) 'Legal Positivism: 5 ½ Myths'. 46(1) *American Journal of Jurisprudence* 199–227, p. 199.

should be drawn between what '*ought*' to be (what is morally desirable) and what 'is' (law which exists): 'black-letter law'. However, legal positivists do subscribe to the idea that law should be changed for moral reasons and that unjust laws should not be obeyed. This section first considers the classical positivism of Bentham and Austin before, second, outlining the modern positivism of Hart as well as, finally, some of its critiques.

Classical positivism: Bentham and Austin

Moved by the spirit of the Enlightenment (discussed in what follows), utilitarian philosopher **Jeremy Bentham** (1748–1832) sought to demystify law, to expose what lay behind it and attack the ideals of natural lawyers. He purported that appeals to natural law were nothing more than private opinion of men self-constituted into legislatures.

Utilitarianism

The object of all legislation is

the greatest happiness for the greatest number.[34]

Utilitarianism is an ethical theory, whereby the best action is one that maximises 'utility'. Bentham described 'utility' as 'that property in any object, whereby it tends to produce benefit, advantage, pleasure, good, or happiness . . . to prevent the happening of mischief, pain, evil, or unhappiness'.[35] Utilitarianism is a version of **consequentialism**, which states that the consequences of any action are the only standard of right and wrong. Proponents of utilitarianism disagree on a number of points. For example, should the acts of individuals conform to utility (otherwise known as 'act utilitarianism')? Or should agents conform to ethical rules (known as 'rule utilitarianism')? Or, alternatively, should utility be calculated as an aggregate ('total utilitarianism') or as an average ('average utilitarianism')?

Liberalism and utilitarianism

The individual liberties utilitarians seek to protect are similar to those of liberals, such as the right to freedom of religion and speech. These liberties were first advocated by John Stuart Mill, who argued that the government may regulate individual behaviour only in cases in which the interests of others would be harmed.[36] Utilitarian's thus succeeded in broadening the philosophical foundations of liberals whilst also providing a clear programme of reformist goals for them to pursue. Consequently, utilitarianism 'allows some to suffer if the suffering is outweighed by the benefits to others'.[37]

---

34 Jeremy Bentham (1789/2015) *Introduction to the Principles of Morals and Legislation*. London: CreateSpace Independent Publishing Platform.
35 Ibid., Glossary.
36 John Stuart Mill (1859/1974) *On Liberty*. Harmondsworth: Penguin Books.
37 Brain Bix (2009) *Jurisprudence, Theory and Context*. London: Sweet & Maxwell, p. 112.

Suggested reading

- Sandel, Michael (2010) *Justice:What's the Right Thing to Do?* London: Penguin.

Following Bentham, **John Austin** (1790–1859) also built a concept of law based upon the commands of a sovereign.[38] The 'command theory' purports that law is a command backed by the sanction. Austin's map of 'law so properly called' embraces two categories: the law of God *and* human laws. It is only positive law that is the proper subject of jurisprudence. Only the commands emanating from the sovereign are positive laws: anything that is not a command of the sovereign is not law. Austin's insistence on law as commands requires him to exclude customary, constitutional and public international law from the field of jurisprudence. This is because no specific sovereign can be identified as the author of his or her rules.

Modern positivism: Hart

Oxford Professor **H.L.A. Hart** (1907–1992) differentiated between 'habits' and 'social rules'.[39] He asserted that habits were just things that we do without thinking (they have an 'external' aspect), whereas social rules have both an external and an 'internal' aspect: for example, we do not move the queen in a certain manner in a chess game merely out of habit; we understand that it is a rule of the game to do so, and, reflecting upon this rule, we either follow it or not.[40] Law, accordingly, has a boundary where some types of behaviour are legal or legitimate and others are illegal or illegitimate, and the same can be said for social norms. Hart's main work, *The Concept of Law*, illuminated the way we think about law and the legal system. For Hart, law was a *social* phenomenon: it can only be understood and explained by reference to the actual social practices of a community. Three key aspects of Hart's concept of law were that, first, there is a 'minimum content of natural law'; second, law requires a 'rule of recognition'; and finally it is made up of 'primary' and 'secondary rules'. These three aspects are further discussed in what follows.

1 Minimum content of natural law

Hart's concept of law was a response to classical positivists; he severed positivism from both the utilitarianism and the command theory of law championed by Austin and Bentham. His formulation of the 'minimum content of natural law' was due to the recognition that for a community to survive, certain rules must exist. Hart was strongly influenced by the work of Hume to affirm that these were necessary consequences of the 'human condition'. For Hart, all societies have 'social rules', which includes those relating to morals, games and the like as well as 'obligation rules' which impose duties or obligations. Obligation rules may be divided into moral rules and legal rules (or law). As a result of our human limitations, there is a need for obligation rules in all societies: in other words, a 'minimum content of natural law'.

---

38 John Austin (1832/2013) *The Province of Jurisprudence Determined*. London: The Classics.
39 H.L.A. Hart (1961) *Concept of Law*. Oxford: Clarendon Press, pp. 56–57.
40 Davies, *surpa* note 1, pp. 12–13.

2 The rule of recognition

The 'rule of recognition' is the essential constitutional rule of a legal system, acknowledged by the officials who administer the law as specifying the conditions or criteria of validity that certify whether a rule is indeed a rule.

3 Primary and secondary rules

As stated, for Hart, obligation rules are divided into moral or legal rules. Legal rules are then divisible into 'primary' and 'secondary' rules. First, primary rules proscribe 'the free use of violence, theft and deception to which human beings are tempted but which they must, in general, repress if they are to coexist in close proximity to each other'.[41] Primitive societies have little more than these primary rules imposing obligations. Second, as a society becomes more complex, there is a need to develop the primary rules into secondary ones to adjudicate on breaches of them and to identify which rules are actually obligation rules. There are three sorts of secondary rules. These are:

1   Rules of change;
2   Rules of adjudication; and
3   Rules of recognition.

Unlike primary rules, the first two of these secondary rules do not generally impose duties but usually confer power.

Two key Hartian debates

1 The Hart/Fuller debate

In 1958, one of Hart's lectures was published in the *Harvard Law Review*, followed by a response by natural law theorist Lon Fuller (see what follows). The Hart/Fuller (positivist/naturalist) debate was over a decision of a post-war West German court. Under the Third Reich (see earlier), a German wife, wishing to be rid of her husband, denounced him to the Gestapo for insulting remarks he made about Hitler. He was tried and sentenced to serve as a soldier on the Russian front (which was certain death). After the war, the wife was prosecuted for denouncing her husband, and she raised the defence that her husband had committed an offence under a Nazi statute of 1934. The court nevertheless convicted her on the grounds that the statute under which her husband had been punished offended 'sound conscience and sense of justice of all decent human beings'.

On the one hand, Hart argued that the decision of the court was wrong, as the Nazi law of 1934 was valid since it fulfilled the requirements of the rule of recognition. Fuller, on the other hand, supported the court's decision, contending that since Nazi 'law' deviated so far from morality it failed to qualify as law. Both Hart and Fuller would have preferred the enactment of retroactive legislation under which the woman could have been prosecuted; however, Fuller refused to regard the system of

---

41 Hart, *supra* note 39, p. 89.

the Third Reich as law, a view rejected by Hart who preferred the simple utilitarian position that laws may be law but too evil to be obeyed.

Suggested reading

○ Hart, H.L.A. (1959) 'Positivism and the Separation of Law and Morals'. 71 *Harvard Law Review* 593–629.
◐ Fuller, Lon L. (1959) 'Positivism and Fidelity to Law – A Reply to Professor Hart'. 71 *Harvard Law Review* 630–672.

2 The Hart/Devlin debate

The Hart/Devlin debate was sparked by a report in 1957 by a British committee under the chairmanship of Sir John Wolfenden. The Wolfenden committee recommended that, although the function of the criminal law was to preserve public order and decency, consensual homosexual acts between adults in private and prostitution be decriminalised. In a series of lectures in 1959, Lord Devlin took issue with the Wolfenden's Committee's position, arguing that society has every right to punish conduct that, in the view of the ordinary members of society, is grossly immoral. The fabric of society is maintained by a shared morality. Social cohesion is undermined when immoral acts are committed – even in private and even if they harm no one. Hart agreed with the recommendations of the Wolfenden report and challenged Lord Devlin's 'social cohesion' argument. He insisted that a society does not require a shared morality; pluralistic, multicultural societies may contain a variety of moral views. Hart did, however, support a paternalistic (overprotective) role for the law. This was at odds with the utilitarian philosophy of Stuart Mill (see earlier), who purported that victimless crimes should not be crimes. Hart acknowledged that there may be circumstances in which the law *ought* to protect individuals from physically harming themselves.

Suggested reading

○ Report of the Committee on Homosexual Offences and Prostitution, Chairman Sir John Wolfenden (The 'Wolfenden' Report) (Cmnd 247).
◐ Devlin, Patrick (1959/2010) *The Enforcement of Morals*. London: Liberty Fund Inc.
● Hart, H.L.A. (1963) *Law, Liberty and Morality*. Stanford: Stanford University Press.

Critique of Hartian positivism

Hans Kelsen (1881–1973) acknowledged that '[t]he legal order is a system of norms'.[42] He stated that law was 'made up of legal norms and legal acts as determined

---

42 Hans Kelsen (1967) *Pure Theory of Law*. Berkley: University of California Press, p. 110.

by these norms'.[43] Influenced by the thinking of Immanuel Kant (see what follows), Kelsen espoused that objective reality can be comprehended only by the application of formal categories, like time and space. These categories do not 'exist' in nature but are used to make sense of the world. Equally, to understand the law, 'we require formal categories in particular the *grundnorm* or basic norm which lies at the heart of the legal system'.[44] Kelsen's legal perspective challenged Hart's because, rather than adopting the Hartian concept of primary and secondary rules, Kelsen adhered to a singular approach. He argued that law does not tell subjects what to do; it tells officials what to do to its subjects.

Immanuel Kant (1724–1804)

Influencing the legal perspectives of Kelsen and others, the thinking of eighteenth-century German philosopher Immanuel Kant was crucial in the history of philosophy. Instead of starting with the proposition that knowledge must conform to its objects, Kant argued that our perception of objects conforms to certain conditions of knowledge that exist in the human mind.

> In essence Kant argued that there are certain laws of the understanding that order our experience. We cannot know things in themselves (*noumena*); we can only know the appearance of things (*phenomena*). This does not mean that there is nothing outside the mind; rather that we do not know things as they are, prior to their appearance in the mind. Knowledge of the world is not gained simply by receiving unedited impressions of it or by having sensations entering our minds. Rather, knowledge of the world is filtered by the laws of understanding . . . The universal laws of the mind provide the conceptual structure of experience and it is based on these laws that we can make objective judgments about our experience and the world.[45]

Suggested reading

O   Scruton, Roger (2001) *Kant: A Very Short Introduction*. Oxford: Oxford University Press.

*   Kant, Immanuel (1929) *The Critique of Pure Reason*. Hampshire: Palgrave Macmillan.

In comparison to the theory of Kelsen, **Joseph Raz** (1939–) argued that identity and existence of a legal system may be tested by reference to three elements. These are:

1   Efficacy;
2   Institutional character; and
3   Sources.[46]

43 Hans Kelsen (1961) *General Theory of Law and State*. New York: Russell, p. 39.
44 Kelsen (1967), *supra* note 42, p. 1.
45 Davies, *supra* note 1, pp. 7–9.
46 Joseph Raz (1979) *The Authority of Law*. Oxford: Oxford University Press.

Thus, law is autonomous: we can identify its content without recourse to morality. Legal reasoning, however, is not autonomous; it is an inevitable and desirable feature of judicial reasoning. For Raz the answer to the question 'what is law?' is always a fact, never a moral judgment, and this 'marks him as a hard or exclusive positivist'.[47]

Another critic of legal positivism, particularly Hart's version, **Ronald Dworkin** (1931–2013) finds the distinction between what law *is* and what it *ought* to be unacceptable. For Dworkin law consisted of the following:

1   Legal rules;
2   Non-rule standards (principles and policies).

Dworkin created an imagery judge, Hercules, to determine that when a court has to decide hard cases it will draw on principles and policies (moral and political standards) to reach the 'right answer'. The answer is 'right' when it 'fits' with the institutional and constitutional history of the law. Judges are like interpreters of an unfolding novel. Dworkin argued that legal argument and analysis are therefore interpretative (or what Dworkin calls, 'interpretive') in character.[48] Dworkin's theory is premised on his concern that the law *ought* to 'take rights seriously'.[49]

John Rawls (1921–2002)

Rawls also regarded utilitarianism as an unsatisfactory means by which to measure justice. In *A Theory of Justice*, Rawls's theory of justice as fairness is rooted in the idea of the social contract.[50] For Rawls, a 'veil of ignorance' prevents people from knowing to which sex, class, religion or social position they belong. Each person represents a social class, but they do not know whether they are clever or stupid, strong or weak. Nor do they know in what period they are living. Rawls's two principles of justice are set out as follows:

1   First principle: 'Each person is to have an equal right to the most extensive total system of equal basic liberties compatible with a similar system of liberty for all'.
2   Second principle: 'Social and economic inequalities are to be arranged so that they are both:

     a)   To the greatest benefit of the least advantaged, consistent with the just savings principle, and
     b)   Attached to offices and positions open to all under conditions of fair equality of opportunity.

Suggested reading

O   Hart, H.L.A. (1961) *The Concept of Law*. Oxford: Clarendon Press. See Chapters 2–5 particularly.

47 Wacks, *supra* note 4, p. 132.
48 Ronald Dworkin (1986) *Law's Empire*. Cambridge, MA and London: Belknap Press.
49 Ronald Dworkin (1977) *Taking Rights Seriously*. London: Duckworth.
50 Rawls, *supra* note 28.

●   John Rawls (1971) *A Theory of Justice*. Cambridge, MA: Harvard University Press. Chapters 1–3.

Renaissance in natural law theory

The twentieth century saw a renaissance in natural law theory, evident from the post–**World War II** recognition of human rights. Many of the international conventions and declarations of the **United Nations** (UN), established in 1945 (such as the **Universal Declaration of Human Rights 1948**, as well as regional treaties like the **European Convention on Human Rights and Fundamental Freedoms 1950**), draw upon the unspoken assumption of natural law. The **Nuremberg Trials** (held between November 1945 and October 1946) of senior Nazi officials also regenerated natural law ideals by applying the principle that certain acts constitute 'crimes against humanity' (see previous chapter for a discussion of the Third Reich). Although the judges in these trials did not explicitly cite natural law theory, their judgments represent recognition of the principle that law is not necessarily determinate of what is right.

During this time, Harvard Professor **Lon Fuller** (1902–1978) developed a secular approach to natural law that regards law as having an 'inner morality': a legal system has the specific purpose of 'subjecting human conduct to the governance of rules'. Fuller devised eight principles by which moral laws should abide. These are:

1   Generality
2   Promulgation
3   Non-retroactivity
4   Clarity
5   Non-contradiction
6   Possibility of compliance
7   Constancy
8   Congruence between declared rule and official action.[51]

Fuller concluded that where a system does not conform to these principles, it is not 'law'. Although Fuller's eight principles seem to be 'moral' they are more procedural guidelines for effective governmental law making: the principles only verify the effectiveness of a legal system, and an evil regime might still satisfy Fuller's test. Certainly, the rulers of apartheid (racial separation between those with 'white' and 'black' skin) in South Africa complied with these procedures, although they enacted discriminatory laws.

In his book *Natural Law and Natural Rights*, **John Finnis** (1940–) revived some of the Aquinian tenets of natural law.[52] Finnis rejected Hume's conception of practical reason because it only informs how best to achieve desires, not what *ought* to be desired. He circumvents the positivist criticism of natural law – that it starts with a description of

51 Lon L. Fuller (1977/2004) *The Morality of Law*. London: Universal Law Publishing Co Ltd.
52 John Finnis (1980) *Natural Law and Natural Rights*. Oxford: Clarendon Press.

the natural world (and 'is') but somehow ends up purporting what law *ought* to be, by arguing that natural law principles are not derived from anything: they are self-evident.

Suggested reading

● Davies, Margaret (2008) *Asking the Law Question*. Sydney: Thompson Law Book Co. chapter 3: Natural Law and Positivism.

Doctrinal analysis of *Begum*

A doctrinal analysis of *Begum*, based on the legal perspectives of natural law theory and legal positivism, would provide a 'black-letter law' analysis focused on primary (the case itself) and secondary sources (books and journal articles). For example, since the House of Lords' judgment, on the one hand, scholars such as Mohammad Mazher Idriss agree with the decision, as it 'effectively maintains the current right of each school to decide its policy on school uniforms'.[53] On the other hand, Russell Sandberg argues that the legacy of *Begum* is a 'flawed precedent that has constrained religious liberty in England and Wales'.[54] This is because *Begum* provides that if the right to manifest one's religion can be exercised elsewhere (for example, in another school) the courts are obliged to find that there has been no interference with the right. Mark Hill and Sandberg criticise the House of Lords' judgment for taking the 'specific situation rule'[55] and 'the impossibility test'[56] out of their original contexts.[57] As stated in the Education Act 1996, being free to attend another school to receive an education is not a contractual choice: there is a statutory duty to provide education to children.[58]

B. Critical perspectives of law

One prevalent view amongst those contemplating a legal education is that law is a discrete object of study, clearly defined and labelled, with distinct boundaries and

---

53 Mohammad Mazher Idriss (2006) 'Dress Codes, the Right to Manifest Religion and the Human Rights Act 1998: The Defeat of Shabina Begum in the House of Lords'. 11(1) *Coventry Law Journal*, 58–78, p. 60.

54 Russell Sandberg (2009) 'The Changing Position of Religious Minorities in English Law: The Legacy of *Begum*' in Ralph Grillo, *et al.* (ed) *Legal Practice and Cultural Diversity*. London, Ashgate, 267–282, p. 267.

55 The European Court of Human Rights (ECtHR) case of *Kalaç v Turkey* [1997] 27 EHRR 552 stipulated that there is no interference with the right to manifest one's religious belief where a person voluntarily accepts employment (or a similar role) which does not accommodate that practice or observance, and there are other means open to practice or observe the religion.

56 The ECtHR, in *Jewish Liturgical Association Cha'are Shalom Ve Tsedek v France* [2000] 9 BHRC 27; [2006] HRLR 21, created an 'impossibility test' that relates to the specific situation rule providing that applicants should not suffer any undue hardship or inconvenience by being prevented from practicing his or her religion or beliefs.

57 Mark Hill and Russell Sandberg (2007) 'Is Nothing Sacred? Clashing Symbols in a Secular World'. *Aut Public Law*, 488–506.

58 See the House of Lords decision decided on the same day, *A v Head Teacher and Governors of Lord Grey School* [2006] 2 WLR 690.

categories . . . But, such a view takes for granted and therefore leaves unanalysed, the ways in which law presents this discrete appearance.[59]

Critical legal theories

A central theme of critical theory is to doubt the prospect of universal foundations of knowledge. Critical legal theorists argue that knowledge is 'a construct of social, cultural, and linguistic contexts and the [associated] mechanisms of power'.[60] As a school of thought, critical theories provide a critique of society and culture. The notion of 'critique' is the product of Enlightenment thinking (see what follows), and this critical activity was, historically, a weapon in the hands of warring religious parties.[61] Prior to providing a discussion of CLS, first, an understanding of sociological and Marxist perspectives of law is required.

Law and social theory: sociological perspectives

The sociology of law is concerned with analysing and interpreting the part played by law and legal administration in effecting certain observable forms of conduct or human behaviour. American sociologist **Roscoe Pound** (1870–1964), for example, emphasised the importance of the distinction between 'law in books' and 'law in action'.[62] For Pound, the task of lawyers and legislators was 'social engineering' in the construction of as efficient a society as possible. Alan Hunt criticised Pound, however, because he 'used sociology [only] when he saw fit'.[63] Undoubtedly, however, Pound exerted a considerable influence upon sociological jurisprudence.

Building on the work of Pound, Austrian sociologist **Eugen Ehrlich** (1862–1922) distinguished 'living law' from 'norms of decision' (rules found in the civil codes, judicial decisions and statutes). 'Living law' was defined as 'the law which dominates life itself'.[64] Ehrlich's ideas are best described by Roger Cotterrell as a 'powerful challenge to lawyers' typical assumptions about the nature and scope of law and of its importance'.[65] David Nelken, however, questions: what, if anything, do the various norms of the 'living law' (relating to families, organisations and business activity) have in common?[66] Nelken asserts that the answers to this question are dependent on the development of 'sociology of norms' rather than a sociology of law.

Deemed the father of sociology, **Émile Durkheim's** (1859–1917) general concern was: what is it that holds society together? Throughout his major works, his preoccupation was with 'social solidarity'.[67] For Durkheim, law plays a significant

---

59 Wade Mansell, *et al.* (2015) *A Critical Introduction to Law*. London: Cavendish Publishing Ltd, p. vii.
60 Davies, *supra* note 1, p. 16.
61 Paul Connerton (ed.) (1976) *Critical Sociology*. Harmondsworth: Penguin, p. 15.
62 Roscoe Pound (1910) 'Law in Books and Law in Action'. 44 *American Law Review* 12–36, p. 12.
63 Alan Hunt (1978) *The Sociological Movement in Law*. London: Palgrave Macmillan, p. 34.
64 Eugen Ehrlich (1936) *Fundamental Principles of the Sociology of Law*. Trans. W. L. Moss. Cambridge, MA: Harvard University Press, p. 493.
65 Roger Cotterrell (1984/2005) *Sociology of Law: An Introduction*. London: Butterworth, p. 31.
66 David Nelken (1984) 'Law in Action or Living Law? Back to the Beginning in Sociology of Law. 4 *Legal Studies*, 157–174.
67 Émile Durkheim (1893/1964) *The Division of Labour in Society*. Trans. George Simpson. London: Collier: Macmillan.

role in the transition from mechanical to organic solidarity; it is an 'external' index which 'symbolises' the nature of social solidarity.

A trained lawyer and German sociologist, **Max Weber** (1864–1920) subjected law to a rigorous and systematic social and historical analysis in his work.[68] Essentially, Weber's project was to explain the development of capitalism in Western societies.[69] A key element in his explanation was the existence of a 'rational' legal order. To this end he employed certain 'ideal types' along with the development of particular concepts of rationality to demonstrate the movement towards capitalism. His starting point was the individual: social action can be understood only by reference to its meaning, purpose and intention for the individual.

Suggested reading

● Pound, Roscoe (1910) 'Law in Books and Law in Action'. 44 *American Law Review*, 12–36.

3 Marxism

[C]laim[s] that human actions and institutions are determined by the law of economics, and that change is about class struggle.[70]

The theories of **Karl Marx** (1818–1883) and **Friedrich Engels** (1820–1895) continue to exert influence on legal theories. Although neither Marx or Engels provided a comprehensive or systematic account of law, they made several observations about the relationship between law and economics.

Historicism

A central feature of Marxist theory was that social evolution could be explained in terms of inevitable historical forces. Marx and Engels argued that each period of economic development has a corresponding class system. For example, under a capitalist system, three principal social classes exist: the landowners, capitalists and wage labourers. Marx, however, foresaw the crystallisation of just two classes: the '*bourgeoisie*' (those who own the means of production) and the 'proletariat' or 'working class' (who are forced to sell their labour). A revolution would eventually occur because the *bourgeois* mode of production, based upon individual ownership and unplanned competition, stands in contradiction to the increasingly non-individualistic, social character of labour production in the factory. The proletariat would seize the means of production and establish a 'dictatorship of the proletariat' that would, in time, be replaced by a classless, communist society in which law would eventually wither away.

---

68 Max Weber (1968) *Economy and Society: An Outline of Interpretive Sociology*. Guenther Roth and Claus Wittich (eds.) New York: Bedminster Press.
69 Max Weber (1954) *Max Weber on Law in Economy and Society*. Trans. Edward Shils and ed. Max Rheinstein. Cambridge, MA: Harvard University Press.
70 Anthony Harrison-Barbet (2001) *Mastering Philosophy*. Basingstoke: Palgrave Macmillan, p. 2.

In *A Contribution to the Critique of Political Economy*, Marx declared that our ideas are the result of economic conditions: we absorb our knowledge from our social experience of productive relations.[71] This provides an explanation of the way in which law comes to maintain the social order that represents the interests of the dominant class. 'Ideological hegemony' is established, which ensures that (educationally, culturally and legally) the dominant set of values prevails, as first explained in the prison writing of the Italian Marxist Antonio Gramsci.[72] Law is a vehicle of class oppression, and in a classless society there is therefore no need for law. This is the essence of Marx's argument in his early writings.[73] In Marxist legal theory, there is nothing special about law; rather it is 'the result of one particular kind of society'.[74] 'Legal fetishism' obscures the origins of the legal system's power and creates the impression that the legal system has a life of its own. Law in this image is the means by which the dominant group maintains its domination. Neither Marx nor Engels addressed themselves explicitly to the nature of rights in a socialist society: they were more concerned to uncover the deception of *bourgeois* ideas and institutions.

Marxist analysis of *Begum*

A Marxist analysis of *Begum* is probably one of the most difficult of the seven legal perspectives to illustrate. That is because a Marxist interpretation of law sees it primarily as an instrument of class domination: the right to manifest one's religion is essentially a *bourgeois* (or middle-class) right. Although Marx articulated 'many demands for social and economic rights that were not secured by capitalism',[75] however, 'the concept of human rights was not a well-developed idea at the time he wrote'.[76] The importance of a Marxist analysis to *Begum* is the influence it has had on the CLS, feminist and CRT perspectives discussed in the following sections. See what follows for an example of a Marxist analysis.

Example

Marx's theory of economics argues that wealth will become concentrated into a few hands. This research project is based on an interpretation of Marx's theory and argues that although the denationalisation of public services in Britain led to more companies being set up in the short term, over a few decades, mergers and buy-outs have resulted in many smaller companies closing. As a result, the wealth of these industries is now in the possession of a smaller number of 'super-companies'. The research hypothesis is that after three decades, seventy-five per cent of the wealth of former British nationalised industries will, in each case, be in the hands of three or fewer super-companies.[77]

71 Karl Marx (1859/2013) *A Contribution to the Critique of Political Economy*. London: The Classics.
72 Antonio Gramsci (1929/2005) *Selections from the Prison Notebooks of Antonio Gramsci*. London: Lawrence & Wishart Limited.
73 See Karl Marx (1875/2009) *The Critique of the Gotha Programme*. London: Dodo Press.
74 Isaac D. Balbus (1977) 'Commodity for and Legal Form: An Essay on the "Relative Autonomy of the Law". 11 *Law and Society Review*, 571–582, p. 21.
75 Micheline R. Ishay (2007) *The Human Rights Reader*. London: Routledge, p. 108.
76 David Fasenfest (2016) 'Marx, Marxism and Human Rights'. 42 (6) *Critical Sociology*, 777–779, p. 778.
77 Cottrell, *supra* note 9, p. 150.

Suggested reading

○   Collins, Hugh (1982) *Marxism and Law*. Oxford: Clarendon Press.
●   Marx, Karl (1848/2004) *Communist Manifesto*. London: Penguin Books.

4 Critical Legal Studies (CLS)

[H]istorically CLS is located at the beginnings of the 'dissolution' or 'integration' of legal theory. . . [which]has moved from somewhat a closed activity, into a multitude of legal theories which are loosely held together by the focus upon law.[78]

CLS is a relatively new movement, and its value as a theory of law is still being assessed. It is called a 'movement' because it is characterised by a continuing 'struggle to break up the rigidity to which understating has reduced everything'.[79] The CLS movement provides a direct attack on the orthodoxy (generally approved beliefs) of legal theory, scholarship and education. Its original focus was on Blackstone's *Commentaries*,[80] the Wagner Act,[81] as well as tort and contract laws. Later it reflected a multi-disciplinary approach that draws upon politics, literary criticism and psychoanalysis and the like to expound its critique of law. According to David Trubeck, there are three important ideas that inform CLS. These are:

1   *Hegemonic consciousness*: a concept derived from the writings of Gramsci, reflecting the idea that only the interests of the dominant elite are supported in society;
2   *Reification*: a Marxist concept asserting that systems of ideas are 'reified' (become material) when presented as essential, necessary and objective; when they are contingent, arbitrary and subjective; and
3   *Denial*: in Freudian psychology (see what follows) legal thought is also a form of 'denial', as it is a means of coping with perceived contradictions that are too painful for us to hold in our conscious minds.[82]

Sigmund Freud (1856–1939)

Austrian psychologist Sigmund Freud first disrupted the classical view of subjectivity. He theorised an irreconcilable division in the mind between the conscious and unconscious sides of the psyche. According to Freud's early thought, this division was formed primarily by repression. In response to Freud's psychoanalysis,

---

78 Davies, *supra* note 1, p. 185.
79 Alan Thompson (1987) 'Critical Legal Education in Britain'. 14 *Journal of Law and Society*, 183–197, p. 184.
80 William Blackstone (1825/2013) *Commentaries on the Laws of England*. London: Waxkeep Publishing.
81 The National Labor Relations Act 1935 (49 Stat. 449) 29 USC.
82 David M. Trubeck (1984) 'Where the Action Is: Critical Legal Studies and Empiricism'. 36(1/2) *Critical Legal Studies Symposium*, 575–622.

Swiss psychiatrist **Karl Jung** (1875–1961), who collaborated with Freud in his early work, developed other psychological concepts, such as the collective unconscious.

Suggested resources

O Freud, Sigmund (1941/2002) *Civilisation and its Discontents*. London: Penguin Books.
● Young-Eisendrath, Polly and Terence Dawson (eds.) (1997) *Companion to Jung*. Cambridge: Cambridge University Press.

Film
● *A Dangerous Method* (2011) Recorded Picture Company.

The CLS movement developed in the US in the 1970s with roots largely in American legal realism as well as influence from the German 'Frankfurt School'. Although the British CLS movement started roughly at a similar time as its American counterpart, it has developed its own context and critique. These three aspects of the CLS movement are now considered in turn. First, the CLS movement of the 1960s and 1970s was influenced by the American legal realism of the 1930s. As Paul Connerton states '[i]f Critical Theory was a creation of the early thirties, it was also a discovery of the late sixties'.[83] With the influence of the writings by scholars such as the Polish philosopher **Leon Petrazycki** (1867–1931), legal realism unsettled American jurisprudence for decades. Under the influence of legal realism, Harvard professor **Duncan Kennedy** (1942–), together with other scholars (most notably, **Roberto Mangaberia Unger** (1947–)), established the CLS movement.[84]

Second, the CLS movement is also influenced by a group of German philosophers known as the 'Frankfurt School'. The term 'Frankfurt School' includes influential scholars who fled from Germany during Hitler's Nazi regime in the 1930s from Frankfurt to New York, such as **Max Horkheimer** (1895–1973), **Theodor Adorno** (1903–1969) and **Herbert Marcuse** (1898–1979) (mentor to the philosopher **Martin Heidegger** [1889–1976]). Members of the Frankfurt School considered Freudian and Marxist theories to be two instances of a single new type of theory, which they called 'critical theory'.[85] The influential theory of German social theorist **Jürgen Habermas** (1929–) draws upon that of the Frankfurt School in his attempt to develop a systematic theory with a view to showing how 'distortion of communication' can be eliminated.[86] Since his concept of 'communicative reason' rests on the principles of freedom and equality, for Habermas the legitimacy of the

83 Connerton, *supra* note 61, p. 12.
84 Kennedy is best known for his critique of American legal education in his essay: Duncan Kennedy (1982) 'Legal Education and the Reproduction of Hierarchy'. 32 *Journal of Legal Education*, 591–615.
85 Raymond Geuss (1981) *The Idea of a Critical Theory: Habermas and the Frankfurt School*. Cambridge: Cambridge University Press, pp. 1–2.
86 Harrison-Barbet, *supra* note 70, p. 3.

law depends crucially on the effectiveness of the process of discourse by which the law was made.

Finally, it is 'only relatively recently that the umbrella term "critical", imported from the US, has come into widespread use in this country'.[87] In his comprehensive historical and theoretical analysis of human rights, British scholar **Costas Douzinas** (1951–) concluded with the following warning:

> [a]s human rights start veering away from their initial revolutionary and dissident purposes, as their end becomes observed in even more declarations, treaties and diplomatic lunches, we may be entering the epoch of the end of human rights.[88]

Originally created to protect the individual from violations by the nation-state, human rights have now become a discourse in their own right.[89] There is an ongoing struggle between, on the one hand, how to analyse human rights and the international human rights system critically and how to attempt to save the human rights project by patching it up where it is needed and, at times, turning a blind eye to shortcomings, on the other.[90]

CLS analysis of *Begum*

Although, as discussed, there are several key themes of CLS scholarship, such an analysis of Begum depends upon the particular perspective selected. Perhaps the most obvious scholar to consider here would be Douzinas, who states that

> religion is the desire of the people. But the paternal function is coming under attack in late modernity and cannot fulfil its role any longer.[91]

Therefore, in relation to Begum, the minority opinion of Baroness Hale is particularly noteworthy. This is because Lady Hale considered Shabina's religious beliefs in detail and drew upon academic literature to discuss the multiple reasons women wear a jilbab. Baroness Hale held that, because of her young age, Shabina was likely to be influenced by her brothers in relation to the garments she wore.[92] For this reason, Lady Hale's opinion has been described as 'paternalistic',[93] which correlates with Douzinas's critical analysis of law and religion.

87 Thompson, *supra* note 79, p. 183.
88 Costas Douzinas (2000) *The End of Human Rights*. Oxford: Hart Publishing, p. 380.
89 For example, Marie-Bénédict Dembour argues that human rights are important because they are 'talked about': Marie-Bénédict Dembour (2006) *Who Believes in Human Rights? Reflections on the European Convention*. Cambridge: Cambridge University Press.
90 Sari Kouvo (2004) *Making Just Rights? Mainstreaming Women's Human Rights and a Gender Perspective*. Uppsala: Iustua Förlag, p. 93.
91 Douzinas, *supra* note 88, p. 330.
92 Begum, *supra* note 12, at para. 93.
93 Antasisa Vakulenko (2007) 'Islamic Dress in Human Rights Jurisprudence: A Critique of Current Trends'. 7(4) *Human Rights Law Review*, 717–739, p. 728.

Suggested reading

   ◈   Douzinas, Costas (2000) *The End of Human Rights*. Oxford: Hart Publishing.

Postmodernism

> The Enlightenment marks a particular episode in the history of thought. Post-modernity marks the end of this episode.[94]

'Postmodernism' was originally a movement in architecture, literature and philosophy and now law. The term was 'first coined by a British historian to refer to the post–World War II era of irrationalism and passim'.[95] Its main proponents are French thinkers such as Jean-François Lyotard, Michel Foucault and Jacques Derrida. For postmodernists 'law' is merely a manipulative apparatus which controls people without them being able to shape it.[96]

The age of Enlightenment

The age of Enlightenment was a broad intellectual and philosophical movement in Europe in the eighteenth century. It essentially comprised the development of liberal democracy and the rise of interest in the sciences and secularism to create an 'enlightened' (or non-superstitious) philosophy. Adorno and Horkheimer argue that the Enlightenment was always inherently irrational as well as rational, producing fascism as well as liberalism.[97] Despite liberalism, Enlightenment values have become associated with a general intolerance to pluralism. What the Enlightenment arguably did produce was a mode of thought built upon a solid European cultural base, which promoted itself as universal.

Modernism

'Modernism' refers to a literary period (roughly between 1890 and 1930) in which writers such as D. H. Lawrence, T. S. Eliot and James Joyce searched for aesthetic (visual) order – outside history and social contexts. In a philosophical sense, it refers to the attempt to find absolute grounds for knowledge, to discover abstract principles that are the foundation for philosophical questioning. The method of Descartes (see earlier), for instance, was to attempt to discover a rational ground for knowledge in the face of all doubt. In legal theory, scholars have attempted to determine a universal basis for the concept of law (Kelsen's *grundnorm* and Hart's rule of recognition; see

---

94 Anthony Carty (ed.) (1990) *Post-Modern Law: Enlightenment, Revolution and the Death of Man*. Edinburgh: Edinburgh University Press, p. 1.
95 Davies, *supra* note 1, p. 331.
96 Carty, *supra* note 94, pp. 6 and 7.
97 Theodor Adorno and Max Horkheimer (1979) *Dialectic of the Enlightenment*. London: Verso.

earlier). The term 'postmodernism' therefore signified that the 'modern' era was over and that a new artistic and philosophical culture had emerged.

In his influential book *The Postmodern Condition*, **Jean-François Lyotard** (1924–1998) defined postmodernism as doubting 'meta-narratives'.[98] Lyotard began his argument by distinguishing between two forms of knowledge scientific and narrative.[99] On the one hand, 'scientific' knowledge comprised mathematical formulas to determine what (according to probabilities) happened. On the other hand, 'storytelling' attempted to formulate a narrative that fits best with the evidence. The central problem for Lyotard is the 'legitimation' of knowledge: what methods do we use, or what assumptions do we make, to claim that something is correct or proven to the requisite degree? Who proves the proof? Lyotard asserted that questions about the foundations of knowledge concern legal philosophers. He highlighted the recognition of heterogeneity of 'discourses' (formal discussions), or what Ludwig Wittgenstein famously called 'language games',[100] to be what Lyotard identified as the 'postmodern condition'. Drawing upon Lyotard's work, modern universal values and 'master narratives' are regarded as meaningless, and the historical developments associated with the Enlightenment are treated with suspicion. The conventional assumption that human 'progress' is 'evolving' toward 'civilization' or some other end is rejected and replaced by an emphasis on individual experience(s).

Nihilism

Postmodernism is not nihilistic (or pessimistic). The point of postmodernism is not to destroy knowledge or even to demonstrate that any point of view is as good as any other. Rather, what we regard as 'true' or 'real' is reconstructed to reveal the possibility of engaging with different discourses or language games to formulate new positions. Traditional knowledge is questioned at its foundations and made to focus on the specific. Law provides a good example of this, since it operates on many levels and on many people differently. Rather than providing a nihilistic approach, the 'postmodern' provides a way of describing the fragmentation of our knowledge and social interactions.

Structuralism and poststructuralism

'Structuralism' is an intellectual approach that questions how language relates to the world and how meaning works. 'Poststructuralism', however, is a rather more nebulous term. It is basically concerned with language and meaning, denying 'the possibility of a [single] discourse . . . and a consequent recognition that there is nothing but discourses, discourses which while they might talk to each other are ultimately untranslatable'.[101] Swiss linguist **Ferdinand de Saussure** (1857–1913), for example,

---

98 Jean-François Lyotard (1984) *The Postmodern Condition: A Report on Knowledge.* Minneapolis: University of Minnesota Press, p. xxxiv.
99 John Leubsdorf (1991) 'Stories and Numbers'. 13 *Cardozo Law Review*, 455–463, p. 455.
100 Ludwig Wittgenstein (1922) *Tractatus Logico-Philosophicus.* London: Routledge.
101 Thompson, *supra* note 79, p. 189.

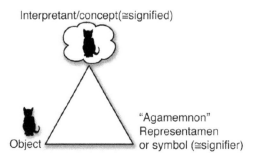

Interpretant/concept(≅signified)

"Agamemnon"
Representamen
or symbol (≅signifier)

Object

Figure 3.3 'Signified' and 'signifiers'[102]

generated a theory to explain that things themselves are not the words we call them. Rather, a thing or an object is 'signified' in the human mind by a 'signifier' (the words or images used to describe it). When we hear certain words we invariably think of a thing or a concept. For de Saussure, the thing or object referred to, the 'referent', remains outside the system of language: it does not determine meaning.

Drawing upon the work of Freud and Saussure, French psychoanalyst **Jacques Lacan** (1901–1981) is regarded as the creator of psychoanalytic semiotics. Lacan claimed that the unconscious is structured like language; it is the repository of knowledge, power and agency. Lacan argued that we do not control what we say; rather, the structure of language is pre-determined by thought and desire. He employed the Freudian conception of the divided human subject (ego, superego and the unconscious) to demonstrate that the 'I' expressed by language can never represent a person's 'true' identity. Rather, Lacan theorised that 'I' am defined through my relations with others and through the complex fabric of discourses which surround me (see also the discussion on communitarianism, earlier).

Michel Foucault (1926–1984)

French thinker Michel Foucault's theories 'have a number of implications for law and [the] legal system'.[103] For Foucault, 'we can know the past only as genealogies . . . merely [as] the field in which the discourses of power compete as rhetoric's'.[104] 'Rhetoric' is basically language used to persuade but lacks any real outcome (**Martti Koskenniemi** (1953–), for example, contends that international law is merely rhetoric).[105]

---

102 Jo Faith, Nick Rossiter and Paul Vickers (2003) 'Understanding Visualization: A Formal Approach Using Category Theory and Semiotics' 19 *IEEE Transaction on Visualization & Computer Graphics*, 1048–1061.
103 Wacks, *supra* note 4, p. 224.
104 Thompson, *supra* note 79, p. 189.
105 Martti Koskenniemi (1990) 'The Politics of International Law'. 1(1) *European Journal of International Law*, 4–32.

Power

For Foucault, power is distinct from either physical force or regulation. Instead, in *Discipline and Punish*, Foucault demonstrated how, beginning in the eighteenth century, the human body was subject to new 'micro-physics' of power through the geography of institutions, hospitals, schools and prisons.[106] Disciplinary power required us to act in ways that we came to think of as natural. We are manipulated and controlled by these 'technologies' to become 'docile' bodies. Foucault referred to Bentham's concept of Panopticon as a paradigm of disciplinary control. This showed how a prison building designed in 1785 permitted an observer to survey inmates without them being aware that they were being observed. This investigation of power led Foucault to question liberalism, with its preoccupation with centralised state power. In *The Order of Things*, Foucault contemplates the fundamental laws of order that determine our perception of the world.[107] Power, for Foucault, is not just something which one holds as a commodity but arises within a system of meaning.

Suggested reading

- Gutting, Gary (2005) *Foucault: A Very Short Introduction*. Oxford: Oxford University Press.

Deconstructing jurisprudence

'Deconstruction' is sometimes used simply as a substitute for the word 'criticism'. French philosopher **Jacques Derrida** (1930–2004) expounded the idea of 'deconstruction' to explain the operation of '*différance*'. Adopting Saussure's semiotics, Derrida concluded that since language emerges from the unstable system of difference, it will always be indeterminate.[108] When we deconstruct jurisprudence, there is an object ('law') that is distinct from other practical and intellectual pursuits. In universities, for instance, law is considered to constitute a different intellectual discipline from history, politics and physics. Law is seen to be in some way self-contained or self-defined: a closed system. Derrida comments on this in 'The Law of Genre' with Avital Ronell by pointing out that the definition of a genre depends upon there being some 'mark' or 'trait' which allows us to distinguish or recognise the genre.[109] There is then a 'law of genre' – basically a 'trait' that sets the limits of any conceptual territory such as law, determining what falls within the genre and what falls outside.

---

106 Michel Foucault (1977/1991) *Discipline and Punish: The Birth of the Prison*. London: Penguin New Edition.
107 Michel Foucault (1966/2001) *The Order of Things: An Archaeology of the Human Sciences*. Trans. London: Routledge.
108 Jacques Derrida (1990) 'The Force of Law: The "Mystical Foundation of Authority"'. 11 *Cardozo Law Review*, 919–1046.
109 Jacques Derrida and Avital Ronell (1980) 'The Law of Genre'. 7(1) *Critical Inquiry*, 55–81.

Suggested reading

● Lyotard, Jean-François (1984) *The Postmodern Condition: A Report on Knowledge*. Minneapolis: University of Minnesota Press.

5 Feminism(s)

> This [section] . . . refers to 'feminisms' in the plural, because the word "feminism", in the singular, tends to suggest that there is a common theoretical approach shared by those who believe that women are marginalised and devalued in society.[110]

As with many of the other legal perspectives, there is difficulty in providing a definition of 'feminism(s)'. One reason for this is that feminism(s) are not only philosophical, political and legal theories but also a form of activism. Similar to law and critical thinking, the debate concerning the status of women in society dates back to the Ancient Greeks. It is, however, the eighteenth-, nineteenth- and early-twentieth-century feminist campaigns 'which mark the origins of contemporary feminist thought'.[111] In agreement with Davies, the term 'feminism(s)' (see earlier quote) seems appropriate and it used in this section to signify the 'range of philosophical, political [and] social . . . projects'.[112] A common theme for feminists is that they all ask the 'women question': a question that aims to reveal 'disadvantage based upon gender'.[113]

In her book *A Vindication of the Rights of Women*, **Mary Wollstonecraft** (1759–1797), for example, famously expressed that women were equally rational to men and thus able to perform the same civic duties.[114] In France, existentialist philosopher **Simone de Beauvoir** (1908–1986) stated in *The Second Sex* that women are the 'Other' (sex).[115] de Beauvoir asserted that the construction of society, language and family all rests on the assumption that the world is male: women are excluded from these constructions. Women, de Beauvoir argued, are socially constructed rather than biologically determined: 'one is not born, but rather becomes, a woman'.[116] Being a woman – the Other – is reflected in law's construction: the subjects of law are male.[117] Feminist jurisprudence, consequently, reflects the demands of women to be recognised as equal parties to the social contract which is underpinned by law and legal systems.

---

110 Davies, *supra* note 1, p. 220.
111 Hilaire Barnett (1998) *Introduction to Feminist Jurisprudence*. London: Cavendish Publishing Ltd, p. 3.
112 Angela Harris (2000) 'Equality Trouble: Sameness and Difference in Twentieth Century Race Law'. 88 *California Law Review*, 1923–2015, p. 293.
113 Yavuz Selim Alkan (2012) 'Feminist Legal Methods: Theoretical Assumptions, Advantages, and Potential Problems'. 9(2) *Ankara Law Review*, 157–174, p. 167.
114 Mary Wollstonecraft (1792/2017) *A Vindication of the Rights of Women*. London: CreateSpace Independent Publishing Platform.
115 Simone de Beauvoir (1949/1989) *The Second Sex*. H Parshley (ed and trans). London: Picador.
116 *Ibid.*, p. 293.
117 Barnett, *supra* note 111, p. 4.

Waves of legal feminism(s)

Feminist legal scholarship is frequently presented as having differing phases or waves, although none of these are totally distinct or isolated from the others. Stating that there are different 'waves' of feminism(s), whilst being a stereotypical approach, is a useful way to start to appreciate the nuances and differences between the various viewpoints. The three different waves of feminism(s) are now considered in turn.

1 First-wave feminism(s)

The first wave of feminism(s) dated from mid-Victorian times to the present time (although most vocal from the 1960s through to the mid-1980s) and was dedicated to unmasking the features which exclude women from public life. Ngaire Naffine has stated that 'the first phase can be characterised by its concern with the monopoly of law'.[118] It is epitomised by the quest for equality, whether in employment, politics or roles in society generally. First-wave feminists worked within the existing system to remove its inequalities without necessarily questioning the system itself. The objections voiced by feminists in this wave were to highlight 'bad laws': law that operates to the exclusion or detriment of women.

Liberal feminism(s)

Feminists who attack 'liberalism' do so because, although liberals insist that the autonomy of individuals be nurtured equally in society, the 'individual' presupposed is male. Liberal laws therefore provide general rules about the rights and responsibilities of male citizens. Supposedly gender-neutral legal rules are seen not to be neutral at all. Examples from homicide law, the offence of rape and employment law evidence the lack of the laws neutrality. These examples are discussed in what follows.

EXAMPLES

Homicide law

Although English law prohibits homicide (whosoever deliberately kills another is charged with murder), it allows for the partial excuses of loss of control and diminished responsibility. A string of English cases in the 1990s highlighted the dilemmas of women who had suffered years of violent abuse and eventually killed their partners.[119] A liberal response, according to feminists, ignored the actual experience of the accused women.[120]

---

118 Ngaire Naffine (1990) *Law and the Sexes*. Sydney: Allen & Unwin, p. 2.
119 See the cases of *R v Ahluwalia* [1992] 4 All ER 889; *R v Thornton (No 2)* [1996] 2 All ER 1033 and *R v Humphrey's* [1995] 4 All ER 1008 leading to the enactment of the Coroners and Justice Act 2009 which repealed the defence of provocation and the need for a 'sudden and temporary loss of self-control' (as provided in *R v Duffy* [1949] 1 All ER 932).
120 See Alan Norrie's (2010) 'The Coroners and Justice Act 2009 – Partial Defences to Murder (1) Loss of Control'. 10 *Criminal Law Review*, 275–289.

The offence of rape

Two further examples can be taken from the law regarding rape. First, for serious crimes no-one is to be held guilty unless it is satisfied beyond reasonable doubt that he or she acted intentionally, or at least recklessly. The House of Lords ruled that this applies to cases of rape, so that if a man honestly believes a victim to be consenting to sexual intercourse, he is entitled to an acquittal.[121] However, a careless belief in consent, even if honestly held, should not exonerate a defendant. One should look at the matter from the point of view of women who are regularly subjected to coerced sex or fear of it.[122]

Second, marital rape (the act of sexual intercourse with one's spouse without their consent) was an exception in English law until the case of R v R[123] in the early 1990s – there was no legal punishment for raping your wife until the twentieth century! During the case Lord Keith held that, 'marriage in modern times is regarded as a partnership of equals, and no longer one in which the wife must be the subservient chattel [property] of the husband'.[124]

Employment law

One of the most crucial issues for liberal feminists is the public–private divide. For Habermas the public sphere is the realm of public authority (such as government and the police), whereas the private sphere is that of individual authority, unobstructed by government (such as family and the home). The division between public and private spheres is a main tenet of liberalism.[125] Formal equality as a political right is of very little value to women, given their economic dependence on men. Equal rights of entry into the professions can do nothing to counteract the social forces that stereotype women as homemakers and child carers (in the private sphere) and hence do not confer to them real equal promotion opportunities (in public spheres).

2 Second-wave feminism(s)

Although first-wave feminists made many remarkable advances for female equality, women still suffer discrimination. Second-wave feminists (who dominated discussions in the late 1970s and 1980) attempted to address the legal and societal structure in which inequality is perpetuated. Here the focus was on understanding 'the deep-seated male orientation which affects all . . . practices'.[126] For second-wave feminists, the root problem with law lay in its pretended impartiality, objectivity and rationality. By assuming gender-neutral language, law masks the extent to which it is permeated by male standards. One key example of this is the concept of the 'reasonable *man*': if women are to be 'reasonable' they must adopt the male standard of reasonableness.[127]

121 See *Director Public Prosecutions v Morgan* [1976] AC 182.
122 Harris, *supra* note 112, p. 295.
123 [1991] 3 WLR 767.
124 Ibid., at p. 616.
125 S. Lukes (1973) *Individualism*. Oxford: Basil Blackwell, p. 62.
126 Naffine, *supra* note 118, p. 2.
127 Barnett, *supra* note 111, pp. 5–6.

Radical feminism(s)

The term 'radical' means 'going to the root or origin'. In the context of gender equality 'origin' means not only first in time but the source from which a thing is derived.[128] 'Radical feminists' therefore see oppression on the basis of sex as the original oppression. In all societies, there has been but one official voice, that of the dominant male, whereas suppression and silencing has been the universal experience of women. The state, law and social institutions are all structured in the interests of one class, men, and against the interest of another class, women. Whether a society espouses liberal or socialist principles, the experience of women is one of relative economic deprivation, sexual objectification and systematic subjection to personal violence by men.[129]

The most influential radical feminist, **Catharine MacKinnon** (1946–), argued that we can characterise the state itself as 'male'. She dismissed the jurisprudence of Austin, Hart and Dworkin as simply expressing a male point of view.[130] For MacKinnon, the primary methodology of feminism(s) should be 'consciousness raising', wherein women share their experiences and thus reveal or construct a specifically feminine point of view. As things are, discourse of all kinds is man-made and has established a concept of a woman as a passive and subservient 'other'.[131] Many writers (feminist or not) today agree with MacKinnon and adopt 'politically correct' terminology to overcome the male preoccupation with 'he' in their writing, by always using the plural or 'she' (redefining the concept of the 'reasonable *man*' to that of the 'reasonable *person*', for example). However, some radical feminists disagree with MacKinnon's grand-scale theorising: African Americans and people with disabilities (both women and men) also suffer at the hands of white or able-bodied people. Furthermore, there is not one single 'woman's view' of female oppression.

3 Third-wave feminism(s)

While accepting the premise of law's maleness, third-wave feminism(s) question whether law and legal systems operate in a consistently sexist manner. The perception of third-wave feminists is that while law is deeply gendered, this does not necessarily mean that law operates consistently, inevitably or uniformly to promote male interests. Rather, law is too complicated a phenomenon to be portrayed in such a holistic manner. What needs to be understood is the way law responds to differing problems, and its operation reveals its well-concealed gender bias. The approach of a third-wave feminist is one that necessarily rejects the 'grand theories' of second-wave feminism(s) and asserts that 'law in the reflection of the society it serves, is as complex as that society'.[132] **Carl Smart**'s analyses of the family, for example, demonstrated

---

128 Davies, *supra* note 1, p. 240.
129 Harris, *supra* note 112, p. 295.
130 Catharine MacKinnon (1983) 'Feminism, Marxism, Method and the State'. 8 *Signs*, 635–658, p. 636.
131 Catharine MacKinnon (1989) *Towards a Feminist Theory of the State*. Cambridge, MA: Harvard University Press, p. 244.
132 Barnett, *supra* note 111, p. 7.

that the law relating to abortion, the law relating to financial provision on divorce and the law relating to domestic violence advanced protection for women unevenly conceals the patriarchal ordering of law and society.[133]

Postmodern feminism(s)

Arising out of the late 1980s and continuing through the 1990s, some feminists adopted postmodernist philosophy that questions all 'meta-narratives' (see the discussion of Lyotard, earlier). Postmodern feminist theory is tormented with doubt, uncertainty and fragmentation. Concepts such as 'equality', 'gender' and even 'women' are treated with profound scepticism. Indeed, the very idea that things have properties themselves (or 'essences') is rejected. This so-called essentialism is detected by postmodern feminists. Leading postmodernist feminist Frances Olsen has drawn upon the work of Derrida and Julia Kristeva to create an 'imaginative universal' that transcends the essentialism of real experience.[134] In her influential essay, Katherine Bartlett attempts to show that in analysing the practice of law by courts and lawyers, at least three 'feminist legal methods' are used. These are:

1   *Asking the women question*: seeking to uncover the gender implications of rules and practices which might otherwise appear to be neutral and objective. Discriminatory rules and practices are thereby revealed and attacked;
2   *Feminist practical reasoning*: challenging the legitimacy of the norms of those who claim to speak, through rules, for the community. In particular, it emphasises a woman's perspective in, say, rape and domestic violence cases; and
3   *Consciousness raising*: an 'interactive and collaborative process of articulating one's experiences and making meaning of them with others who also articulate their experiences'. In other (simpler) words, it attempts to understand and reveal their oppression.[135]

In seeking appropriate feminist epistemology, Bartlett argues for what she calls 'positionality' which recognises the possibility of feminine values and knowledge.

Difference feminism(s)

Difference feminism(s) (also known as 'cultural feminism(s)) reject a formal equality that undermines the differences between men and women, seeking to uncover, instead, the unstated premises of the law's substance, practice and procedure. In her influential work In *a Different Voice*, **Carol Gilligan** showed how women's moral

133   Carol Smart (1989) *Feminism and the Power of Law*. London: Routledge.
134   Frances Olsen (1990) 'Feminism and Critical Theory: An American Perspective'. 18 *International Journal of the Sociology of Law*, 199–215; and Jacques Derrida and Julia Kristeva (1990) 'The Doubly-Prized World: Myth, Allegory and the Feminine'. 75 *Cornell Law Review*, 643–698.
135   Katherine T. Bartlett (1990) 'Feminist Legal Methods'. 103 *Harvard Law Review*, 829–888.

values tend to stress responsibility, whereas men emphasise rights.[136] She argued that women endorse an 'ethic of care' which asserts the morality of caring and nurturing. Gilligan's theory has been criticised, however, for its essentialism: for treating characteristics as natural when they are a consequence of male domination. This criticism aside, feminist legal theorists have used Gilligan's insights to strengthen their argument that the law tends to reflect masculine values.

Women, multiculturalism and sexuality

As stated, one criticism directed at early second-wave feminism(s) is that they assume that there is a single feminine experience and take the position of white heterosexual and privileged women to be the standard case. Not only do white feminism(s) ignore issues of race, they also ignore its own racial positioning and are based upon a universalist approach to knowledge. **Susan Moller Okin**, for example, has discussed the tenuous relationship between multicultural and feminist theories.[137] One concern about accommodating cultural and religious diversity, raised by Moller Okin, is that women do not have adequate choices. She argues that multiculturalism is 'bad' for women because accommodation of cultural and religious diversity includes accepting sexist practices and values. Since Moller Okin's famous contribution to the literature on liberal multiculturalism, a great deal of nuanced and critical work has been written by postcolonial and multiculturalist feminists.[138] For example, rather than being separate realms, both culture and religion are themselves inter-woven experiences – as scholars such as Aziah Al-Hibri observe.[139] Consequently, Moller Okin's opposition essentialises the various and diverse reality of human experiences.

Queer theories

Another site of difference relates to sexuality. Historically, there have been some points of tension between feminism(s) and theories concerning sexuality. For example, the discrimination experienced by lesbians and gay men was marginalised by mainstream feminism(s) in the 1970s and 1980s. Carl Stychin and Didi Herman argue that a liberal approach to sexuality and law accepts that the categories (if not the experience) of sexuality that already exist and holds that law is a neutral, rational medium for promoting change – for instance, by getting same-sex couples equal rights to relationship recognition through legislation on gay marriage or civil partnerships. But queer theories incorporate a range of approaches to critique liberal assumptions, such as the presumed normality of the heterosexual family form.[140]

136 Carol Gilligan (1982) In a Different Voice: Psychological Theory and Women's Development. Cambridge, MA: Harvard University Press.
137 Susan Moller Okin (1999) 'Is Multiculturalism Bad for Women?' in Susan Moller Okin, et al. (eds.) Is Multiculturalism Bad for Women? Susan Okin Miller with Respondents. Princeton: Princeton University Press, 7–47.
138 See Anne Phillips (2007) Multiculturalism Without Culture. Princeton: Princeton University Press and Vakulenko, supra note x.
139 Aziah Y. Al-Hibri (1999) 'Is Western Patriarchal Feminism Good for Third/World Minority Women?' in Susan Moller Okin, et al. (eds.) Is Multiculturalism Bad for Women? Susan Okin Miller with Respondents. Princeton: Princeton University Press, 41–46.
140 Carl Stychin and Didi Herman (eds.) (2000) Sexuality in the Legal Arena. London: Athlone Press.

International law and feminism(s)

Of the several blind spots in the early development of the human rights movement, none is so striking as that movement's failure to give violations of wom-
en's (human) rights the attention, and in some respects the priority, that they
require.[141]

International feminist scholars such as **Hilary Charlesworth** and **Rebecca Cook**
(1994) argue that human rights mechanisms fail to be universal because the disadvantages experienced by women are not adequately addressed by them.[142] After years
of drafting and discussions, the Convention for the Elimination of Discrimination
of Women (CEDAW) was adopted by the UN General Assembly in 1979. CEDAW
is an international bill of rights for women. The Convention, basically, defines what
constitutes discrimination against women and sets up an agenda for national action
to end such discrimination. CEDAW is one of the most widely ratified human rights
treaties; however, seven countries have not ratified or acceded to the Convention: Iran,
Palua, Somalia, South Sudan, Sudan, Tonga and even the US. Although the UK signed
CEDAW in 1981, it did not ratify the Convention until 1986, and the Optional Protocol entered into force in 2005. Since then, there have only been two cases against
the UK: *Salgado v UK* and[143] *NSF v UK*.[144] In the *Salgado* case a woman complained that
UK law prevented her from passing on her British nationality to her Colombian-born
son (by then fifty-two years old). The Committee declared her application inadmissible because the facts of the case occurred before the Optional Protocol entered into
force and because the applicant had not exhausted all domestic remedies pursuing
the complaint. In the *NSF* complaint, a woman claimed that her purposed deporta-
tion to Pakistan put her back at risk from her violent husband. To this the Committee declared her application inadmissible because she had, again, not exhausted all
domestic remedies.

Feminist analysis of *Begum*

Maleiha Malik provided a feminist judgment of *Begum* as part of the influential UK–
based Feminist Judgments project.[145] In her judgment, Malik argues that focus should
remain on whether a woman has made a choice in wearing a *jilbab*. Malik argues that
rather than creating a conflict for Shabina between her choice of religious dress (as a
member of a religious group) and her choice of preferred school (as a British citizen
and a member of the wider community), state law should enable both the recognition of her culture and religion *and* her access to education, which are important to
her individual autonomy.

141 Henry Steiner, Philip Alston and Ryan Goodman (2008) *International Human Rights Law in Context: Law, Politics and Morals: Text and Materials*. Oxford: Oxford University Press, p. 166.
142 Rebecca Cook (ed.) (1994) *Human Rights of Women; National and International Perspectives*. Philadelphia: Philadelphia University of Pennsylvania Press.
143 CEDAW/C/37/D/11/2006, 22nd January 2007.
144 CEDAW/C/38/D/10/2005, 12th June 2007.
145 Maleiha Malik (2010) 'Judgment: R (SB) v Denbigh High School' in Rosemary Hunter, Clare McGlynn and Erika Rachley (eds.) *Feminist Judgments: From Theory to Practice*. Oxford: Hart Publishing, 336–344.

Suggested reading

○ Walters, Margaret (2005) *Feminism: A Very Short Introduction*. Oxford: Oxford University Press.

⬤ Davies, Margaret (2008) *Asking the Law Question*. Sydney: Thompson Law Book Co. chapter 6: Feminisms and Gender in Legal Theory.

● Kennedy, Helena (1993) *Eve Was Framed: Women and British Justice*. London: Vintage.

6 Critical race theories (CRTs)

> For people of color . . . modernist conceptions of truth, justice, and objectivity have always been both indispensable and inadequate.[146]

CRTs are 'the heir to both [CLS] and traditional civil rights scholarship'.[147] The privileged position occupied by mostly white, middle-class academics is perceived by CRTs scholars as a significant obstacle to the exposure of the racism that permeates the law and its rules, concepts and institutions. 'Racism' is the presumption that race determines characteristics such as intelligence, work ethic and moral fibre. Specifically, it is the presumption that white people are naturally or biologically superior. Ideas about race are reinforced, historically, through slavery and, today, by general social disadvantage. In recent times, explicitly discriminatory laws have been dismantled, and it has become common to regard racism as individual ignorance or prejudice. These developments aside, racism remains prevalent in society.

One important feature of CRTs scholarship is the use of autobiography to analyse and criticise social and legal relations. **Patricia Williams**, for example, in *The Alchemy of Race and Rights*, combined legal analysis with personal narrative to criticise legal subjectivity.[148] Williams explored 'how both literary knowledge . . . and legal knowledge are produced to make possible a postcolonial mimicry of these dominant discourses'.[149]

Colonialism

In his famous work *Orientalism*, **Edward Said** considered the study of the Orient as just an idea and 'not an inert fact of nature'.[150] It is not really there, just as the Occident (Europe) is not just there either.[151] In other words, European discourses (literary, political, religious, *etc.*) created a theoretical object out of an enormously disparate

---

146 Angela Harris (1994) 'The Jurisprudence of Reconstruction *Symposium: Critical Race Theory: Foreword.*' 82(4) *California Law Review*, 741–786, p. 744.

147 *Ibid.*, p. 743.

148 Patricia Williams (1991) *The Alchemy of Race and Rights*. Cambridge, MA: Harvard University Press.

149 Wacks, *supra* note 4, p. 373.

150 Edward Said (1978) *Orientalism*. London: Penguin Books.

151 *Ibid.*, p. 4.

reality, labelled the 'Orient. Said's endeavour was not to describe the material facts of colonialism but rather to consider the Western/colonial representation of the Orient as other and the way that this discourse gave (and still gives) the West power over its object, justifying Western imperialism.

EXAMPLES

America

In the US, between 1790 and 1952, only 'free white persons', not slaves, could be naturalised as citizens, leading to an extensive jurisprudence on the meaning of whiteness. Although African Americans were citizens by birth since the passing of the Fourteenth Amendment in 1868, the practice of racial segregation was not regarded as opposing the 'equal protection' provision until the Supreme Court decision of *Brown v Board of Education*[152] in 1954. The civil rights movement in the US is the most well-known example of a broad anti-racist movement which aimed to ensure equality before the law.

Australia

Upon the colonisation of Australia, Indigenous people became British subjects receiving, however, little and meaningless protection from the law. For much of the twentieth century many statutes established land reserves upon which Indigenous people were forced to live and work while being denied wages and citizenship. They also required the removal of 'half-caste' children from Indigenous communities in order to assimilate them into white society.

Britain

In the past decade, British scholars of race have noticed the emergence of a new form of racism, labelled 'neo-racism' or 'cultural-racism'. Tariq Modood, for example, has argued that during the 1980s there was a growing presence of a British 'new racism' that accentuated the incompatibility of cultural groups living in close proximity to one another.[153]

CRT analysis of *Begum*

In his review of *Begum*, for example, Boris Johnson (Conservative MP) affirms that the case was really about 'militant Islam'.[154] Johnson raised one of the most worrying aspects of Shabina's case: her brothers' alleged connection with the extremist

---

152 (1954) 347 US 483.
153 Tariq Modood (1997) '"Difference", Cultural Racism and Anti-Racism' in Pnina Werbner and Modood (eds.) *Debating Cultural Hybridity: Multi-Cultural Identities and the Politics of Anti-Racism*. London: Zed Books, p. 154.
154 Boris Johnson 'The Shabina Begum Case Never Had Anything to Do with Modesty' *The Telegraph*. 23rd March 2006. Available at www.telegraph.co.uk/comment/personal-view/3623879/The-Shabina-Begum-case-never-had-anything-to-do-with-modesty.html.

Islamic organisation Hizb-ut-Tahrir.[155] Such arguments support Samuel Huntington's clash-of-civilisations thesis, which asserts that the survival of the West depends upon an inevitable clash with other civilisations (such as Chinese, Muslim, Latin-American etc.).[156] Adopting this image of such cases, the ECtHR was wrong to uphold the discretion of educational institutions in matters of religious dress (see the cases of *Dahlab v Switzerland*[157] and *Şahin v Turkey*).[158]

Suggested reading

* Williams, Patricia (1991) *Alchemy of Race and Rights*. Cambridge, MA: Harvard University Press.

7 Legal pluralism(s)

As a method for studying the relationship between law and society legal pluralists provide: 'a metaphor within the traditional legal vocabulary for exploring the role of [normative orders]'.[159]

The question, 'what is legal pluralism?' has occupied the attention of scholars for a number of decades. There is difficulty in answering the question because the literature and studies into situations of legal pluralism are vast. For example, alternative definitions include 'legal polycentricity'[160] or 'inter-legality'.[161] Legal pluralism is variously regarded to be an 'ethos'[162] or an 'analytical concept'.[163] Moreover, the study of legal pluralism occurs in a wide range of contexts, which include tribal cultures,[164] industrial societies[165] and the global society.[166] In agreement with **Roderick Macdonald** (1948–2014), legal pluralism is an essential 'analytical tool' that provides a metaphor to discuss law as a multi-sited social phenomenon.[167] It is a way to 'write-in' the

155 See also Shabina Begum. Live dialogue number 569, 17th March 2005. Available at www.islamonline.net/livedialogue/english.
156 Samuel P. Huntington (2002) *The Clash of Civilisations and the Remaking of World Order*. London: Simon and Schuster.
157 [2001] Appl. No. 42393/98.
158 [2005] Appl. No. 44774/98.
159 Roderick A. Macdonald (1998) 'Metaphors of Multiplicity: Civil Society, Regimes and Legal Pluralism'. 15(1) *Arizona Journal of International and Comparative Law*, 69–92, p. 70.
160 Hanne Petersen and Henrik Zahle (1995) *Legal Polycentricity: Consequences of Pluralism in Law*. Aldershot: Dartmouth.
161 Bonaventura de Sousa Santos (2002) *Towards a New Legal Common Sense: Law, Globalization, and Emancipation*. London: Butterworth's.
162 Margaret Davies (2005) 'The Ethos of Pluralism'. 27(1) *Sydney Law Review*, 87–112.
163 Franz von Benda-Beckmann (2002) 'Who's Afraid of Legal Pluralism?' 47 *Journal of Legal Pluralism and Unofficial Law*, 37–74.
164 Peter Fitzpatrick (2001) 'Magnified Features: The Undeveloped Law and Legitimation' in Italo Pardo (ed.) *Morals of Legitimacy: Between Agency and System*. Oxford: Berghahn Books, 157–176.
165 Sally Falk Moore (1973) 'Law and Social Change: The Semi-Autonomous Field as the Appropriate Subject of Study'. 7(4) *Law and Society Review*, 719–746.
166 Paul Schiff Berman (2007) 'Global Legal Pluralism'. 80(6) *Southern Californian Law Review*, 1155–1237.
167 Macdonald, *supra* note 159, p. 70.

normativity of social associations occurring from a variety of different situations into law's narrative(s).

Current jurisprudential textbooks mention little about legal pluralism.[168] This is due to the assumption that legal pluralism(s) produce only a 'vague and wholly indeterminate conception of legality';[169] whereas the possibilities of a pluralistic legality are not 'indeterminate' (indefinite or uncertain) or infinite (leading to a 'nihilistic' outcome – see earlier). Rather, as people are locked into what poststructuralists call 'discourses' (see earlier) or Wittgensteinian 'language games', there are sets of established ideas or principles that we draw upon in order to create our own notions of normativity. In this sense law is ultimately 'phenomenological' (in other words, connected to human consciousness and lived experiences). Moreover, scholars such as Brian Tamanaha argue that there is difficulty in creating a generalisable definition of legal pluralism because legal pluralists diverge on their underlying concept of law.[170] However, doctrinal scholars also provide a multitude of definitions of 'law' (as for Hart, law is social ordering based upon a rule of recognition and the establishment of primary and secondary rules, whereas Fuller acknowledged the importance of official enactments of law as well as human conduct).[171] Due to the varying definitions given to situations of legal pluralism, the types of social contexts studied and concepts of law supported, it can be said that a 'plurality' of legal pluralism(s) exists.[172] The present section discusses four pluralistic perspectives, which are now considered in turn.

Institutional legal pluralism

In his seminal article, **John Griffiths** clarifies a definition of legal pluralism suitable for studying various social scenarios. Griffiths defined legal pluralism as 'that state of affairs for any social field, in which behaviour pursuant to more than one legal order occurs'.[173] Griffiths challenged the doctrinal (or 'legal centralist') assumption that law is only legislation interpreted and enforced by state institutions (called 'state law'). Instead, Griffiths fills the (doctrinal) normative vacuum between legislator and legal subjects by theorising a plurality of legal orders active in a social field by following **Sally Falk Moore**'s notion of 'semi-autonomous social fields' (or 'normative orders').[174] For Griffiths, 'law' is the self-regulation of normative orders. Therefore, adopting Griffiths's definition state law, school uniform and university plagiarism policies are law(s).

---

168 For example, see J. W. Harris (2004) *Legal Philosophies*. Oxford: Oxford University Press; Penner and Melissaris, *supra* note 1 and Wacks, *supra* note 4.

169 Emmanuel Melissaris (2009) *Ubiquitous Law: Legal Theory and the Space for Legal Pluralism*. Bodmin: MPG Books Ltd, p. 5.

170 Brian Tamanaha (2000) 'A Non-Essentialist Version of Legal Pluralism'. 27(2) *Journal of Law and Society*, 296–321.

171 Lon L. Fuller (1969) 'Human Interaction and the Law'. 14 *American Journal of Jurisprudence*, 1–36.

172 Amy R. Jackson and Dorota A. Gozdecka (2011) 'Caught Between Different Legal Pluralisms: Muslim Women as the Religious 'Other' in European Human Rights Discourses'. 64 *Journal of Legal Pluralism*, 91–120.

173 John Griffiths (1986) 'What Is Legal Pluralism?' 24 *Journal of Legal Pluralism*, 1–55, p. 2.

174 Falk Moore, *supra* note 165.

Griffiths distinguished between normative orders that are incorporated and excluded from state law, called 'weak' and 'strong' legal pluralism. An example of a situation of 'weak' legal pluralism is Parliament delegating the decision-making power of uniform policies to state schools. However, **Emmanuel Melissaris** has argued that the distinction between strong and weak legal pluralism is arbitrary as, for example, marriages conducted to meet the requirements of Islam must registered to become a legal marriage in English state law (as required under Marriage Act 1949).[175]

Another criticism of Griffiths's approach is that he perpetuates the doctrinal image of law that he aims to oppose because his definition accedes to an institutional notion of law.[176] This is because a school, for example, can be viewed as a normative order *because* it holds the capacity to generate its own norms (such as a uniform policy) that it can enforce (by disciplining pupils if they fail to comply with these norms). This limitation aside, an institutional legal pluralist analysis of a particular social situation is a useful analytical tool to expose the operation(s), interaction(s) and conflict(s) between a multiplicity of normative orders, including state law.

Cultural and religious legal pluralism

An additional criticism of Griffiths's definition of legal pluralism is that he fails to account for cultural and religious diversity. **Prakash Shah** argues that legal pluralism has received a 'more complex' articulation of the inter-cultural world by **Masaji Chiba**.[177] Chiba conceives a three-level system of law (which consists of official law, unofficial law and legal postulates). First, 'official law' (or state law) is the norms sanctioned by state institutions. For Chiba, religious laws (such as Canon law and Islamic law), unsanctioned by state institutions, are examples of 'unofficial' laws that may complement, modify and even undermine official law. Unofficial laws can become state law. In this respect Chiba's image correlates with Griffiths's notion of situations of weak (or incorporated) and strong (or excluded) legal pluralism. Finally, the term 'legal postulates' (another aspect unconsidered in Griffiths's approach) describes the moral principles found in a legal system. Examples of these principles are natural law, justice and equity.

Chiba adds that a cultural and religious legal pluralist approach highlights personal identity (subjectivity) – an aspect also omitted by Griffiths's perspective. When people encounter situations of legal pluralism, they are not passive recipients of legal regulations; rather, they are active agents who choose to adopt a particular legal rule from the multiplicity of rules that exist. **Werner Menski** adds to Chiba's dynamic and subjective articulation of law by formulating a notion of hybrid laws, such as '*Angrezi Shari'a*' law.[178] Following conception, a person is perceived to be an active agent who chooses to follow both English law and their traditional customs simultaneously.

175 Emmanuel Melissaris (2004) 'The More the Merrier? A New Take on Legal Pluralism'. 13(1) *Social and Legal Studies*, 57–79.
176 Martha-Marie Kleinhans and Roderick A. Macdonald (1997) 'What Is a Critical Legal Pluralism?' 12(2) *Canadian Journal of International Law and Society*, 25–46.
177 Prakasah Shah (2009) 'Transforming to Accommodate? Reflections on the Shari'a Debate in Britain' in Raplh Grillio *et al.* (eds.) *Cultural Diversity and Legal Practice*. London: Ashgate 73–93, p. 86 and Masaji Chiba (ed.) (1986) *Asian Indigenous Law in Interaction with Received Law*. London: KPI. Ltd.
178 Werner Menski and David Pearl (1998) *Muslim Family Law*. London: Sweet and Maxwell.

The attention of cultural and religious legal pluralism dramatically increased following **Rowan Williams**'s (former Archbishop of Canterbury) lecture on the transformative accommodation of *shari'a* councils into English law.[179] Shah classified Williams as a legal pluralist because he implies that the use of *shari'a* councils in England to obtain a religious divorce by some members of the Muslim community, which is a situation of strong legal pluralism.[180] Cultural and religious legal pluralism, however, is criticised for essentialising cultural, gendered and religious experiences of Muslim women. For instance, **Samia Bano** criticised Williams's comments by highlighting the heterogeneity of British Muslim identity.[181] During her study, for example, one participant stated that

> I do identify myself as both British and Muslim, so I don't want to support initiatives that mean that I have to choose between one kind of legal system. . . . Reality is a lot more difficult than choosing between one or the other! [Parveen, Birmingham].[182]

Although Bano documents the heterogeneous identities of British Pakistani Muslim women, her discussion is limited because it centres on how legal subjects, subjected to the rules of normative orders, perpetuate institutional normativity: Bano does not consider whether legal subjects construct the law(s) they follow.

Critical legal pluralism

> When Martha-Marie and I appropriated the word 'critical' for our article we were less thinking about CLS and more thinking about the Frankfurt School.[183]

In their radical critique of legal pluralism, **Martha-Marie Kleinhans** and **Roderick Macdonald** locate law in the human imagination: what is law, within a particular social situation, is found in the imagination of people.[184] Kleinhans and Macdonald criticise 'traditional' legal pluralists, such as Griffiths, for perpetuating an institutional image of law. They argue that pluralistic definitions offer no criteria to distinguish normative orders from other forms of social ordering (such as morals, etiquette, fashion *etc.*). **Sally Engle Merry**, for example, contends that the lack of such criteria creates the dilemma 'where do we stop speaking of law and find ourselves simply describing social life?'[185] Her criticism can be overcome by acknowledging the

179 Rowan Williams (2008) 'Civil and Religious Law in England: A Religious Perspective'. 10(3) *Ecclesiastical Law Journal*, 262–282.
180 Shah, *supra* note 177.
181 Samia Bano (2012) *Muslim Women and Shari'ah Councils, Transcending the Boundaries of Community and Law.* London: Palgrave Macmillan.
182 Samia Bano (2008) 'In Pursuit of Religious and Legal Diversity: A Response to the Archbishop of Canterbury and the 'Sharia Debate' in Britain'. 10 *Ecclesiastical Law Journal*, 282–309, p. 304.
183 Roderick Macdonald as cited in Amy Jackson (2008) *How Might Legal Pluralist Methods Lead to a Better Understanding of the Role of Other Actors in Public International Law?* University of Sussex: Unpublished LLM Dissertation, p. xii.
184 Klienhans and Macdonald, *supra* note 176.
185 Sally Engle Merry (1988) 'Legal Pluralism'. 22(5) *Law and Society Review* 869–896, p. 896.

differences between normative orders, for example, Chiba's distinction between official and unofficial law.

Another criticism vested on traditional legal pluralists by Kleinhans and Macdonald is that they tend to question: '[w]hich legal order has jurisdiction over a given legal subject in a given situation at a given time?'[186] This is the type of question that Williams posed, for example, in relation to the use of shari'a councils in England. Kleinhans and Macdonald argue that to ascertain to which normative order a legal subject feels (and/or judges) he or she belongs, a complementary question should be asked: '[w]ithin which legal order does the particular legal subject perceive himself or herself to be acting – whether resisting or sustaining?'[187] Simply adding this complementary question is problematic, however, as a legal subject is required to identify him- or herself as belonging to some external normative community. Bano, for example, illustrates the point by arguing that '[c]learly there is a sense of belonging to a Muslim community, which the women in this study expressed'.[188] By simply adding the complementary question, there remains the problem that legal subjects' are 'subsumed under one (or even several) homogeneous labels [such as 'British' or 'Muslim'] instead of being allowed to persist as heterogeneous, multiple creatures'.[189] On this basis, people constantly construct (and re-construct) their identities by drawing upon their own interpretations of normative, cultural, gendered and religious commitments. Questioning within which normative order a legal subject perceives himself or herself to be acting merely focuses on how they perpetuate institutionalised norms. Accordingly, the types of questions legal pluralists should pose are: how are legal subjects constructed by law? and what laws do legal subjects construct as law?

Autopoiesis

> If a tree falls down in the woods and there is no one there to hear it, does it make a sound?[190]

Kleinhans and Macdonald posit a way of reconstructing law similar to the 'autopoietic' theory developed by **Günter Teubner** (1992). Teubner's notion is based upon the 'social systems theory' of German sociologist **Nikolas Luhmann** (1927–1998).[191] In the Greek language, the term 'autopoiesis' means 'self-creation' or 'production'. In short, legal autopoiesis describes the internal operations of self-production of a system (what Hart calls 'secondary rules'). Legal communications occur when people express their behaviour in terms of being lawful/unlawful or legal/illegal. This means that '[a]ny act or utterance that codes social acts according to the binary code

---

186 Klienhans and Macdonald, supra note 176, p. 36.
187 Ibid.
188 Bano, supra note 182, p. 306.
189 Klienhans and Macdonald, supra note 176, p. 36.
190 Bishop George Berkley (1710/1982). Treatise Concerning the Principles of Human Knowledge. London: Hackett Publishing Co.
191 Günter Teubner (1992) 'Two Faces of Janus: Rethinking Legal Pluralism'. 13(5) Cardozo Law Review, 1443–1462.

of lawful/unlawful may be regarded as part of the legal system, no matter where it is made and no matter who made it'.[192] Binary codes, such as lawful/unlawful, also distinguish which communications are to be included within the boundaries of the legal system and which are not. Consequently, by drawing upon an autopoietic approach, law is perceived as a communication system of meaning. As explained by **Michael King**, 'structural coupling' occurs when two communication systems become environments for one another:[193] the communication systems of 'law' and 'religion', for example. Recently **Russell Sandberg** concluded that Luhmann's social systems theory overcomes 'fundamental flaws' of legal pluralism[194] and that legal pluralists need to turn their attention 'from groups to discourses'.[195] The call to abandon the pluralistic endeavour in favour of social systems theory (or autopoietic approach to law), however, rests on three key misunderstandings. These are:

1   First, just as autopoiesis views the legal system as one of meaning, under Klienhans and Macdonald's critical legal pluralist approach, 'law' is 'meaning and not machinery'.[196] Concepts such as the 'state', 'society' and 'community' are all 'hypothetical institutions within which subjects are shaped by the knowledge they inherit, create and share with other subjects';[197]

2   Second, unrealistic power is granted to communication (or legal) systems. As remarked by Raymond Wacks, by adhering to social systems theory, '[d]o we not risk abandoning the power of human beings to control and change legal norms?'[198] In other words, one could purport: 'the "system" (rather than its vanguards) told me to do it!';[199] and

3   Finally, an autopoietic system of law *is* anti-humanist because it focuses on phenomena or essences rather than the creativity of the human imagination. Luhmann asserts that people are simply 'living systems',[200] leading King to contend that 'systems, not people, make society happen'.[201] Sandberg maintains that social systems 'theory does not deny human agency; it simply does not focus on it'.[202] This argument is unconvincing, however, as the creative capacity of the human mind enables even the most rigid of social systems to be bent,

192 Michael King (1993) 'The "Truth" About Autopoiesis'. 20(2) *Journal of Law and Society*, 218–236, p. 218.
193 Michael King (2009) *Systems, Not People, Make Society Happen*. Edinburgh: Holcombe Publishing (e-book).
194 Russell Sandberg (ed.) (2015) *Religion and Legal Pluralism*. Farnham: Ashgate; see also Brian Tamanaha (2001) *A General Jurisprudence of Law and Society*. Oxford: Oxford University Press, p. 171.
195 See also Günter Teubner (1997) 'Global Bukowina': Legal Pluralism in the World Society' in Günter Teubner (ed.) *Global Law Without a State (Studies in Modern Law and Policy)*. Aldershot: Dartmouth Publishing Co., p. 4.
196 Klienhans and Macdonald, *supra* note 176, p. 42.
197 See Benedict Anderson (1991) *Imagined Communities: Reflections on the Origin and Spread of Nationalism*. London and New York: Verso.
198 Wacks, *supra* note 4, p. 230.
199 See the discussion of the 'Milgram experiment' in the previous chapter.
200 Michael King and Chris Thornhill (2003) *Niklas Luhmann's Theory of Politics and Law*. Basingstoke: Palgrave Macmillan, p. 7.
201 King (2009), *supra* note 193.
202 Sandberg (2015), *supra* note 194, p. 255.

broken or defeated. The privilege Kleinhans and Macdonald's approach provides the imagination of the human mind is what is novel about their pluralistic approach. Thus, the potential emancipatory, liberating and creative power of law is realised as it is connected to the imaginations of each and every person. Supporting 'Hui Neng's Flag Story' in Buddhist philosophy, that makes the following point:

> [t]wo monks were arguing about the temple flag waving in the wind. One said, 'the flag moves'. The other said, 'the wind moves'. They argued back and forth but could not agree. The Sixth Ancestor said, 'gentlemen! It is not the wind that moves; it is not the flag that moves; it is simply your mind that moves!

For Kleinhans and Macdonald, as law(s) exist in the human imagination, any attempt to capture law (in an objective sense) will fail because it has no independent existence outside the human mind. Kleinhans and Macdonald point to dialogical approaches, first articulated by Taylor, as best representing how critical legal pluralism accounts for law-inventing and law-abiding subjects (see 'communitarian' section earlier).[203] Legal subjects are to be viewed as a multiplicity of selves as perceived by the 'modern self'. For these reasons, Kleinhans and Macdonald's approach turns the traditional agency pattern inside out. Unlike doctrinal perspectives, whereby legal subjects abide the law of the state and have liberties endowed upon them from above, the image of law is shifted to a different symbolic signifier, from a linear representation to that of a circle by viewing legal subjects as law inventing, not simply law abiding. In Macdonald's words,

> the theory of legal pluralism raises the hypothesis that non-conforming behaviour . . . may be the reflection of an alternative conception of legal normativity.[204]

Indeed, Macdonald argues that '[t]he best response to the inevitable existence of informal [law] is not to suppress it. . . [r]ather . . . give it a productive institutional outlet'.[205] For these reasons, the best account of law is one that is, consequently, autobiographical.[206]

One criticism with Kleinhans and Macdonald's approach is the presupposition that, by locating law within the human imagination, law exists everywhere. Melissaris, for example, argues that a critical legal pluralist approach produces only a 'vague and wholly indeterminate conception of legality'.[207] His criticism is based upon the assumption that every person, out of approximately seven and half billion in the world, will have their own ideas about what law is. As a result, it is questioned whether Kleinhans and Macdonald's critical legal pluralist approach says anything meaningful about the concept of law.

---

203 Taylor (1994), *supra* note 28.
204 Macdonald, *supra* note 159, p. 79.
205 Macdonald, for example, provides an excellent autobiographical account of his personal experiences of Canadian Public Law in: Roderick A. Macdonald (2002) *Everyday Lessons in Law*. Montreal & Kingston: McGill-Queen's University Press, p. 28.
206 *Ibid.*
207 Melassaris (2009), *supra* note 169, p. 5.

Subjective legal pluralism

Kleinhans and Macdonald contend that there are many ways of conveying critical legal pluralism in the legal imagination. They call for an autobiographical account of law, and their approach is inspired by the methodologies of 'hermeneutics'[208] and 'narratives'.[209] One limitation of Kleinhans and Macdonald's legal pluralist approach is that many judges, lawyers and academics cannot draw upon their own personal experiences to provide an autobiographical account of various situations of legal pluralism.

In order to overcome this limitation, a 'subjective' legal pluralist perspective seeks to capture and analyse the narrative account of legal subjects. Sandberg contends that there is currently a 'subjective turn' in academia and contemporary identity politics,[210] that 'people are constantly constructing and re-constructing their identities':[211] after all, as Taylor states: 'each of us has an original way of being human'.[212] The stance of 'positionality'[213] correlates with this perspective as there is some form of knowledge 'out there' (for example, a legal subject's perspective of law), but this is open to change, and it depends on the person being asked. A subjective pluralistic perspective contends that 'law, like religion, is whatever we believe' it to be:[214] in other words, 'law' is a subjective belief. In this sense 'law' is phenomenological. A phenomenological approach stresses the analysis and interpretation of the structure of conscious experiences of the relationships of people.[215] A subjective legal pluralist perspective follows the dialectical–phenomenological tradition of the German philosopher Hegel.

Georg Wilhelm Friedrich Hegel (1770–1831)

Hegel's account of the 'master–slave dialectic' has been highly influential (see Taylor, earlier). In his immensely difficult work the *Phenomenology of Spirit*, Hegel attempts to outline the fundamental nature of human knowledge.[216] He contended that our consciousness is always pulled in two directions. On the one hand, our senses give us a certain kind of evidence about the world, whereas on the other, categories of

208 Used to interpret human action, see Kristen Gjesdal (2011) *Hermeneutics*. New York: Oxford University Press.
209 Used to interpret how people construct narratives and stories, see Catherine Kohler Riessman (1993). *Narrative Analysis*. Newbury Park: Sage Publications.
210 Russell Sandberg (2014) *Religion, Law and Society*. Cambridge: Cambridge University Press, p. 161.
211 Russell Sandberg (2014a) 'The What, the Why and the How' in Marie-Claire Foblets *et al.* (eds.) *Belief, Law and Politics: What Future for a Secular Europe?* Farnham: Ashgate, p. 113.
212 Taylor (1989), *supra* note 30, p. 30.
213 Bartlett, *supra* note 112.
214 Amy Codling (2015) 'What Do You Believe? Taxonomy of a Subjective Legal Pluralism' in Russell Sandberg (ed.) *Religion and Legal Pluralism*. Farnham: Ashgate, 199–212, p. 210.
215 Robert Sokolowski (2000) *Introduction to Phenomenology*. Cambridge: Cambridge University Press.
216 Georg Wilhelm Friedrich Hegel (1807/1976) *The Phenomenology of Spirit*. Oxford: Oxford University Press.

language tell us what the input of our senses means. The fact that a difference exists between our perceptions and the meaning we give to them gives rise to a feeling of uncertainty or scepticism. We strive to find sense and certainty in situations, and this entails a learning process. Hegel calls this process *understanding*, the highest mode of consciousness.[217] Hegel asserted that there is a collective component to knowledge, and this influences communitarian aspects of Taylor's work.[218] Another influence for Taylor is the philosophies of novelist Iris Murdoch,[219] who in *Metaphysics as a Guide to Morals* claimed that consciousness is itself internally structured by a notion of the 'good', and she advocated a return to the Platonic forms.[220] Murdoch endorsed the moral phenomenology of the Hegelian tradition and crucially stated that '[w]e need a moral philosophy in which the concept of love, so rarely mentioned now by philosophers, can once again be made central'.[221]

Suggested reading

O Singer, Peter (2001) *Hegel: A Very Short Introduction*. Oxford: Oxford University Press.

● Taylor, Charles (1993) *Human Agency and Language*. Cambridge: Cambridge University Press.

● Murdoch, Iris (1993) *Metaphysics as a Guide to Morals*. New York: Penguin Press.

The idea that law, like religion, is a subjective belief requires the narrative accounts of people to be captured and analysed to interpret elucidations of normativity. I conducted a study, for example, in the form of focus group discussions with Muslim women who wear a *hijab* (headscarf) or *niqab* (face veil) and live in Britain to capture their views and experiences of the practices because currently excluded from the debates on religious dress in Britain are the voices of women who wear the garments themselves.[222] From my findings, I define wearing of a *hijab* or *niqab* as a 'subjective' normative order. The practice is subjective (rather than institutionalised) when a woman describes herself as having freely chosen to adopt the practice and merges it with her other legal, cultural, gendered, religious, professional and similar commitments. Accordingly, the human imagination is influenced by a person's relationships with others and holds a consciousness and creative capacity to overcome normative conflicts (between, for example, cultural, gendered, religious and Western values *etc.*). One limitation of a subjective legal pluralist approach is that the role of a researcher is reduced to interpreting people's normative interpretations: it provides the subjective

---

217 R. A. Stern (2013) 'Taylor, Transcendental Arguments, and Hegel on Consciousness' 34(1) *Hegel Bulletine*, 79–97.

218 Charles Taylor (1972) 'The Opening Arguments of the Phenomenology' in Alasdair MacIntryre (ed.) *Hegel: A Collection of Critical Essays*. Notre Dame: Notre Dame University Press, 151–188.

219 Maria Antonaccio (2001) 'The Virtues of Metaphysics: A Review of Iris Murdoch's Philosophical Writings'. 29(2) *Journal of Religious Ethics*, 309–335.

220 Iris Murdoch (1993) *Metaphysics as a Guide to Morals*. New York: Penguin Press.

221 Iris Murdoch (1965/2015) On 'God' and 'Good' in Marjorie Grene (ed.) *The Anatomy of Knowledge*. London: Routledge Library Editions: Epistemology.

222 Amy R. Jackson (2012) *What Is Law? Unveiling a Subjective Legal Pluralism*. University of Reading: Unpublished Thesis.

study, analysis and interpretation of subjective norm(s). However, this criticism does not undermine the impact of the approach to scholars studying situations of legal pluralism. This is because a subjective legal pluralist, following the stance of positionality, acknowledges that they are unable to transcend their own perspective but that they can improve it by stretching the imagination to identify and understand the perspectives of others.

A subjective legal pluralist perspective contends that 'law' is subjective belief. A legal subject's belief in law can be accessed from a person's narrative account and is subject to daily construction, re-construction, re-imagination and resistance. Subjective legal pluralism overcomes Melissaris's critique of legal pluralism, because it is not that *each* and *every* person in the entire world will have their own beliefs about what the law *is*; rather, there are sets of established ideas that people draw upon to create their own notions of normativity and identity. This is because, as law is located in a person's narrative account or discourse, with only so many words to describe what exactly it *is* (or what it means to people), an authoritative statement of what law is does not have to be endowed on people from above or by a certain set of institutions; indeed, it could be other people or come out of a person's own imagination or be a mixture of all of these influences. What then becomes important, as Macdonald contends, is the *reasons* behind rules:[223] hence the importance of the question, what do *you* believe 'law' is?

Legal pluralist analyses of *Begum*

Institutional legal pluralism

An analysis of *Begum* influenced by an institutional legal pluralist approach draws the attention to the multiplicity of normative orders that operate, interact and conflict with one another. For example:

- Several laws can be seen to be *operating* in *Begum*, such as the human rights law on which Shabina's initial claim was made and the school's uniform policy;
- The case also details particular *interactions* between the various normative orders, for instance, *Begum* upholds a situation of weak legal pluralism by enabling headteachers and governors of schools discretion over their uniform policies; and
- Finally, an institutional legal pluralist analysis of *Begum* also discusses the *conflicts* occurring between normative orders, like the conflicting interpretations of Islamic scholars on the issue of religious dress.

Cultural and religious legal pluralism

In his cultural and religious analysis of *Begum*, for example, Shah highlighted the unequal power relationship between state law and unofficial, personal and religious law. He contended that *Begum* 'illustrates that we are working within a framework

---

223 Macdonald (2002), *supra* note 205, p. 89.

which attempts to cope with legal pluralism in the context of Britain's cultural diversity'.[224] His analysis exposed that the challenge for the English legal system 'is the recognition of difference'.[225]

Critical legal pluralism

Kleinhans and Macdonald assert that the questions legal pluralists should be posing are: how are legal subjects constructed by *and* what do legal subjects construct as law(s)? In answer to these questions related to *Begum*, the case illustrates *how* arguments about veiling are being constructed: as one of human rights under Article 9 ECHR. For this reason, *Begum* forms part of the 'juridification'[226] process of the practice of veiling. The legacy of *Begum* is, however, that claims of religious dress will no longer be successful under the provisions of Article 9.

A critical legal pluralist analysis of *Begum* also questions *what* Shabina viewed as law. However, under the doctrinal image of law, Shabina's voice is silenced: *her* reasons for wearing a *jilbab* are unknown, so they can only be assumed. At the time of her case, it was reported by the media that Shabina stated that 'I feel it is an obligation upon Muslim women to wear the *jilbab*, although there are many other opinions'.[227] By describing wearing a *jilbab* as something she *ought* to do, Shabina appears to elucidate that, for her, there is an element of normativity behind the practice.

Subjective legal pluralism

The findings from my subjective legal pluralist study suggest English courts should adopt a different approach in religious dress cases, such as *Begum*. Judges in religious dress cases should scrutinise a religious believer's narrative account – either by writing a witness statement or by making one in court, thus establishing situations of weak legal pluralism, as state law would privilege legal subjects' narrative accounts. Supporting a situation of weak legal pluralism does not undermine a subjective pluralistic perspective because it acknowledges that normative orders (such as state law, religious law, human rights law and uniform policies or employment dress codes) are all law(s) that exist in the human imagination: what law is depends on a person's subjective belief, accessible in a legal subject's narrative account. The reasoning of judges in cases such as *Begum* could be enriched and enhanced to include an element of self-reflection as to the reasons *why* they have come to their particular decision.

Suggested reading

Institutional legal pluralism

● Griffiths, John (1986) 'What Is Legal Pluralism?' 24 *Journal of Legal Pluralism (and Unofficial Law)*, 1–56.

---

224 Prakash Shah (2005) *Legal Pluralism in Conflict: Coping with Cultural Diversity in Law*. London: Glasshouse Press, p. 177.
225 *Ibid.*
226 Russell Sandberg (2011) *Law and Religion*. Cambridge: Cambridge University Press.
227 BBC News. 'School Wins Muslim Dress Appeal'. 22nd March 2006. Available at http://news.bbc.co.uk/1/hi/education/4832072.stm.

Cultural and religious legal pluralism

- Shah, Prakash (2005) *Legal Pluralism in Conflict: Coping with Cultural Diversity in Law*. London: Glasshouse Press.

Critical legal pluralism

- Kleinhans, Martha-Marie and Roderick Macdonald (1997) 'What is a Critical Legal Pluralism?' 12(2) *Canadian Journal of Law and Society*, 25–46.

Subjective legal pluralism

- Codling, Amy R. (2015) 'What Do You Believe? Taxonomy of a Subjective Legal Pluralism' in Russell Sandberg (ed.) *Religion and Legal Pluralism*. Farnham: Ashgate. Chapter 12.

Key points

The present chapter has provided the following:

- An introduction to the chronology of the development of seven legal perspectives; and
- Outlining the response of one legal perspective to another (for example, positivist reactions to natural law theory and critical legal perspectives to doctrinal legal perspectives).

How these different legal perspectives could be integrated into your own legal discussions is considered in the second part of TCAL, focused on thinking critically about law in practice.

Part II

Thinking critically about law in practice

Chapter 4

Putting critical thinking into legal practice

Chapter contents

Chapter aims

The three key aims of the present chapter are to:

● First, introduce the critical reading and writing process;
● Second, explain how to develop and demonstrate your critical thinking in the classroom; and
● Finally, describe beyond the classroom, extra-curricular activities.

While studying at university, you are expected to develop critical thinking skills to gain a deeper understanding of subjects, such as law. Being able to demonstrate the ability to think critically is an important part of the transition from studying at school or college to the expectations at university. The chapters in the previous part of TCAL focused on the theoretical and philosophical aspects of thinking critically about law. The following four chapters concentrate on practical guidance for improving your critical thinking process. This chapter looks at ways to put critical thinking into legal practice, ranging from unpacking the critical thinking process to providing techniques for how to read and write critically. The following chapter, Chapter 5, focuses on how to demonstrate critical thinking in assessments, from essays to exams, working as a team and creating posters and presentations. Chapter 6 then moves on to discussing an important aspect of thinking critically about law, namely how to think ethically about law, before discussing working experience as well as working in the legal field and other career options.

Ahead of this, the present chapter is divided into three parts. The first builds upon the discussion in Chapter 2 to introduce TCAL's critical thinking process. In Chapter 2 it was concluded that thinking critically about law is a two-stage process, and a working definition is that it is an 'intellectually disciplined process of thought whereby you develop your own informed legal opinions or arguments on a particular issue'. This part of the chapter outlines how to read legal authorities (see introduction) and write about them as part of the critical thinking process. The second part of the chapter discusses how to develop and demonstrate your critical thinking abilities in the classroom, whether it be in a lecture, seminar, tutorial or round-table discussion session. Finally, your critical thinking beyond the classroom is considered as part of extra-curricular activities.

I. The critical reading and writing process

Reading and writing should be conducted together rather than in isolation from one another. The process of critical reading and writing can be broken down into bite-sized, manageable chunks. The first is to consider the question: what is 'legal research'?

Legal research

Critical thinking 'is one of the more sophisticated forms of thinking as it requires you to undertake a good deal of *research*'.[1] But what is 'research'?

---

1 Lisa Webley (2016) *Legal Writing*. London: Routledge, p. xiii. Emphasis added.

What *is* 'research'?

In order to answer your essay or problem question effectively, you will need to research the relevant law. Basically, there are two types of research:

1   **Applied research**: the ability to identify and find relevant sources; and
2   **Analytical research**: the ability to analyse, criticise, sift and synthesise to gain a better understanding of a legal phenomenon.

Critical thinking as a two-stage process

As previously stated in Chapter 2, thinking critically about law is a two-stage process that involves six steps:

Stage 1: Applied research

1   Knowing the information: such as the relevant statutes, cases and academic opinions on a legal topic;
2   Understanding information: for example, what does the wording of a statute mean? How has it been interpreted by the courts?
3   Application: applying the relevant statute, case or academic opinion to the question posed;

Stage 2: Analytical research

4   Critical analysis: split up an argument into its component parts and weigh up the pros and cons;
5   Reflection: reflect on whether an argument works; and
6   Creative thinking: produce a new and original argument solution.

King George III is reputed to have said that lawyers do not know much more information than other people, but they know better where to find it. The observation is still true today, as the sources of law become more and more diverse, and it is still an essential part of legal learning that you know how and where to find relevant law.[2] For academic study and professional life, supporting evidence for your arguments or claims must come from 'reputable sources' (or 'authorities'). A reputable source is basically one that

* has credibility: it can be believed with a high degree of certainty;
* is based on research, first-hand knowledge or expertise; and
* is recognised in the field or academic discipline as an authority.[3]

Tip

Critical thinking requires concentration, so try to find a quiet place to study and do it in 'bite-sized' chunks, giving yourself breaks between.[4]

---

2 Glanville Williams (2016) *Learning the Law*. London: Sweet & Maxwell, p. 206.
3 Stella Cottrell (2011) *Critical Thinking Skills: Developing Effective Analysis and Argument*. Basingstoke: Palgrave Macmillan, p. 129.
4 Open University (2008) *Thinking Critically*. Milton Keynes: Open University p. 11.

Primary and secondary sources

Reputable sources can be 'primary' or 'secondary' source materials. Primary source materials are basically those that originate from the time and place of the events being investigated. Primary sources include

● witness testimonies;
● responses of participants to surveys and questionnaires.

For example, as TCAL includes responses of law students, teachers and those in the profession, it includes primary research. Primary source materials are original materials that 'present and report discoveries, or share new ideas or information'.[5] In comparison, secondary sources are materials that are written or produced about an event, usually sometime later. These include

● books, articles, web pages; and
● papers and reports using the results of surveys, questionnaires and experiments.

You need to examine secondary sources critically to decide whether, for your purposes, they are likely to be sufficiently

● trustworthy
● recent
● relevant.[6]

Secondary sources, therefore, are books, journal articles or pieces of journalism about 'someone else's opinions, research or writings' that are written in 'hindsight'.[7]

Online sources

Today, a whole host of sources are accessible online. Simply google[8] a particular phrase (such as 'murder UK') and a whole list of results appears. The first to come up is usually a link to Wikipedia.[9] Although it is a great website for aiding your own knowledge and understanding, it is not a reputable authority. Therefore, it should not be cited in your assessments. In comparison to Google, useful legal databases include

● **WestLaw:** national and European legal sources, as well as an international law section.

---

5 Martin Cohen (2015) *Critical Thinking Skills for Dummies*. Chichester: John Wiley & Sons Ltd, p. 185.
6 Ibid., p. 128.
7 Ibid., p. 185.
8 Colloquial phrase meaning to put a search term into the Google search engine: www.google.co.uk.
9 *Wikipedia.com*.

- **LexisNexis:** global provider of legal, regulatory and business information.
- **JStor:** a digital library of primarily journals in the humanities.
- **Heinonline:** an essential international journal archive.

Avoid!

Avoid citing sources such as Wikipedia in your assessments.

The critical thinking process

As previously stated in Chapter 2, Stella Cottrell views critical thinking as a 'process of thought'.[10] TCAL's critical thinking process, involving five key steps, is set out as shown in Figure 4.1 in what follows.

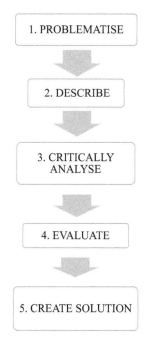

Figure 4.1 The critical thinking process of thought

1 Problematising

First, a key part of the critical thinking process is 'problematising'. Problematising a question or issue requires you to turn it into or regard it as a problem requiring a solution. When first reading an assessment, ask yourself: what is the main problem or issue(s) at hand? Then consider how and in what ways the issue you have found could be resolved.

---

10 Cottrell, *supra* note 3, p. 2.

EXAMPLES

The following are examples of problematising assessment questions.

Table 4.1 Problematising questions

Question	Problem
1 'Consider and critically evaluate the ruling of the Privy Council in *Attorney General for Jersey v Holley* [2005] 3 WLR 29'.	• Should the mental characteristics of the defendant be taken into account when assessing the objective of loss of self-control?
2 'Discuss whether the absence of a human rights commission undermines the effectiveness of the Human Rights Act 1998 in protecting individual rights'.	• Should a human rights commission be established to protect individual rights?
3 'Critically assess the concept of the failed state in international law'.	• Is the concept of the failed state useful for international lawyers?

2 Describing

Second, once you have clearly identified the key problem or issue(s) at the heart of the question, then you need to set out, in simple terms, the main points of the argument(s). To do this, you need to provide a definition of any key terms. This is important because '[i]t is typical in critical thinking to define any terms used in the line of reasoning that might be open to more than one interpretation'.[11]

EXAMPLES

Following the examples provided in Table 4.1, the following are key terms:

1 **'Loss of self-control' and 'mental characteristics':** Under section 54(1)(c) of the Coroner's and Justice Act 2009 to avoid a conviction of murder it must be proven that a person of the defendant's age and sex with the normal degree of tolerance and self restraint would have acted the same way.

2 **'Human Rights Commission':** The Equality and Human Rights Commission (EHRC) was established by the Equality Act 2006 and has responsibility for the protection and enforcement of equality in England, Scotland and Wales.

3 **'Failed state':** Gerald Helman and Steven Ratner assert that the indicative element of the 'failed state' is the collapse of state institutions (such as the police and judiciary), resulting in the paralysis of government and the break-down of law and order.[12]

11 *Ibid.*, p. 170.
12 Gerald B. Helman and Steven R. Ratner (1992) 'Saving Failed States'. 89 *Foreign Policy*, 3–20, p. 5.

3 Critically analysing

Third, critically analysing the question or problem requires you to break down an argument or idea to its component parts and assess or weigh up the pros and cons. For example, what are the advantages and disadvantages of the new defence of loss of self-control under the Justice and Coroner's Act 2009? What are the costs and benefits of the EHRC since it was established in 2006? Are there any pros and cons that can be attributed to Helman and Ratner's concept of the failed state?

4 Evaluating

Fourth, evaluation (or assessing the validity of an argument) also requires an element of 'weighing up' the pros and cons. However, this is not just an evaluation of the pros and cons of the argument or idea as required for the previous step of critical analysis but also of your own thinking: what are the limits of your own thoughts?

5 Creative thinking/solution to a problem

Finally, in the creation of a solution, 'you must be willing to *creatively* reconstruct your thinking'.[13] To do this, consider: is there anything that particularly stands out to you that needs to be considered in the solution to the problem or issue(s)? Do you agree or disagree with the opinions or suggestions put forward by others to resolve the problem at hand, whether academics or institutional bodies such as the Law Commission? One way to resolve a problem or issue is to agree with a solution put forward by an academic or institutional body, such as the Law Commission. For example, the Law Commission extensively considered what mental characteristics of a defendant should be taken into account in its recommendations for the establishment of the new defence of loss of self-control.[14] You could simply agree with such recommendations when putting forward a solution to a problem or issue(s). However, this type of resolution is more fitting with 'applied' rather than 'analytical' research (see earlier) because you are simply applying recommendations to form a solution rather than creating your own. To demonstrate you have thought 'creatively' about resolutions, there are two creative outcomes that you can achieve. The first is creating a quasi-original solution in the form of putting two previously suggested or recommended solutions together or, second, creating your own original solution.

a. Creating a quasi-original solution

To put forward a quasi-original solution rather than simply applying the recommendations of others (such as the Law Commission) to a problem or issue(s), you look at two or more suggestions, evaluate (or weigh up their pros and cons) and then put together a new solution based on the best parts of both. For example, one

---

13 Richard Paul and Lisa Elder (2014) Critical Thinking: Tools for Taking Charge of Your Learning and Your Life. London: Pearson, p. 1.
14 For example, see Law Commission (2004) Partial Defences to Murder. Law Comm No 290. London: TSO.

reason for introducing a Human Rights Commission stated by Former Education Secretary Baroness Shirley Williams is the importance of educating citizens about the need of protecting their rights.[15] While the education of the public about their rights is important, the establishment of a Human Rights Committee (such as the EHRC) would have better built-in institutional support mechanisms to support those whose rights have been infringed – rather than an individual simply knowing that their rights have been infringed, they can be supported to bring a claim, such as by being able to have the power to 'act as a friend of the court'.[16]

b. Creating an original solution

Alternatively, creating an original solution requires the 'ability to produce work that is both novel (i.e. original, unexpected) and appropriate (i.e. useful, adaptive concerning task constraints)'.[17] For example, rather than supporting Helman and Ratner's concept of the failed state, putting forward the alternative concept of 'collapsed government' is an original solution to the problem and one that does not carry the negative connotations of the concept of the 'failed' state. In this regard, critical thinking 'provides more than creative solutions; it provides emancipation and a sense of freedom'.[18] An emancipatory (or liberating) sense of freedom comes from the ability to think for yourself and create your own solutions to perceived problems or issues.

A. Critical reading

To become a 'critical reader', you need to understand not only the meaning of a text but also how the subject matter is portrayed, recognising how each and every text is unique to every author.

> Taking a reflective, enquiry-based approach to your study helps you delve deeper into the materials you read. It requires you to keep an open mind, ask questions and reflect on the answers you might come up with.[19]

As illustrated in Figure 4.2, the learning process is circular and generally consists of four elements. These are:

1   **Asking questions:** What do you need to know to answer the question?
2   **Investigating solutions:** What solutions have been put forward by others, and what would you like to suggest to resolve the problem or issue?

---

15 Hansard (3rd November 1997) *Human Rights Bill*, at 844.
16 Joint Committee on Human Rights (2002) 'The Case for a Human Rights Commission'. 6th Report. VI (HL 67; HC 489).
17 Robert J. Sternberg (ed.) (1999) *Handbook of Creativity*. Cambridge: Cambridge University Press, p. 3.
18 Mike Metcalfe (2006) *Reading Critically at University*. London: Sage Publications, p. 3.
19 Open University, *supra* note 4, p. 11.

Figure 4.2 Enquiry-based learning cycle[20]

3   **Creating knowledge:** What sources do you need to look at to answer the question?
4   **Reflecting on results:** Has what you have found helped answer the question and/or resolve the issue(s) at hand?

TASK NINE   *Capturing the author's position[21]*

Read through the following passage and identify the author's position:

● Skim quickly over the passage and note your first impressions, aiming to capture the author's position (the main message of the passage).
● Follow up your rapid read by closer reading to check if you were right. This will give you an idea of how accurately you capture the message when reading at speed.
● Check your answers in the 'Task answers' section.

Passage

Barristers do not have much direct contact with their clients, but it is possible to find a legal job that suits your preferences for court work. However, if an aspiring barrister wants to spend time in court, they need to select a field carefully to see if the work patterns associated with it match their preferences. Every field is different. Criminal lawyers may spend most of their time in court. Tax lawyers, on the other hand, may spend only a day a month or less in court. Advocacy work requires less time in a court than in the office.

20 Ibid.
21 Cottrell, *supra* note 3, p. 39.

Further activity

- Read the introduction and conclusion of three books or articles on your subject.
- How well does the introduction present the author's position: is it clear what the author is trying to persuade you to accept?
- How well does the conclusion make it clear what the author's position is?

How to make 'critical' notes

When reading, it is always useful to make notes on the materials that you are looking at. These can be handwritten or typed up on your laptop or iPad. Note-taking is important because

- If done properly, it breaks up continuous reading tasks into many shorter reading sessions alternated with note making. This rests the eyes and parts of the brain involved in reading. This is especially useful given the intense reading activity used for critical reading.
- Many people find it easier to recall information that is written in their own handwriting.
- Selecting what to write rather than writing everything means greater interaction with the material, which helps us recall it in the future.[22]

Tip

Develop the habit of using a particular coloured pen, such as red, blue or green, for any copied text such as quotations. This will make it immediately obvious to you, when you read your notes at a later date, what you have copied and what are your own words.[23]

TASK TEN   *Making 'critical' notes*[24]

Use the following table the next time you read a source material to direct the notes you make about it.

Topic:
Source: (e.g. author, book title, page number, edition)
Description:

---

22 Ibid., p. 153.
23 Ibid., p. 154.
24 Open University, *supra* note 4, p. 18.

Claim:	
Evidence for claims: Strengths:	Weaknesses:
Questions and Queries:	
Links to Other Topics:	

In addition to using the example table to organise your notes on a source material, you may wish to make your own notes on a text, organising the information in a more visual way and using your own words, as shown in the following example:

Example

There are various ways of dividing up the domain of justice. The most famous distinction is probably Aristotle's, between 'corrective justice' and 'distributive justice'. Corrective justice involves rectification between two parties, where one has taken from the other or harmed the other. Modern discussions of corrective justice often occur within the context of arguing about appropriate standards within tort law and contract law. Distributive justice involves the appropriate distribution of goods among a group ('giving each person his or her due'). Most of the better-known modern discussions of justice, which usually treat justice primarily as about the proper structuring of government and society, are basically discussions of distributive justice.[25]

Brian Bix (2009) *Jurisprudence, Theory and Context*. London: Sweet & Maxwell

p. 107

Aristotle = <u>*Corrective Justice*</u> +   <u>*Distributive Justice*</u>

Rectification between parties: *Distribution of goods among a group.*

- *Where someone has taken from the other; or*
- *harmed the other.*

Modern discussions on the structuring of gov & society.

Tort & Contract law contents.

---

25 Paragraph taken from Brain Bix (2009) Jurisprudence, Theory and Context. London: Sweet & Maxwell, p. 107.

How to read legal authorities

As stated in the introduction, there is a 'hierarchy of legal authorities' (see earlier). These are: first, treaties, conventions and statutes, that state the wording written by international bodies (such as the UN) or Parliament, which are, second, interpreted by the courts such as the ECtHR or Supreme Court in case law and, finally, commented upon by academics and institutional bodies (such as the Law Commission). How to read each of these sources critically is considered in the following sub-sections.

1 Legislation

The first source on the hierarchy of legal authorities is international and domestic legislation, such as treaties, conventions and statutes. It is important that you actually find and read for yourself the wording of legislation rather than looking at it from secondary sources such as journal articles, textbooks and lecture notes. If you do not have a statute book on a particular field of law, legislation can be found online by the following ways. First, UK legislation is published on the official www.legislation.gov.uk website. Here you can browse all legislation on the database or search for a particular piece by entering the title or key words. Second, you can search for legislation on legal databases such as www.legalresearch.westlaw.co.uk and www.lexisnexis.com/uk/legal. Both Westlaw UK and LexisLibrary offer browse and search facilities for current as well as historic versions of legislation. Third, there are a number of ways to search for international and European legislation. One of the easiest ways is to use the Westlaw international database (www.westlawinternational.com/), although you can look on the institution's own website, such as the UN treaty collection (www.treaties.un.org) and EUROPA, the main website for the European Union (www.europa.eu). Once you have located the particular international, European or domestic legislation you are looking for, paraphrase the meaning of an article of a treaty or convention or section of a statute using your own words, as shown in the following example.

EXAMPLE

Article 9 ECHR

1   Everyone has the right to freedom of thought, conscience and religion; this right includes freedom to change his religion or belief and freedom, either alone or in community with others and in public or private, to manifest his religion or belief, in worship, teaching, practice and observance.

2   Freedom to manifest one's religion or beliefs shall be subject only to such limitations as are prescribed by law and are necessary in a democratic society in the interests of public safety, for the protection of public order, health or morals, or for the protection of the rights and freedoms of others.

Paraphrase

Article 9 ECHR provides for private, personal beliefs and religious affiliations. It is a qualified right, which means that prohibitions on the right to religious freedom are not justified unless there are special grounds that validate an interference (such as health and safety concerns or contraventions to the rights of others).

TASK ELEVEN *Paraphrasing a statute*

Following this example, paraphrase the meaning of the following section using your own words.

Section 76 of the Sexual Offences Act 2003: Conclusive presumptions about consent

(1)   If in proceedings for an offence to which this section applies it is proved that the defendant did the relevant act and that any of the circumstances specified in sub-section (2) existed, it is to be conclusively presumed –

    (a)   that the complainant did not consent to the relevant act, and
    (b)   that the defendant did not believe that the complainant consented to the relevant act.

(2)   The circumstances are that –

    (a)   the defendant intentionally deceived the complainant as to the nature or purpose of the relevant act;
    (b)   the defendant intentionally induced the complainant to consent to the relevant act by impersonating a person known personally to the complainant.

2 Cases

The second source of legal authorities is cases. English law is known to have a 'common law system', which means that law is derived from customs and judicial precedents rather than legislation. The common law system is beneficial because it combines local customs and case law. It can be detrimental, however, if judges overstep their capacities to become judicial lawmakers. The courts form an important part of the legal system, as '[w]ithout a set of institutions to enforce legal rules, there would be no legal system'.[26]

---

26 See Edgar Bodenheimer (1976) 'Hart, Dworkin, and the Problem of Judicial Lawmaking Discretion'. 11 *Georgia Law Review*, 1143–1172.

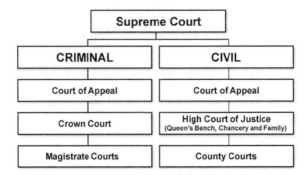

Figure 4.3 The English court system

Doctrine of precedent

There is a hierarchy of the English court system (Figure 4.3). Sitting above the domestic courts are international and European courts (such as the International Court of Justice and ECtHR). The courts at the top of the English hierarchy are more important than the lower courts. The doctrine of judicial precedent is based on the principle that *like cases should be treated alike*. This means that once a decision has been reached on a particular case, it stands as good law and should be relied upon in other cases.[27]

The *ratio decidendi* of a case

The '*ratio decidendi*' of a case is the reason or rule of law on which a judicial decision is based. Importance of the *ratio decidendi* (or simply '*ratio*') of a case cannot be understated. If you remember anything about a case rather than the facts, it should be the *ratio*. The *ratio* of a case should be stated as simply and succinctly as possible.

EXAMPLE

Brief facts of *R v Miller*[28]

The defendant fell asleep while smoking a cigarette in a squat and simply moved to another room when the mattress he was sleeping on caught alight. The question of law put to the court was whether the *actus reus* of the offence of arson was present when the defendant accidentally started a fire (under section 1 and 3 of the Criminal Damage Act 1971).

Ratio decidendi

• A person who initiates a sequence of events and then fails to do anything to stop it should be regarded as having caused the whole sequence in a single continuing act.

---

27 Emily Finch and Stefan Fafinski (2015) *Legal Skills*. Oxford: Oxford University Press, pp. 131–132.
28 [1983] AC 161.

Additional Example

See the 'Case Summary of *Begum*' in the first part of the previous chapter.

TASK TWELVE *Reading* Brown

Read the case of *R v Brown*[29] and complete the following case summary points:

Brief facts of the case:	•
Ratio decidendi:	•
Summary of the majority opinion:	• • •
Summary of the dissenting opinion(s):	• •
Your own opinion of the case:	•

Paraphrasing a quote from a judgment

When using a quote from a judgment in your work to evidence a point or argument you are making, where possible, paraphrase the statement using your own words, as this helps demonstrate the you have thought critically about what you have selected. Where possible, include references to additional authorities (such as other cases) to further support the point or argument you are making. See what follows for an example.

Example

For example, Lord Mackay R v *Adomako*[30] stated that

> the ordinary principles of the law of negligence apply to ascertain whether or not the defendant has been in breach of a duty of care towards the victim who has

---

29 [1994] 1 AC 212. See the alternative judgment of the case in the UK Feminist judgments project: Robin Mackenzie (2010) 'Feminist Judgment of R v Brown' in Rosemary Hunter, Clare McGlynn and Erika Rachley (eds.) *Feminist Judgments: From Theory to Practice*. Oxford: Hart Publishing. Chapter 14.
30 [1994] 3 WLR 288; [1995] 1 AC 171 at p. 187.

died. If such a breach is established the next question is whether that breach caused the death of the victim. If so, the jury must go on to consider whether that breach of duty should be characterised as gross negligence and therefore a crime.

From Lord Mackay's judgment, in order for a charge of gross negligence manslaughter to succeed, four elements need to be established. These are:

1   That there is a duty of care between the defendant and victim (*Capro Industries v Dickman*);[31]
2   The duty of care has been breached (*R v Litchfield*);[32]
3   Risk of death – causing D to die (*R v Misra & Srivastaava*);[33]
4   and a jury finds the breach serious enough to be a crime (*R v Bateman*).[34]

TASK THIRTEEN — *Paraphrasing a quote from a judgment*

Following this guidance, in your own words, paraphrase the following quote from a famous judgment.

Lord Aitken's neighbour principle in *Donoghue v Stevenson*:[35]

You must take reasonable care to avoid acts or omissions which you can reasonably foresee would be likely to injure your neighbour. Who, then is my neighbour? The answer seems to be persons who are so closely and directly affected by my act that I ought reasonably to have them in contemplation as being affected when I am directing my mind to the acts or omissions which are called in question.

(at para 80)

_____

_____

_____

_____

Suggested reading

- Barnard, Catherine, Janet O'Sullivan and Graham Virgo (2011) *What About Law? Studying Law at University*. London: Hart Publishing.

31 [1990] 2 AC 605 per Lord Bridge at pp. 617–618.
32 [1998] Crim LR 507.
33 [2005] 1 Cr App R 328 per Judge LJ at para 52.
34 [1925] 19 Cr App R 8.
35 [1932] AC 562.

3 Academic opinions

The third source of legal authorities is academic opinions. These can be in the form of journal articles or books or reports by institutional bodies such as the Law Commission. These are considered to be secondary rather than primary sources because they are commentaries written about legislation and case law (see what follows for a further discussion about primary and secondary sources). The following sub-section considers how to read journal articles, books and reports critically.

Journal articles

In what ways could your understanding of critical thinking be improved?

By reading articles/journals.[36]

Journal articles are an important resource because they keep up to date with any relevant changes in the law. They are also a source of academic criticism and commentary on legal developments. Practitioner journals contain shorter articles than academic ones but are published on a weekly or bi-weekly basis. They provide useful information that is easily digestible and are a great place for you to start to understand a particular area of law, legal argument or issue. Practitioner journals include:

- New Law Journal
- Solicitors' Journal
- Law and Society Gazette

In comparison to practitioner journals, generalist academic journals contain lengthy articles based upon extensive academic research. Key generalist journals are:

- Legal Studies
- Oxford Journal of Legal Studies
- Modern Law Review

In addition to generalist journals, specialist journals focus on academic commentary and review of a particular area of law. For example:

- Criminal Law Review
- Family Law
- Journal of Legal Pluralism

Most of these journals can be found via the legal databases listed earlier (see the 'Online Sources'). These secondary sources offer comments, reviews and criticisms of the law but are not 'law' themselves. Browsing the abstracts of journal articles is a useful way of gaining a sense of recent research conducted in a particular field. Article abstracts summarise the main point(s) of the argument, research methods, findings and conclusions stated in the article. Reading these will help you decide whether the article is one that is worth reading in depth. Sections that summarise the background literature of the study can provide important leads for your own research.[37]

---

36 First-year student, Cardiff.
37 Cottrell, *supra* note 3, p. 128.

TASK FOURTEEN *Reading a journal article*[38]

Complete the following table when next reading a journal article to aid your critical understanding of the text.

Names of author(s):
Full title of article:
Full title of journal:
Year published: **Month:**
Volume number: **Issue number:**
Hypotheses: What is the paper setting out to prove? Are research hypotheses supported?
What is the theoretical position underlying the research? Type of theory?
What is the key literature used as background to the article or paper?
Which research methods are used?
What kind of sample is used?
Key results: Key conclusions and recommendations
Strengths of the research: How does it advance our understanding of the subject or how to research it? Are there appropriate hypotheses, sample sizes or types, controls or variables, recommendations? Consideration of ethics?
Weaknesses of research: In what ways is it limited? When and where would it not apply? What, if any, are the flaws in the research, in the hypotheses, research design and methods, sample size and type, conclusions drawn on the basis of the results?

Books

In comparison to the up-to-date nature of journal articles, due to the developing nature of law, books are generally out of date as soon as they are published. Textbooks collect, analyse and criticise the law in particular areas.[39] Examples of textbooks are:

● **Land law:** Mark Thompson and Martin George (2017) *Thompson's Modern Land Law.* Oxford: Oxford University Press.

38 *Ibid.*, p. 157.
39 Finch and Fafinski, *supra* note 27, p. 150.

- **Public law:** Mark Elliot and Robert Thomas (2017) *Public Law*. Oxford: Oxford University Press.
- **Criminal law:** Jeremy Horder (2016) *Ashworth's Principles of Criminal Law*. Oxford: Oxford University Press.

You should be given a range of textbooks to look at in your course materials and find the textbook that best suits you. Make sure that the textbook you are using is the latest edition so that it includes any changes or developments in the law. In comparison to textbooks, cases and materials books contain a collection of key cases, statutes, reports, articles and book extracts on a particular area of law. Such books are useful, as they collect and arrange key materials from one area of law. However, the extracts that are considered key are selected by the book's editor, so some other materials may be missing. Therefore, simply relying on such books demonstrates uncritical thinking. Examples of cases and materials books are:

- **Public law:** Helen Fenwick and Gavin Phillipson (2016) *Text, Cases and Materials on Public Law and Human Rights*. London: Routledge.
- **European law:** Paul Craig and Gráinne de Búrca (2015) *EU Law Text, Cases and Materials*. Oxford: Oxford University Press.
- **International law:** David Harris and Sandesh Sivakumaran (2015) *Cases and Materials on International Law*. London: Sweet & Maxwell.

Monographs are detailed written studies of a single specialised topic. They offer greater depth on a subject area than a general textbook. Examples of monographs on the subject of criminal law include:

- Martin Innes (2003) *Investigating Murder*. Oxford: Oxford University Press.
- Itzhak Kugler (2002) *Direct and Oblique Intention in Criminal Law*. Abingdon: Ashgate.
- Richard Stone (1999) *Offences Against the Person*. London: Cavendish.

Many students, generally those who are 'strategic learners' (see Introduction), learning information on a 'need to know basis' for assessments and exams, use revision guides. Used in the right way, these guides can be useful as the first stage in the building blocks of your knowledge on a particular area of law or actually used as a revision aid at the end of your studies, before an exam. They should not be used in isolation from attending lectures and seminars and undertaking your own research on a particular topic. This is because revision guides do not provide the level of depth required on a topic to demonstrate critical thinking.

When reading a book, whether it is a textbook or monograph, first, undertake a preliminary skim of the material, as this will give you a feel for what information it contains. The best place to start this is to look at the book's contents. Second, scan the introduction for an indication of the author's overall argument. Finally, scan the concluding chapter, as it summarises the main arguments contained in the book.

TASK FIFTEEN *Reading a book[40]*

Next time you read a book, use this table to aid your creation of concise critical notes.

Names of author(s):	
Full title of book:	
Author of chapter:	
Chapter title:	
Year published:	**Edition:**
Publisher:	**Place published:**
Theoretical position or type of theory?	
Essential background information	
Key arguments:	
Reasons and evidence to support the arguments:	
Strengths of the arguments:	
Weaknesses in the argument:	
Comparison or contrast with other sources:	

Reports

Reports include official publications by governmental bodies (such as the Law Commission) as well as independent bodies (such as charities like Amnesty International). The Law Commission, for example, was established under the Law Commission Act 1965 with the purpose of promoting law reform. Its reports provide reasons and insights behind the need for law reform in a particular area. One of the key areas of reform in criminal law in recent times has been to the partial defences of murder, resulting in the enactment of the Coroner's and Justice Act 2009.

B. Critical writing

This section discusses the mechanics of how to write critically. Writing critically, as opposed to descriptive writing (which involves simply setting out the definitions of

---

40 Cottrell, *supra* note 3, p. 156.

key terms or ideas), requires you to refuse to accept the conclusions of others without undertaking an evaluation of the arguments and evidence they provide. Rather than factually explaining the law as it is, critical legal writing requires you to add a value judgment, persuade others to agree with your argument or point of view and/or evaluate a particular area or topic of law.

Samples of uncritical and critical writing

In what ways could your understanding of critical thinking be improved?

[T]o look at numerous amounts of papers that are successful in thinking critically, where certain paragraphs or statements are highlighted to demonstrate what good critical thinking is.[41]

The following are examples of uncritical and critical writing taken from my own work as a student.

EXAMPLES

Uncritical statements

Accordingly, in his dissent, Lord Carswell argues that 'the distinction between the two [limbs] of the objective [requirement] is difficult and confusing'[42] for jurors to comprehend. In light of [this] discussion of the dissenting argument in *Holley* is supported.

61% So evaluate – do you agree?

In any event, at least '[t]he fundamental human rights of individuals. . . [are now] *common place* in international law'.[43] Fundamentally, 'individuals are participants . . . part and parcel of the fabric of international law'.[44]

66% Ok, but what does this mean? What is the effect of participation? How does it differ from the classical view? What, if anything, does it add to that view? . . . I consider that there was considerably more scope for critical analysis than you undertook, and I have included some relevant questions/comments on the hard copy.

Critical statements

In conclusion, I submit that legally and constitutionally the absence of a Human Rights Commission does not undermine the [Human Rights] Act (HRA). There is no need for a statutory body to be established to give effect to the Act. This is because there is no assurance a Commission would have

---

41 Second-year student, Reading.
42 *Attorney General for Jersey v Holley* [2005] 3 WLR 29.
43 *R v Bow Street Magistrate ex parte Pinochet (No 3)* [2000] AC 147 per Lord Millet at p. 275.
44 Rosalyn Higgins (1994) *Problems and Process: International Law and How We Use It.* Oxford: Clarendon Press, p. 16.

sufficient power to enforce the law or enough influence to put an end to Parliament's 'illegitimate' acts of conflicting laws, which *do* undermine the HRA in the protection of individual rights.

64% Excellent critical evaluation of a commission in your conclusion

'Three particular points are raised in order to critically analyse Koskenniemi's main argument'.[45] First, the critique of the analogy of the international system to municipal law is examined to relay that more emphasis could be given to this point. This is followed by analysing Koskenniemi's omissions to discuss both the development of Security Council legislation and future creation of a pluralistic system of international law'.

80% [I]t is clear that the candidate is highly engaged in the issues raised by the Koskenniemi article and is sufficiently confident to engage in a highly critical and challenging analysis of the work.

Table 4.2 provides additional examples of descriptive ('uncritical') statements compared to those that are critical.

Table 4.2 Deceptive and critical statement examples

Descriptive Statements	Critical Statements
1 Murder in England is an offence under the common law of England and Wales.	Murder is undermined in England and Wales by being an outdated common law offence rather than being provided a current and modern meaning in statute law.
2 The definition of oblique settled in *R v Woollin*[46] is that a jury is not entitled to find the necessary intention for murder unless death or serious bodily harm was a virtual certainty of the defendant's act.	Following the *Woollin* direction, juries are provided the opportunity to expand or contract the reach of the law of murder by being entitled to find, or not, the defendant's intention to kill or cause serious injury as the case may be.
3 The Court of Appeal held in *R v Bree*[47] that 'a drunken consent' to sexual intercourse 'is still a consent' to the act.[48]	Cases such as *Bree* demonstrate that section 74 of the Sexual Offences Act 2003 requires a more drastic interpretation: a drunken consent is *not* a consent when the person is very drunk.[49]

45 Martti Koskennieni (2005) 'International Legislation Today: Limits and Possibilities'. 23 *Wisconsin International Law Journal*, 61–87.
46 [1998] WLR 382.
47 [2007] EWCA Crim 804.
48 *Ibid.*, per Sir Igor Judge at para. 32.
49 Shlomit Wallerstein (2009) '"A Drunken Consent Is Still Consent" – Or Is It? A Critical Analysis of the Law on a Drunken Consent to Sex Following *Bree*'. 73(4) *The Journal of Criminal Law*, 318–344.

TASK SIXTEEN — *Developing 'critical' statements*

Following these examples, change these descriptive statements into critical ones:

Descriptive Statements	Critical Statements
1 The modern meaning of recklessness was established in *R v G*.[50]	
2 Lord Lane stated the test for dishonesty in *R v Ghosh*.[51]	
3 In the law of negligence, the neighbour principle stated by Lord Atkin in *Donoghue Stevenson*[52] provides the basis on which to resolve questions of duty of care.	
4 The case of *R v Brown*[53] demonstrates that the defence of consent cannot be relied upon for section 47 and 20 offences under the OAPA 1861.	
5 The House of Lords held in *Begum*[54] that there had been no infringement of the student's right protected under Article 9(1) ECHR, and, if there had been such an infringement, this was justified under Article 9(2).	
6 The British government triggered Article 50 of the Treaty on the European Union 2007 on 29 March 2017.	

How to make an argument

In what ways could your understanding of critical thinking be improved?

Teaching people how to counter argue, rather than just saying you have to do it. Show how it can be dome smoothly, because a lot of people find it difficult to be precise.[55]

When you think critically, you weigh up all sides of an argument and evaluate its strengths and weaknesses. Thinking critically about an argument entails

- actively seeking all sides of an argument;
- testing the soundness of the claims made; and
- testing the soundness of the evidence used to support the claims.[56]

---

50 [2004] 1 AC 1034.
51 [1982] 3 WLR 110, at p. 1064.
52 (1932) AC 562.
53 Brown, *supra* note 29.
54 *R (on the application of Begum) v Headteacher and Governors of Denbigh High School* [2007] 1 AC 100; [2006] UKHL 15; [2006] 2 WLR. 719; [2006] HRLR 21.
55 Final-year student, Cardiff.
56 Open University, *supra* note 4, p. 7.

But, what is an 'argument?' In everyday language, an 'argument' suggests poor communication, a difficult relationship, hard feelings and, possibly, aggression; however, this is not the case with an argument as part of critical thinking. For the purposes of academic study, an argument can be broadly defined as:

> **Argument:** the identification of one or more claims supported by logical reasoning and evidence which lead to a justified conclusion.[57]

In relation to critical thinking, an argument is 'akin to [a] legal argument or reasoned debate, not quarrelling; its purpose is to validate knowledge claims'.[58] An argument is when reasons are presented to support a position or point of view. If other people accept your reasons, they are more likely to be persuaded by your point of view. The key ingredients of an argument are a position or point of view, an attempt to persuade others to accept that point of view and reasons given to support the point of view. The word 'argument' is used in two ways in critical thinking. These are:

● **The overall argument** (or thesis): is composed of contributing arguments, or reasons. The overall argument presents the other's position. The term 'line of reasoning' is used to refer to a set of reasons, or contributing arguments, structured to support the overall argument.

Table 4.3 Overall and contributing arguments examples[59]

The Overall Argument	Contributing Arguments
1 Longer prison sentences should be introduced.	• Heavy punishments deter crime. • Current penalties for crime are too lenient and do not deter criminals. • Since prison sentences were reduced, crime has increased. • Victims need to see that perpetrators of crimes are punished.
2 Increasing the prison sentences is not the way to prevent crime.	• Crime was high even when punishments were more weighty. • Prison teaches people how to be more skilled as criminals. • Criminals who are imprisoned are more likely to take part in increasingly serious crime when released. • Most crime is committed by people who are illiterate and lack work-related skills. • Education rather than punishment is required.

57 Cottrell, *supra* note 3, p. 29.
58 Metcalfe, *supra* note 18, p. 14.
59 *Ibid.*

- **Contributing arguments** (or reasons): individual reasons as referred to as 'arguments' or 'contributing arguments'.[60]

Examples of overall and contributing arguments are set out in Table 4.3.

TASK SEVENTEEN *Overall and contributing arguments*

Following the first example supplied, write the contributing arguments to these overall arguments:

The Overall Argument	Contributing Arguments
1 The law of murder in England and Wales is in urgent need of reform.	• • •
2 There is no need for consent to sexual intercourse to be reformed under the Sexual Offences Act 2003.	• • •
3 The law is not currently satisfactory in relation to religious dress in the UK.	• • •

EXAMPLE

Set out below is a famous and influential legal argument. The argument is effective not because it is brilliant and complex but because it offers simple answers to difficult questions.

Defending human rights[61]

The big issue: In practice, arguments for the 'reality' of certain human rights hinge on legal precedents. This makes sense, because the idea of a 'right' is essentially legal. The US Bill of Rights is one text people often think of when they consider the issues of human rights. It's the name for the first ten amendments to the United States Constitution that attempt to limit the central government's power and guarantee some personal freedoms, such as that unfortunate one about the 'right to keep and bear arms'.

---

60 Cottrell, *supra* note 3, p. 38.
61 Cohen, *supra* note 5, p. 331.

The flaw: Legal rights are all very well, but they only survive because people think that the law is protecting something more fundamental. The law has to fit with public perceptions of what's right and wrong.

Alas, people's views differ so widely that what is a 'human right' in one place is completely illegal in another, and *vice versa.* Eating your grandparents seems pretty bad to most people today (rather chewy, for a start!), but some historical societies considered it the responsible thing to do. In some countries today, homosexuality is against the law, and gays are barred from jobs and can even be executed. In the UK and lots of other places, by contrast, homosexuals are protected from workplace discrimination and can marry and adopt children.

TASK EIGHTEEN   *Justice for TV watchers*[62]

Have a look at this argument:

In Britain, every household pays the same amount for their televisions, regardless of how rich the household is or how many TVs they have – or how much they watch them! Surely this is unfair. Instead, TV should be made a subscription service so that those who watch the most pay the most. This wouldn't only be fairer but could also bring in more revenue.

Which of the following arguments uses the same principle as the previous one?

(Hint: The question isn't about whether the argument is a good one but rather the structure).

a)   Things should only be available free to people if they can't afford them otherwise.

b)   Discounts on bus and train fares should be available to people who travel the most.

c)   Rich people should pay a surcharge on their houses to help the poor who don't have a home at all.

d)   Television channels should be funded by general taxation so that the richer you are, the more you pay.

e)   Internet sites that make a lot of money from advertising shouldn't be able to charge for access.

- See the answer in the 'Task answers' section.

62 Ibid., p. 74.

Suggested reading

○ Garner, Bryan A. (2013) *Legal Writing in Plain English*. London: University of Chicago Press.
● Samuelson, Pamela (1984) 'Good Legal Writing: Of Orwell and Window Panes'. 46(1) *University of Pittsburgh Law Review*, 149–169.

II. Critical thinking in the classroom

Traditionally, university students know little about a subject area prior to learning about it in the classroom. Usually, the first phase of the learning process takes place during a large lecture or small-group teaching in the form of a seminar or tutorial. This is to be followed up by the second stage of the learning process that involves you undertaking your own independent research on a field. Starting the critical thinking process at the very start of your understanding will only benefit the outcome.

Critical listening and speaking skills

Critical thinking requires good communication skills. The classroom environment provides a space for you to develop your critical listening and speaking skills. First, critical listening skills require you to know what information to listen to and retain. This will help you with time- and information-management skills, as rather than noting down information verbatim you will have a better idea of what to note down and when. Second, critical speaking skills are developed in the classroom environment so that your questions, answers and queries can be put across in an effective manner. Ways to develop your critical listening and speaking skills during lectures, seminars and tutorials as well as round-table discussions are considered in turn.

Lectures

Lectures introduce you to a particular subject or topic. They generally 'make a point, then expand upon the point and then provide evidence to back it up and further explanation to illustrate it'.[63] Attending lectures is important because

● they outline the 'basics and essentials' provided of the subject;
● a lecturer can emphasise important aspects, in comparison to a textbook; and
● a lecturer can bring textbooks up to date.[64]

One way to make it easier to think critically during a lecture is to read the required reading for the lecture prior to it rather than afterwards. You can find the reading for lectures in your course handbook.

---

63 Webley, *supra* note 1, p. 79.
64 Williams, *supra* note 2, p. 80.

Note-taking

As part of the listening critically process, you do not need to write down word for word what is stated during a lecture – in any event, it will be hard to keep up with everything that is said! Instead, consider the overall meaning of the point being discussed and take note of any supporting evidence. So rather than noting everything, make a judgment as to what is important to note down and why it is. Another way to write quick and effective lecture notes is to use shorthand.

Shorthand[65]

H Husband	W Wife
T Tenant	L Landlord
Er Employer	Ee Employee
C Claimant	D Defendant

TASK NINETEEN	*Self-assessment checklist after a lecture*[66]

Complete the following table after you attend your next lecture.

	(Please tick one or more columns as appropriate for each row)	This is what I did	I would have liked to do this but didn't manage it	I didn't think this necessary	This just was not possible for me	I'll do this next time
1	I've looked through my notes to check I understood everything.					
2	I've re-read the handout and made extra notes on it to help me to remember what seemed clear at the time.					
3	I've jotted down questions where, I don't yet understand something, onto notes and handout for me to follow up later.					

---

65 Ibid., p. 81.
66 Adapted from Phil Race (2010) *Making Learning Happen*. London: Sage Publications.

(Please tick one or more columns as appropriate for each row)	This is what I did	I would have liked to do this but didn't manage it	I didn't think this necessary	This just was not possible for me	I'll do this next time
4 I've filed my notes carefully where I can find them easily later.					
5 I've followed up reading suggestions made by the lecturer.					
6 I've noted down for revision purposes the three most important things from the lecture.					
7 I've looked back at the course outline to see how this lecture fits into the programme as a whole.					
8 I've looked forward on the course outline to see what will be coming up in the next lecture.					
9 I've made sure that the intended learning outcomes for the lecture are included in or with my notes.					
10 I've checked how well I reckon I've already achieved each of the intended learning outcomes and marked these decisions against the outcomes for future reference.					
11 I've asked my fellow students for their reactions to what we learned in the lecture.					

(Please tick one or more columns as appropriate for each row)	This is what I did	I would have liked to do this but didn't manage it	I didn't think this necessary	This just was not possible for me	I'll do this next time
12 I've compared my notes with those of at least one fellow student and added in things I missed.					
13 I've self-tested myself on what I remember from the lecture.					

Seminars or tutorials

In what ways could your understanding of critical thinking be improved?

Encouraging debate in tutorials is helpful, but that depends on everyone preparing for discussion.[67]

Following a lecture, it is useful to consolidate the information you received by preparing for the seminar or tutorial on the topic. Using the information you have received to answer questions on the topic will help you in the critical thinking process. Seminars and tutorials usually take place in small groups and provide you with the opportunity to discuss and ask questions about the materials you are learning. Tutors act as facilitators of the sessions, being led by you rather than supplying you with another mini-lecture on the topic. They are designed to help you establish your own informed thinking on a particular topic or issue. During the session, you may find other students who agree with your point of view or perspective and others that disagree. Either way, try not to take this personally; rather remember that it is your argument or line of reasoning that is being accepted or rejected by others. Just because you cannot get someone else to agree with your point of view does not mean that it is not valid. Consider the reasons someone disagrees with your perspective.

Tip

The importance of proper preparation for tutorials cannot be understated. For example, feedback from my own student report form in my first year states

Better preparation for tutorials would help Amy to feel able to express her views and apply a more critical approach to the topics discussed

67 Lecturer, Reading.

After the tutorial, it is likely that some of the discussion points will stick in your mind. These could be those that you agree with or, just as likely, those you disagree with. So engaging in debate with your fellow students provides you with an opportunity to practice and strengthen your critical thinking skills. It also helps you think through particular issues that might come up during assignments and examinations.[68]

Reluctance to critique experts

Stella Cottrell asserts that 'some students can find it alien, rude or nonsensical to offer criticism of practitioners they know to be more expert than themselves . . . Researchers and lecturers expect students to question and challenge even published material'.[69] The problem is highlighted in the following exchange between a student and teacher:

Student: I want you (the expert) to give me the answers to the questions; I want to know the right answer.
Teacher: I want you to become critical thinkers, which means I want you to challenge the experts and pursue your own answers through active reasoning. This means lots of hard work.[70]

To this Cottrell states '[i]f it was not hard work' to think critically and develop your own answers to the questions posed, then 'you would not be developing your thinking skills into new areas'.[71]

TASK TWENTY *Using critical thinking in a tutorial*[72]

Imagine that your tutor presents your group with the following set of words and asks you to consider the question: 'What is an emotion?' Spend a few moments considering how you think this question could be answered.

nausea	hunger	love
disgust	fear	jealousy
cowardice	being startled	joy
feeling cheerful	nostalgia	sadness

● See 'Task answers' section for the result.

---

68 Open University, *supra* note 4, p. 27.
69 Cottrell, *supra* note 3, p. 12.
70 Brenda S. Cowell, *et al.* (1995) 'Coping with Student Resistance to Critical Thinking: What the Psychotherapy Literature Can Tell Us'. 43(4) *College Teaching*, 140–145, p. 140.
71 Cottrell, *supra* note 3, p. 12.
72 Open University, *supra* note 4, p. 26.

TASK TWENTY-ONE	*Assessing the quality of teaching*[73]

Select a class you are in now or that you have taken in the past that you think involved high-quality teaching. What precisely does/did the teacher do that led to deep, long-term learning? What can you do as a student to deepen your learning in every class you take? How can you learn as you learned in the best class you took by taking initiative in all your other classes? Or do you think the teacher determines how much you learn and you have little to do with it?

Problem-based learning feedback sessions

Traditional teaching methods follow the lecture, seminar or tutorial and independent research model. Problem-based learning (PBL) provides an alternative approach to learning. Here, rather than learning information and then being assessed on your answer to a problem scenario, either in an written assessment or exam, you are provided with a problem upfront to work through the solution in order to gain understanding and a critical insight into the topic or area of law. Following the Maastricht 'seven-jump' model, PBL operates in several major steps, summarised into three major stages, namely: first, the initial stage, second, the PBL stage and the final stage:

1   First, in the initial stage, the first activity is the formation of a group, which is presented with a problem and begins to analyse and understand the issue(s) involved, formulating learning objectives of the task, identifying knowledge gaps and defining concepts to be learned; then

2   Second, the PBL stage requires independent self-study to identify a solution to the problem and the reasons it is adequate to resolve the issue, this is then shared with the other members of the group; and

3   Finally, the group presents the findings during round-table discussions to a facilitator to evaluate their work.[74]

The PBL process aids the development of critical thinking skills by enabling you to have a practical insight into the problem at hand. The problem and solution are context specific. 'Critical' aspects to consider while undertaking PBL include:

●   Who is the problem addressing?
●   Why do they want to know the information?
●   What evidence is there to support this solution, and what are its pros and cons?

As well as providing you with a practical exploration of a problem and its resolution, PBL also lends itself to reflection on the outcomes.

---

73 Paul and Elder, *supra* note 13, p. 165.
74 Alias Masek and Sulaiman Yamin (2010) 'Problem Based Learning Model: A Collection from Literature'. 6(8) *Asian Social Science*, 148–156.

III. Extra-curricular activities

In addition to attending lectures, seminars and tutorials or roundtable discussions and undertaking your own research on a topic, you can also develop and practice your critical thinking skills by being involved in extra-curricular activities. Such activities include pro-bono work and mooting. These are considered in the following sub-sections.

Pro-bono work

'Pro-bono' work is short for the Latin phrase *pro bono publico* that refers to professional work that lawyers undertake without payment. As well as being a rewarding experience in its own right, pro-bono experience is something that potential employers (legal or otherwise) increasingly look for evidence of during your academic studies. This is because they help you develop the practical skill graduates need to develop early in their careers.

Citizen's Advice Bureau training

If you have a social conscience, you can satisfy it handsomely (and can earn useful experience and points for your curriculum vitae in the process) by taking part in your local legal advice centre or Citizen's Advice Bureau (CAB).[75] The CAB is an independent charity that runs throughout the UK and provides people with free and independent advice on issues ranging from debt to employment and benefit rights. You may have the opportunity to train as an assessor in a local CAB. If the opportunity to train as an assessor is not available at your institution, simply contact your local bureau to ask about availability (even before you start your undergraduate studies).[76]

Mediation training

Mediation is an effective way of resolving disputes without the parties involved needing to attend court. The process involves an independent third party – a mediator – to help both sides come to an agreement that both are happy to accept. Training opportunities as a mediator are available through charitable organisations such as Resolve.[77] Resolve is a national mediation provider that provides easy access to the service. Such training provides the opportunity to develop mediation and communication skills and gain a National Open College Network qualification in mediation.

Other pro-bono activities

A number of pro-bono opportunities are available at a number of institutions and charities on a yearly basis. These can be accessed through your school or department or by you getting in contact with the organisation, either prior to, while you are at or

---

75 Williams, *supra* note 2, p. 238.
76 Available at www.citizensadvice.org.uk.
77 Available at www.resolveuk.co.uk.

after graduating from university. Pro-bono opportunities are generally available with charitable organisations such as:

- Amnesty International (www.amnesty.org.uk)
- Age Concern (www.ageuk.org.uk)
- Red Cross (www.redcross.org.uk)

Mooting

Mooting provides an excellent opportunity to enhance your practical application of critical thinking skills. 'Mooting' is the oral presentation of a legal issue or problem against an opposing counsel and before a judge. It involves the art of legal persuasion. Moots are legal problems in the form of hypothetical cases, which are argued by two student 'counsellors' (one leader, the other a junior) on each side, with a bench of judges (usually one or more).[78]

Mooting forms a compulsory part of certain law courses while remaining a voluntary opportunity in others. As well as providing evidence of advocacy skills, mooting also helps you develop confidence in public speaking and provides you with extra time to progress your independent research skills and practice how to put forward complex information succinctly as well as develop and practice your oral presentation skills. Other professional advantages of mooting, apart from practice, include:

- professional presentation skills;
- excellent etiquette;
- thorough research skills;
- good time-keeping;
- attention to detail;
- broaden legal knowledge; and
- affirmation of career goals.[79]

Fluency and clear enunciation are particularly important for the lawyer when our forensic practice is largely oral. Although you will be given training in this at the professional stage, there is no reason you should not participate in the activities of public speaking well before then. Taking part in moots will help you in these respects and also give you experience in the art of (legal) persuasion and putting your case succinctly and intelligibly. Mooting not only gives you practice in court procedure but helps to develop the aplomb that every advocate should possess.[80]

Tip

Remember to read the rules of the moot court competition itself as well as the rules of law you intend to submit to the court!

---

78 Ibid., p. 194.
79 Lisa Cherkassky, *et al.* (2011) *Legal Skills.* Basingstoke: Palgrave Macmillan, p. 316.
80 Williams, *supra* note 2, p. 194.

Mock trials

A mock trial differs from a moot in that it is a mock jury trial, with a jury and witnesses, not an argument on law. The proceedings may be somewhat humorous; witnesses may dress themselves up, and court and counsel wear robes (if procurable). The audience may consist of non-lawyers, who, of course, come simply to be entertained. Since the trial is unrehearsed, it requires a high standard of forensic ability on the part of the student 'counsel'; and the proceedings should either be leavened by humour or present an intellectual problem of the 'whodunit' type.[81]

Suggested reading

○ Snape, John (2010) *How to Moot: A Student Guide to Mooting*. Oxford: Oxford University Press.
◉ Baskind, Eric (2017) *Mooting: The Definitive Guide*. London: Routledge.
● Waller, Bruce (2011) *Critical Thinking. Consider the Verdict*. London: Pearson.

Key points

Three key points discussed in this chapter were that:

● The critical reading and writing process should be undertaken simultaneously;
● Critical thinking in the classroom requires you to develop your critical listening and speaking skills; and
● You can develop and practice critical thinking skills by being involved in extra-curricular activities, such as pro-bono work and mooting.

The next chapter discusses how you can put your critical thinking into practice in your assessments.

---

81 *Ibid.*, p. 203.

Chapter 5

Thinking critically about assessments

Chapter aims

The present chapter discusses thinking critically about assessments in three key ways:

- First, writing critical essays;
- Second, how to think critically about exams; and
- Finally, thinking critically about group assessments.

This part of TCAL focuses on thinking critically about law in practice. The previous chapter discussed how to put critical thinking into your legal practice as a student, first, in the reading and writing process; second, while in the classroom and finally, when participating in extra-curricular activities. The present chapter discusses how to think critically about assessments. It is important to recognise that 'assessments are a way of indicating your current level of knowledge and skill'.[1] Assessments can be undertaken by you working autonomously while writing critical essays and exams as well as by you working with others in a group. They can be in the form of essays or exams. This chapter is divided into three parts. The first part discusses suggestions and tips for thinking critically about essays, whether these be analytical or reflective ones or answers to problem questions. Longer essays, in the form of dissertations and theses, are also considered in this part. The second part of the chapter discusses how you can think critically about exams, either by writing an analytical essay or answer to a problem question under exam conditions or multiple-choice questions (MCQs). The final part of the chapter provides guidance and tips for how to think critically about group assessments. Two of the main ways your knowledge and understanding of the law are assessed by working in a group are by making presentations or designing posters. Some of the common challenges and pitfalls of group working are discussed in this part. Before discussing how you can think critically about your assessments, how do students and staff state that critical thinking could be demonstrated in your assessments?

How could critical thinking be demonstrated in your assessments?

'Using your own words to explain something or to express your point of view on a subject'.[2]

'Asking questions and finding problems and solutions other students may not'.[3]

'Arguments for and against something and then critique those arguments including your personal viewpoint'.[4]

'Engaging with appropriate and relevant academic commentary in the area in question, and synthesising that commentary. I often explain it as "who said what,

---

1 Lisa Webley (2016) *Legal Writing*. London: Routledge, p. 1.
2 First-year student, Reading.
3 Second-year student, Cardiff.
4 Final-year student, Cardiff.

and why? What do we think about those arguments? Are they persuasive? Why or why not? What are the counterpoints?" '5

Law students and staff state that critical thinking can be demonstrated in assessments in a variety of ways, from considering the arguments and perspectives of others to providing 'critical' rather than 'deceptive' statements in your work. Some of these comments and suggestions are considered in the present chapter.

I. Writing critical essays

In what ways could your understanding of critical thinking be improved?

Maybe if we had learned more tips for applying "critical thinking" in our essays.[6]

Essays are basically 'exercises in critical thinking'.[7] They are designed to provide you with the ability to demonstrate your knowledge and understanding of a problem or issue, drawing upon your critical analysis of and engagement with source materials and a range of theoretical perspectives. You are generally given time from a few months to a couple of days or hours to plan, prepare, write and review your argument in an essay. They generally have a word or page limit, which requires you to put your argument and answer forward succinctly and efficiently. This requires you to allocate the majority of space in your essay to a critical evaluation of the argument and sources of evidence you have found rather than simply describing them (see the previous chapter for a discussion of the distinction between 'critical' and 'descriptive' statements). There are different types of essays. The main types of legal essays are analytical essays, reflective writing and answers to problem questions. Longer analytical essays are called dissertations and theses. These main types of legal essays are discussed in this part of the chapter and now considered in turn.

A. Analytical essays

An analytical essay requires you to make an argument. The core aim of the argument is called a 'thesis'. The thesis is your main claim, stated succinctly in one sentence. The most difficult stage of writing is to begin.[8] Good planning and preparation often leads to a clear argument or thesis and a good grade for your work. Your planning and preparation then feeds into the key elements of the essay. These are: content, structure and language. Tips for incorporating these into the introduction, main body and conclusion of an essay are provided along with a discussion of how to turn these into longer analytical essays such as dissertations and theses.

---

5 Lecturer, Leeds.
6 Final-year student, Reading.
7 Stella Cottrell (2011) *Critical Thinking Skills: Developing Effective Analysis and Argument*. Basingstoke: Palgrave Macmillan, p. 181.
8 Webley, *supra* note 1, p. 15.

Planning and preparation

Planning and preparation are essential for writing a good analytical essay, as this will help you think critically about the content and structure of your work. There are several ways to go about planning and preparing your work. Listed here are preparation tools for you to plan and prepare for writing analytical essays in four easy steps:

1   First, checking the marking and assessment criteria for the essay;
2   Second, deconstructing the question so that you fully understand what is being asked;
3   Third, knowing the audience your answer or argument needs to address; and
4   Finally, visualising the structure and content of your essay by doodling, using mind maps, diagrams and charts.

These preparation tools are considered in the following sub-sections.

1 Checking the marking and assessment criteria

At the outset, it is important to be clear what the marker is expecting you to deliver in your assessments. As stated in the introduction, it is worth checking your school or department's marking criteria, particularly the requirements for a first-class degree (see Figure 1.2 First-class triangle). In addition to the overall criteria for attaining a first-class law degree, each assessment that you undertake should have its own marking guidance available to you. This is basically your ingredients list, a list of requirements to tick off when you are planning, formulating, writing and editing your work.

Assessment criteria for coursework assessed by essay[9]

In this assessment the student should write an essay plan and an essay in answer to the question. In the essay students should:

*   address the question asked;
*   identify the relevant areas with precision;
*   demonstrate a thorough knowledge and understanding of the relevant principles, including an analysis of them;
*   show evidence of research and reading;
*   present a coherent argument for the position taken;
*   present work that is well structured; and
*   correctly reference others' work where used.

2 Deconstructing the question

Before you start your essay, make sure that you deconstruct the question. Essays set for students are usually carefully worded so as to encourage a focus on a particular

---

9 Webley, *supra* note 1, p. 5. These are generic assessment criteria adapted from those used by the University of Westminster LLB for public law level 4 assessments (first-year undergraduate).

complex or controversial issue. Before launching into an essay, look carefully at the wording of the title so as to do the following:

- Tease out how many parts or sub-sections there are to the essay and relative weighting of each. If there is a word limit, consider how many words you can allocate to each section. This will, in turn, give you a sense of how much time to spend on each.
- Identify the main focus of the essay: what is it that the tutors want you to address? If it is not clear, it may become so once you have read around the subject.

Consider which theoretical perspective or schools of thought to call upon to explore the issues – you will be expected to engage in a 'critical dialogue' with these. Again, this may not be evidence until you start reading around the subject.[10]

Academic key words used in essay titles[11]

Analyse   Examine in very close detail; identify important points and chief features.

Compare   Show how two or more things are similar. Indicate relevance or consequences of these similarities.

Contrast   Set two or more items or arguments in opposition so as to draw out differences. Indicate whether the differences are significant. If appropriate, give reasons why one item or argument may be preferable.

Critically evaluate   Weight arguments for and against something, assessing the strength of the evidence on both sides. Use criteria to guide your assessment of which opinions, theories, models or items are preferable.

Describe   Give the main characteristics or features of something, or outline the main events.

Discuss   Write about the most important aspects of (probably including criticism); give arguments for and against; consider the implications of.

Distinguish   Bring out the differences between two (possibly confusable) items.

Examine   Put the subject 'under the microscope', looking at it in detail. If appropriate, 'critically evaluate' it as well.

Explain   Make clear why something happens or why something is the way it is.

Justify   Give evidence which supports an argument or idea; show why decisions or conclusions were made, considering objections that others might make.

---

10 Cottrell, *supra* note 7, p. 181.
11 Ibid., p. 182.

Outline	Give only main points, showing the main structure.
To what extent	Consider how far something is true or contributes to the final outcome. Consider also ways in which the proposition is not true, (the answer is usually somewhere in between 'completely' and 'not at all').

Do not simply tell the reader what you are interested in about the question; rather, tell them what they want to know. The question provides a good indication of what that is.[12] Everything in your essay should relate to answering the question. For instance, if the question asks you to 'compare and contrast' two different approaches, you will know that you have to devote some of your word count to one approach and some to the other. Likewise, if the question asks you to 'Assess the value of . . . to our understanding of. . .' you will have two points of focus in your answer.[13]

Example

Essay Title: **In light of decided cases, to what extent, if at all, do you consider the law of implied terms has permitted the court to promote the principles of fairness and justice in the resolution of disputes?**

Deconstruction of the Question: **To what extent** – consider how far it is true that the law of implied terms has helped the promotion of 'fairness and justice' in contract law.

Creating your own essay title

If you are set the task of creating your own essay title, you need to ensure that you set one that encourages you to work in the same way as for an essay title set by your tutor:

- Decide on the key issue that you want the essay to address;
- Ensure that there are multiple perspectives on the issue, each of which presents good arguments and evidence; and
- Ensure that there is a good range of quality reading material on different perspectives.

Also, beware of creating an essay title in which there is good reading material or evidence only for one perspective – this will not help you to demonstrate your own critical judgments well.[14]

3 Knowing your audience

Once you have deconstructed the question and are clear about what you are being asked to do, it is worth spending time planning and preparing your essays, as this will help you think critically about the content and structure of your work (see what follows). A key part of the preparation of critical writing is knowing your audience. The term 'audience' refers to whoever receives the message you are conveying by being

---

12 Martin Cohen (2015) *Critical Thinking Skills for Dummies.* Chichester: John Wiley & Sons Ltd, p. 206.
13 Open University (2008) *Thinking Critically.* Milton Keynes: Open University, p. 19.
14 Cottrell, *supra* note 7, p. 181.

a viewer, reader or listener either through conversation, books, television or other medium. Questions to consider are:

- Who are you writing this for?
  - A lecturer or tutor?
  - Another lawyer?
- What information do they need to know?
  - What do they already know?
  - How much detail do they require?
- Why do they need to know the information?
  - Are they assessing your knowledge and understanding on a topic?
  - Do they need to make a decision?

Types of audiences[15]

Here are some general approaches for particular types of writing aimed at specific audiences:

✓ **Academic studies and report writing:** A summary usually starts this kind of writing, and the main body of the report usually follows a set pattern: a section outlining the problem, a section that explains what people have already said about it and the all-important research methods section. This latter section is where the author explains why he's chosen to go about exploring the issue, whatever it might be, in a certain way. The bulk of the report then concerns an account of 'what was found out' using this method, and the final sections concern the conclusions being drawn from the research.

✓ **Journal articles:** Usually begin with a separate summary called the synopsis, and the main body starts off by looking at the context of the issue and examining several possible positions, all taken with very detailed referencing. The final paragraph may well be called 'Conclusion', and that's what it is – drawing together the threads of what has been discussed earlier. The synopsis and the conclusion of many academic journal articles are very similar.

4 Using visual aids

One way to think creatively about law is to get creative! When asked, many students report that they are 'visual learners'.[16] In response to this, a host of pictures, videos, charts and diagrams are used to convey information to you during lectures. Your visual learning does not need to stop there. In the planning and preparation stage of an essay you can always try to visualise the message, argument or answer you wish to convey. This sub-section discusses doodling, creating mind maps, diagrams and

15 Cohen, *supra* note 12, p. 209.
16 See Cedar Reiner and Daniel Willingham (2010) 'The Myth of Learning Styles'. 42(5) *Change: The Magazine of Higher Learning*, 32–35.

charts as a way to visualise the information you are learning and how to convey your message, argument or answer to your audience.

Doodling

Research into doodling suggests that people who doodle retain and can recall more information than those who do not.[17] Doodling can range from creating your own doodles on a topic to interpreting the images, diagrams and charts of others. Doodling can be useful during lectures, seminars, tutorials and round-table discussions and can also help your knowledge retention when planning, preparing and undertaking research for your essay. Doodling is effective while learning because '[l]anguage taps only a tiny proportion of the power of the human mind, and doodling can draw on some of the rest'.[18] As a law student, you do not need to show your doodles to anyone else if you do not want to. They just need to work for you by helping you be able to understand, retain and remember information. Simply draw whatever images or symbols come to mind when listening to or reading information.

Example

Figure 5.1 Law and justice doodle[19]

17 Jackie Andrade (2009) 'What Does Doodling Do?' 24(1) *Applied Cognitive Psychology*, 100–106.
18 Cohen, *supra* note 12, p. 231.
19 © Crystal Home/Shutterstock.

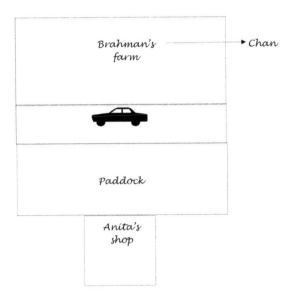

Figure 5.2 Land law doodle example

Tip

Doodling the scenario of a complex analytical issue or problem question can really help you to understand and grapple with the key legal issue. See an example from a Land Law problem question in what follows.

EXAMPLE

Figure 5.2 is a doodle of the following land law scenario:

Anita owns the freehold in a shop and a paddock behind it. Brahman, a farmer, is the freehold owner of a neighbouring plot of land which he bought six months ago from Chan. Anita has been parking a car on a small part of Brahman's land, which is immediately behind her paddock, which he says is preventing him from growing any crops. Brahman seeks your advice as to whether Anita can be required to remove her car, which she says she uses for her delivery business. Anita claims that she cannot conveniently park anywhere else, and she has been parking her cars there for more than ten years.

Mind maps

Another way to aid your understanding of a complex problem or issue and unleash your creative thinking is by mind mapping. Mind maps use doodling but in a more constructive way. Tony Buzan, the inventor of mind mapping, states that it is 'a technique based on memory and creativity and comprehension and understanding, so when [a] student . . . uses the mind map they are using their brain in a way their brain was designed to be used, and so the mind helps them in all learning and cognitive skills'.[20] The aim of a mind map is 'literally to map out your thoughts, using associations, connections and triggers to stimulate further ideas'.[21] The suggested steps to undertake to create your own mind map on a question or topic are set out in what follows.

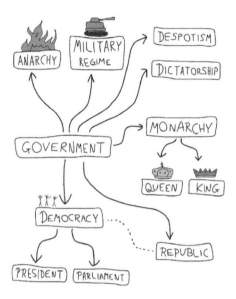

Figure 5.3 Mind mapping[22]

EXAMPLE

Seven steps to making a mind map[23]

1   First, turn your piece of paper sideways to maximize your creative space;
2   Second, place in the centre on the page a topic for your mind map using an image or a picture to convey the central idea, because this will help stimulate your imagination;
3   Third, use colours for your mind map, as this will aid your memory recall on what is on the page;
4   Fourth, connect your main branches of your map to the central image, and connect your second- and third-level branches to your images for the first and second levels, as this helps your brain to work by association to remember information more efficiently;
5   Fifth, curve your branches rather than using straight lines, as this will help stimulate your brain;
6   Sixth, only use one key word per line, as this adds power and flexibility to your map; and

20 Tony Buzan (2009) *The Mind Map Book: Unlock Your Creativity, Boost Your Memory, Change Your Life*. London: BBC Active, p. 20.
21 Cohen, *supra* note 12, p. 136.
22 © Tupungato/Shutterstock.
23 Available at www.tonybuzan.com/about/mind-mapping/.

7   Finally, use images throughout your mind map, as these images, like the central image of your map, help the brain remember and make associations.

Diagrams

If doodling and mind mapping are not for you, drawing diagrams provides another way to get creative about information to stimulate your understanding and memory. Rather than drawing pictures or images, diagrams are generally more technical, symbolic representations of information.[25] One of the most well-known diagrams is the spider diagram (see Figure 5.4 below), which basically works similar to mind mapping without the drawings. Simply place the topic, question or theme of the diagram in the centre of a piece of paper and write down everything that you can think of associated with that topic. You can make your spider diagram more complex if you wish by inserting another level to each of the 'legs' with words associated with the first level.

Charts

The key characteristic of a chart is that the information 'flows', with more focus given to the flow of the information than to the concepts the chart contains.[26] Charts help you to visualise what is happening in a situation and thereby aid your understanding of a process to find its flaws or weaknesses. Flowcharts are one useful example. Some flowcharts specify where things start ('inputs' into the system) or where they end (known as 'outputs'). Others may have no start or end points; rather, they describe the flow of information in terms of self-contained cycles.[27]

Figure 5.4 Law spider diagram[24]

24 © Marigranula/Shutterstock.
25 See William A. Kealy and James M. Webb (1995) 'Contextual Influences of Maps and Diagrams on Learning'. 20(3) *Contemporary Education Psychology*, 340–358.
26 Cohen, *supra* note 12, p. 140.
27 See Figure 4.3 'The English Court System' for an example of a flowchart.

Key elements of analytical essays

Once you have planned and prepared your essay by being clear about the marking and assessment criteria, deconstructing the question, knowing who your audience is and using visual aids, where appropriate, to help you understand the important and complex aspects involved, you need to incorporate your preparation into the writing up of your work. There are three key elements to writing an analytical essay. The key elements of essay writing are:

a First, the content of the essay;
b Second, making sure you have a clear and rational structure for your argument or answer; and
c Finally, that you are using appropriate language and style for your audience.

These three elements of essay writing are now considered in turn.

a. Content

The content of an essay should be relevant to the question posed. Questions to ask yourself about your essay content are:

- Does my essay cover enough depth and breadth (see Chapter 2) of the question or topic?
- Have I found sufficient supporting evidence to back up my arguments or claims?
- Do my conclusions match the arguments or claims made in the main part of my essay?

Supporting evidence

As stated, an important aspect of demonstrating your critical thinking skills, as well as achieving a high grade for your work, is incorporating supporting evidence into your essay. Make sure you think critically about the supporting evidence you use in your assessed work. Choose the quotes you use carefully and sparingly. Select a few quotations that:

- In a secondary source, sum up a point well in a few words;
- In a primary source, provide evidence for your argument; and
- are relevant and the best.[28]

Keep your quotes short and to the point. Quotations should be the first place to look for cuts during the editing process, particularly where you are over the word or page limit for your work.

Correct referencing

Plagiarism is basically 'taking someone else's words or someone else's ideas without stating the sources from which you got them'.[29] It is the fraudulent representation of

28 Cottrell, *supra* note 7, p. 154.
29 Webley, *supra* note 1, p. 113.

the work of another as that of your own. This could be purchasing an essay from the internet and passing it off as your own or cutting and pasting large chunks of text from books or websites and putting them into your essay without including correct references. However, accusations of plagiarism may result from carelessness, poor practice or lack of understanding. Avoiding unintentional plagiarism means knowing how and when to reference, understanding how to get the balance right between your own arguments and your research and being meticulous about noting details when you are doing research. Basically, to avoid accidental plagiarism, make sure to reference the sources in your work accurately. Check with your school or department's guidelines as to how they want you to cite your work. There are several ways to reference the work of others (such as using the Harvard or London style of referencing). Law schools and departments generally prefer you to use London-style footnotes, and the Oxford University Standard Citation of Legal Authorities (OSCOLA) guidelines indicate the use of footnotes.

b. Structure

Using a logical structure to display your answer. For example, there could be more than one answer to a question, which requires your essay to be structured to make sense of this. As well as an introduction and conclusion, your essay requires a main body. As a general idea, it is worth your time to work on the rule of three. Consider: what are the three key points or issues the question or problem posed deliberates? See the coming section on the 'Key elements of an essay' for more of an indication.

Sub-headings

Sub-headings are the headings given to a sub-section of a piece of writing. Short answers to legal questions or problems do not require you to use sub-headings. However, they are useful in longer essays in order to signpost and highlight the main arguments or points in your answer.

c. Language

When writing analytical essays, it is best to use plain English. Provide definitions when using legal jargon or Latin phrases, such as 'oblique intention' (which covers situations whereby it is a 'virtual certainty' of a defendant's act(s) that death or serious injury will ensue)[30] or *mens rea* (meaning the mental element of a crime), for example. Use short sentences that get to the point quickly. Start a new paragraph when you are making a new point or discussing a different issue.

Key Words

✓   Key words flagging up another argument in support of a view:
     Similarly, equally, again, another, in the same way, likewise

---

30 See R v *Woollin* [1998] WLR 382.

✓ Key words flagging up alternative perspectives and arguments:
On the other hand (that's one of my favourites!), yet, however, but
✓ Key words to tell the reader that you're about to draw some conclusions (get ready!): *Therefore, thus, for this reason, because of this, it seems that*[31]

Using qualifiers[32]

Avoid using qualifiers such as

All, every	most, many, some
Always	usually, generally, often, in most cases, so far, haven't
Never	rarely in few cases, it is unlikely that
Proves	the evidence suggests, indicates, points to, it would appear

Signposting

Use linking words and signposting to connect your ideas. These make clear to your reader both how your argument progresses logically from one point to the next and how each new point is relevant. Examples include:

● Drawing attention to certain points: 'equally importantly'; 'furthermore'.
● Indicating cause and effect progression: 'this results in'; 'consequently'.
● Indicating progression within an argument: 'therefore'; 'however'; 'nevertheless'.[33]

Key elements of an essay

Introduction

1 Description
2 Critical Analysis
3 Suggestion(s) for Reform

Conclusion

Introduction

The introduction of an essay should set the scene for your reader. It should be succinct, precise and brief. Depending on your word or page limit, sometimes being as short as a paragraph but no longer than a tenth of your overall essay. The following aspects should be stated clearly to your reader during your introductory comments:

● The core issues considered in your essay;

---

31 Cohen, *supra* note 12, p. 211.
32 Cottrell, *supra* note 7, p. 179.
33 Open University, *supra* note 13, p. 23.

- Key legal perspectives (as discussed in Chapter 3); and
- The direction of your argument.[34]

The introduction provides the opportunity for you to set out the background issues of the question or problem. You also need to identify the purpose or focus of your essay. This will help you show that you have considered the depth and breadth of the issue by briefly stating all the aspects that you could have discussed and then considering the two or three that are most relevant to your position on the problem or issue. Set out the direction of your argument by indicating the structure of the main body of your essay – generally made up of three distinct sections as follows.

1 Description

First, the descriptive section of your essay should describe any key concepts, principles or current areas of law. In this short section, show that you have considered questions such as: How did this come to be so? What is the historical background and reasons for the ways things are now? What is the supporting evidence for the way things are?

2 Critical Analysis

Second, following the short description of the reasons for the current situation, the analytical section of your essay should form the main bulk of your word or page limit. In this section, you should outline your critical analysis of the question or problem posed. Examples of how to make sure that your writing demonstrates a critical appreciation of the assignment, rather than a deceptive one, is set out in Table 5.1.

3 Suggestion(s) for reform

Once the critical assessment of the question or problem posed has been undertaken, finally, you can put forward suggestions for reforming or reformulating the particular topic or area of law under investigation. See the 'Critical thinking process' diagram (Figure 4.1) in the previous chapter for how to come up with an original or quasi-original solution to a question or problem.

Conclusion

To conclude your essay, make sure you summarise the main points of your argument without raising any new ones at this final stage. Your conclusion should:

- Draw together the most compelling reasons that support your position;
- Refer, if relevant, to strengths and weaknesses in the evidence; and
- Describe, if relevant, what specifically needs to be researched further in order to better clarify the issues or strengthen the arguments.[35]

---

34 Cottrell, *supra* note 7, p. 184.
35 *Ibid.*, p. 186.

Table 5.1 Descriptive versus critical assignments[36]

Descriptive Assignment	Critical Assignment
X States the case study facts	✓ Analyses potential offences in the scenario
X Describes potential offences	✓ Dismantles specific offences
X Lists injuries/breaches	✓ Matches applicable areas of law into injuries
X States opinions of judges	✓ Examines the opinions of judges
X States the arguments	✓ Weighs and criticises the arguments
X Provides defence information	✓ Analyses and applies defences
X States a conclusion	✓ Draws a conclusion from the evidence
X Describes theories	✓ Critically assesses the theories

TASK TWENTY-TWO *Planning the key elements of an analytical essay*

Use the following to plan out the key elements of your latest essay.

Introduction

-
-
-

1 Description

-
-
-

2 Analysis

-
-
-

3 Suggestion(s) for Reform

-
-
-

36 Lisa Cherkassky, et al. (2011) *Legal Skills*. Basingstoke: Palgrave Macmillan, p. 109.

Conclusion

-
-
-

TASK TWENTY-THREE   *On submitting your first essay on a course*[37]

Complete the following table once you have submitted your first essay on a course.

(Please tick one or more columns as appropriate for each row)	This is what I did	I would have liked to do this but didn't manage it	I didn't think this necessary	This just was not possible for me	I'll do this next time
1	I started thinking about this essay in plenty of time.					
2	I started to collect my reading materials well in advance.					
3	I discussed the ideas associated with this essay with someone, virtually or live, prior to starting writing.					
4	I had a timetable in mind for pre-reading, planning, drafting, writing, checking, doing the references.					
5	I planned out the structure of the essay logically, so my train of thought was continuous.					

---

37 Adapted from Phil Race (2010) *Making Learning Happen*. London: Sage Publications.

(Please tick one or more columns as appropriate for each row)	This is what I did	I would have liked to do this but didn't manage it	I didn't think this necessary	This just was not possible for me	I'll do this next time
6	I made reasonable efforts to clear the decks for the actual writing of the essay.					
7	I made referencing easy for myself by properly noting all of my sources as I did the reading.					
8	I showed someone a draft of my essay before I completed it.					
9	I acted on feedback I received to make my essay better.					
10	I wrote a summary/ abstract that encapsulated my key points succinctly.					
11	I checked my work over carefully for obvious mistakes, and I used a spellchecker.					

How to use essay feedback critically

The main aim of providing you with feedback on your non-assessed and assessed essays is improvement. It is important because feedback helps to improve your performance, research, dedication, quality and marks.[38] For example, if your essay was missing 'critical analysis', your lecturer or tutor can tell you what it is and how to successfully incorporate it into your next assessment. You will receive more detailed feedback on an essay than you will on an exam. Many students make the mistake of

38 Cherkassy *et al.*, *supra* note 36, p. 233.

simply looking at their grade and disregarding the comments made by the marker. These comments are important because they are tailored to help you improve your work on your next assignment.

TASK TWENTY-FOUR	Reflecting on tutor feedback on your essay[39]

Use the table below to reflect upon the feedback you receive on your next essay.

(Please tick one or more columns as appropriate for each row)	This is what I did	I would have liked to do this but didn't manage it	I didn't think this necessary	This just was not possible for me	I'll do this next time	This did not apply in this case
1 I read the tutor's comments carefully.						
2 I read my essay again to see how the tutor's comments applied.						
3 I noted things I needed to do for the next assignment.						
4 I looked back at the assignment brief to see the extent to which my essay had complied with it.						
5 I shared my feedback with one or more other students to see how my commentary compared with theirs.						

39 Adapted from Race, *supra* note 37.

(Please tick one or more columns as appropriate for each row)	This is what I did	I would have liked to do this but didn't manage it	I didn't think this necessary	This just was not possible for me	I'll do this next time	This did not apply in this case
6	I considered aspects of my approach on which I would especially ask for feedback next time.						
7	I asked my tutor for further clarification on comments which I didn't understand.						

Suggested reading

○ Bailey, Stephen (2015) *The Essentials of Academic Writing for International Students*. London: Routledge.

● Rowe, Suzanne E. (2000) 'Legal Research, Legal Writing, and Legal Analysis: Putting Law School into Practice'. 29(4) *29 Stetson Law Review*, 1193–1216.

● Rylance, Paul (2012) *Writing and Drafting in Legal Practice*. Oxford: Oxford University Press.

Dissertations and theses

Longer analytical essays are called 'dissertations' and 'theses'. Depending on the requirements of your school or department, a dissertation is usually a compulsory or voluntary final-year undergraduate project and part of the master's programme, whereas a thesis is usually required to attain a doctorate. Dissertations can be anything from seven to twenty or thirty thousand words, whereas a thesis is generally ninety thousand words in length. The expectation for both a dissertation and theses is that you create your own question for investigation, conduct your own independent research on the topic and choose a method for undertaking the study. The same guidance provided generally for analytical essays is relevant to the research and writing of both dissertations and theses. However, this section discusses additional elements required for researching and writing dissertations and theses. These include writing literature reviews, choosing a legal method or methodology for your work and a discussion of qualitative and quantitative data gathering methods. These are now considered in turn.

Literature reviews

In an analytical essay, emphasis is placed upon the development of your own argument on a subject rather than summarising the positions of others. However, it is common when writing a dissertation or thesis to start by conducting a literature review. Sometimes you are required to conduct a literature review as an exercise prior to starting your dissertation or thesis. Whether this is a requirement at your school or department or not, dissertations and theses generally contain a literature review section. A literature review provides a brief critical overview of the background field of your study. It generally accounts for ten per cent of the overall piece you are writing. To think critically about your literature review, you need to identify:

- which two or three pieces, theories, perspectives or previous research articles provide the most significant background information for your own research; and
- how, if at all, these pieces of research are linked to each other. Usually, this will be in chronological order.[40]

Write the most about two to five pieces of research, drawing out their key points and how they support the need for your research in the field. Succinctly ensure that your reader understands the significance of the research and its relevance to the rest of your dissertation or thesis. Other pieces of research can be discussed briefly.

Legal methods and methodologies

As well as undertaking a literature review, dissertations and theses also require a section in which you outline your methods or methodology for your study. The legal method or methodology you choose depends upon the topic you select and your own interests and preferences. Legal methods are the set of techniques that you use to analyse and apply the law as well as to determine the appropriate weight that should be attributed to different sources of law. Examples of legal methods include rule-based reasoning (in which you take a statute or case and apply it to a set of facts); distinguishing cases (in which you argue that the facts of the precedent case are not like the facts of the present case and so do not apply) and inductive reasoning (in which you reason from the specific to the general by looking for similarities between precedent cases). In comparison to a legal method, legal methodologies comprise the theoretical analysis of the principles associated with a particular branch of knowledge. A methodology does not seek to set out to provide solutions to a problem like a method does. Instead, methodologies offer the theoretical underpinning for understanding which perspectives can be applied to a specific case (see the discussion of legal perspectives in Chapter 3). The majority of undergraduate dissertations are 'doctrinal' or 'black-letter'. They use interpretative tools or legal reasoning to evaluate

---

40 Cottrell, *supra* note 7, p. 172.

legal rules and suggest recommendations for further development of the law.[41] However, non-doctrinal approaches to studying law in the broader social and political context use a range of methods taken from other disciplines in the social sciences and humanities (perspectives such as Marxist, CLS, feminist, CRT and legal pluralist).

Qualitative and quantitative data

As stated in the previous chapter, legal research requires attention to be given to reputable legal authorities from primary and secondary sources. Primary sources (also known as empirical studies) can be made up from two distinct data-gathering techniques, called 'qualitative' and 'quantitative' data. On the one hand, qualitative data gathering is generally used by '[p]eople whose research involves more than mere measurements'.[42] Researchers here are essentially assessing the 'quality' of an argument, assumption or claim. But on the other hand, quantitative data gathering involves measuring and 'quantifying' data, which results in the creation of statistics or charts. The empirical studies undertaken in TCAL, for example, employ a mixture of these techniques: qualitative data to assess law students and staff's understanding of the phrase 'critical thinking' (see Chapter 2) and quantitative data in the creation of graphs to illustrate the importance of it to the number of those asked (see Chapter 1).

TASK TWENTY-FIVE   *Looking for the robber*[43]

Try this problem out. Here's the data:

✓   A census classifies eighty-five per cent of men in a city as 'European' and fifteen per cent as 'indigenous'.
✓   A witness to a street robbery identifies the assailant as 'indigenous'.
✓   The court tests the reliability of the witness, and he's able to identify correctly people as being either 'European' or 'indigenous' eighty per cent of the time, but he mistakes people's origins up to twenty per cent of the time.

Without being prejudiced one way or the other (of course), but having limited resources, in which community should the police prioritise their search for the street robber?

●   See answer in 'Task answers' section.

---

41 Mike McConville and Wing Hong Chui (2007) *Research Methods*. Edinburgh: Edinburgh University Press, p. 4.
42 Cohen, *supra* note 12, p. 152.
43 Ibid., p. 36.

Suggested reading

○ Salter, Michael and Julie Mason (2007) *Writing Law Dissertations: An Introduction and Guide to the Conduct of Legal Research*. London: Longman.

● Watkins, Dawn (2013) *Research Methods in Law*. London: Routledge.

B. Reflective writing

You may be required to undertake a piece of reflective writing as part of your undergraduate or postgraduate law course. This could be a stand-alone piece of work or form part of a portfolio project. If you are involved in any skills- or practice-based modules these sometimes involve a reflective element. According to John Dewey, reflective thought is '[a]ctive, persistent, and careful consideration of any belief or supposed form of knowledge in the light of the grounds that support it, and the further conclusions to which it tends'.[44] Critical reflective writing, for academic purposes, is a structured, focused and conscious process with the purpose of developing our understanding.

> It is not sufficient to simply have an experience in order to learn. Without reflecting upon this experience it may quickly be forgotten, or its learning potential lost.[45]

Typical characteristics of reflective writing include:

1   *Selection:* select an aspect of experience, learning or professional practice for analysis.
2   *Changing perspective:* analyse experience from different angles and different levels of detail.
3   *Returning to experience:* once, periodically or frequently, as best fits the issue.
4   *Analysis of own role:* look at reasons for and consequences of your own actions rather than those of others.
5   *Drawing upon received wisdom:* make use of theory, research, professional knowledge.
6   *Deepening your understanding:* look actively for meaning, recognising what is significant, and learn from this.
7   *Using insights to effect change:* use your new understanding to do things differently in the future – ideally to benefit others as well as yourself.[46]

---

44 John Dewey (1933/1991) *How We Think: A Restatement of the Relation of Reflective Thinking to the Educative Process*. New York: Prometheus Books, p. 6.

45 Graham Gibbs (1998) *Learning by Doing: A Guide to Teaching and Learning Methods*. London: Further Education Unit.

46 Cottrell, *supra* note 7, p. 208.

Suggested reading

- McMillian, Kathleen (2013) *How to Improve Your Critical Thinking and Reflective Skills.* Harlow: Pearson Education.

C. Problem questions

Generally problem questions relate to 'applied' rather than 'analytical' research (as discussed in the previous chapter). This means that you simply have to know, understand and apply the correct legal authority accurately to the problem scenario presented – the first of the two-stage critical thinking process. The best way to approach a problem question is to pretend that you are already a practicing lawyer advising a client. The client will want to know as efficiently and succinctly as possible the advice you have to give on a particular legal issue, with as few digressions as possible. Here your task is simply to apply the current law and legal precedents to the scenario at hand.

IPAC

Issue
Principle
Application
Conclusion

> ### EXAMPLE
>
> Ben bumped into his ex-girlfriend, Claire, when he attended a reunion at his secondary school and the pair exchanged contact details. Following their meet-up, Ben was bombarded with emails, texts and telephone calls from Claire. Her messages said that *'I cannot stay away, I cannot fight it because for me, it is not over'*. When Ben did not reply he started to receive silent telephone calls with heavy breathing down the line. He thought that he saw Claire standing outside his home and sitting in her car outside his office, but whenever he went to confront her, she was nowhere to be seen. Ben started having panic attacks, became depressed and began to regularly phone in sick to work in order to hide at his home. Advise Ben on Claire's criminal liabilities.
>
> **Issue:** Ben has a potential claim for protection against harassment against Claire due to the alarm, distress and fear she has caused him.
>
> **Principle(s):**
>
> – Section 2 of the Protection from Harassment Act 1997 prohibits harassment by stalking (defined as following, contacting or spying on a person).
>
> – Following *Lau v Director of Public Prosecutions*[47] a course of conduct is required, which means that at least two separate incidents over a period of months is required.

---

47 [2000] 1 FLR 799.

– The House of Lords held in *R v Ireland; Burstow*,[48] that in relation to silent phone calls, defendants that cause their victim psychological injury can be prosecuted for causing actual or grievous bodily harm under sections 47 and 20 of the OAPA 1861.

Application:

– If it can be proven that Claire has contacted Ben via email, texts and calls on at least two separate occasions over a period of months (as held in *Lau*), her conduct will amount to harassment under the 1997 Act.

– Depending on the level of psychological injury sustained by Ben (in the form of panic attacks and depression – making him regularly phone in sick to work) from the silent phone calls from Claire, she may face prosecution under either section 47 or 20 OAPA 1861.

Conclusion: If found guilty under the provisions of the 1997 Act, Ben can impose an injunction, and Claire is liable to pay damages for her behaviour. If she breaches the injunction, Claire may face prosecution for up to five years imprisonment. Claire may even face imprisonment for a term not exceeding seven years if found guilty for causing actual or grievous bodily harm to Ben for making silent telephone calls.

Sometimes extra marks can be awarded for demonstrating your own critical thought on an issue. For instance, in relation to the example, you could also say that this area of law has been recommended for review by the Law Commission and could be subject to change. It is best to check with your tutor or module leader as to whether additional marks will be awarded for such 'critical' claims; otherwise they are not necessary and simply eat up your precious word count.

Suggested reading

* Holland, James and Julian Webb (2016) *Learning Legal Rules*. Oxford: Oxford University Press.

II. How to think critically about exams

Although there are similarities between writing critical essays and exams, the nature and process of exams changes the expectations and outcomes. This part of the chapter discusses how to think critically about exams in their preparation, in the exam room and in the reflection of feedback.

Thinking critically about revision

Revision is an important part of the exam process. Make sure you are clear, before you start preparing for your exams and revising, how many exam questions you will be expected to attempt and the time allocated. You can usually find this information in the module description form or module handbook. If you are unable to find this information, contact your subject leader or tutor. Three key revision steps are:

1   First, consolidate your notes;
2   Second, remember the necessary information; and
3   Finally, practice attempting exam questions.

48 [1997] 3 WLR 534.

The first step of revision is to make sure that your notes are legible, accessible and memorable. The best way to do this is to make sure they are when you start writing them. After each lecture, seminar, tutorial and round-table discussion, make time to note down any key elements onto a note card or small paragraph. This will make it easier for you to start actually revising, rather than learning, during the revision process. Make sure you fill any gaps in your notes by doing your own reading or by asking a classmate. The second step of revision requires you to make sure that you can remember the information. Using some of the ways discussed in the previous section (such as doodling, creating mind maps, spider diagrams or flowcharts) may be a way to aid your memory in an exam. The final step in the revision process is then to make sure you are able to apply the information you remember to an exam question. Most universities have exam paper archives so that you can, first, practice planning an answer until you can remember all the points you want to discuss and then write it out as under exam conditions.

Exam tips

- Look at past exam papers and see whether there are any commonalities between questions – are there certain topics that come up every year? Do exam questions correlate to your discussions in seminar or tutorials?
- Plan generic answers to common questions. For example, what information do you need to remember if a question appears on criminal law defences? Or the implied terms of a contract? Tailor your generic answers to the questions when in the exam room.

The majority of exams are 'unseen' papers: you do not know the questions before entering the exam room; however, 'seen' exam questions are a growing trend, which enable you to prepare some materials in advance of the exam. You are generally allowed to take a dictionary and statute book into the exam room for your reference, although these should not contain any annotations. Once in the exam room, exam questions are generally either analytical essay-based questions, problem questions or multiple-choice questions (MCQs). These are now considered in turn.

Analytical exams

As with analytical essays (see earlier), analytical exam questions require planning and preparation. This requires four main steps: the first step is to make sure that you are clear about the marking and assessment criteria of the exam; the second, deconstruct the question to understand its meaning; third, make sure you keep in mind the marker of your work; and finally, visual aids (doodles, mind maps, spider diagrams or flowcharts, for example) could be useful to recall and plan your answer. Remember the three key elements of analytical essays. These are first, an introduction on the background of the topic and structure of your argument or answer; second, the main body usually includes three distinctive sections (a descriptive section, a critical analytical section and finally a section that discusses your suggestions for reform or reformulating the topic or issue). Finally, a conclusion that summarises the key points or arguments of your answer. In comparison to analytical essay assignments, essays written under exam conditions do not require you to use footnotes. Instead, place your supporting evidence in the main text of your work. See what follows for an example of citing legal authorities in analytical essay assessments and exams.

Example

Essay: According to the famous maxim of criminal law '*actus reus non facit mens sit rea*' a 'person is not guilty [of a crime] unless his mind is also guilty'.[49]

Exam: Lord Hailsham has stated that the famous maxim in criminal law '*actus reus non facit mens sit rea*' means that a person is not guilty of a crime unless his mind is also guilty (Haughton v Smith (1975)).

Problem questions in exams

Problem questions assess your ability to apply knowledge rather than your analytical skills. Although analytical questions lend themselves to critical thinking, you can still think critically about answering problem questions (see earlier). Answering problem questions under exam conditions requires you to 'disentangle a mass of interwoven facts . . . to make a determination about the legal liability of the parties by applying current law to the factual situation'.[50] In exam conditions, make sure that you understand what the legal problem in the problem scenario you are undertaking involves. Once you are clear about the question, use IPAC to state the issue, principle(s), application and conclusion for your answer. See the example of how to attempt a problem style question (note the difference of referencing legal authorities in exam conditions). Figure 5.5 outlines the different requirements of essay and problem questions in exams.

Multiple-choice exam questions

In comparison to analytical essay and problem-style questions, for multiple-choice questions (MCQs) 'you are set a series of questions and have a choice of answers for each question. You select the most appropriate one (or other as stated on the paper)'.[51] MCQs therefore do not require you to write anything but rather to select an answer from a list of possibilities. They could be used for an end of term revision quiz, as part of a law module or interview process for a legal job. See the example of an MCQ that follows.

Example

● What is 'Natural Law Theory'?

    A. A doctrine that actions are right if they are for the benefit of the majority.

    B. A legal perspective which contends that certain values are inherent by virtue of human nature.

---

49 Per Lord Hailsham in *Haughton v Smith* [1975] AC 476, at p. 491.
50 Emily Finch and Stefan Fafinski (2015) *Legal Skills*. Oxford: Oxford University Press, p. 378.
51 Webley, *supra* note 1, p. 152.

C. An ethical position that judges the morality of an action on its adherence to rules.

D. A legal perspective that insists on the distinction between human and moral law.[53]

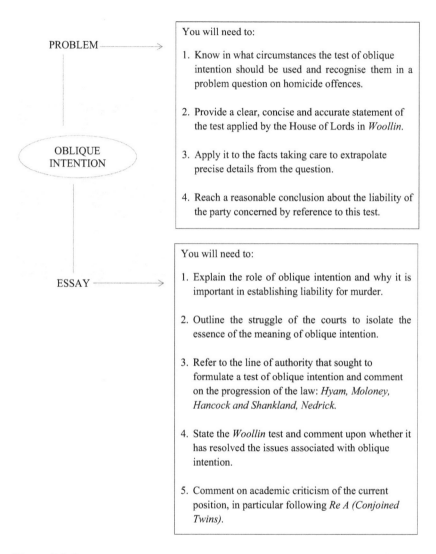

PROBLEM ⟶

You will need to:

1. Know in what circumstances the test of oblique intention should be used and recognise them in a problem question on homicide offences.

2. Provide a clear, concise and accurate statement of the test applied by the House of Lords in *Woollin*.

3. Apply it to the facts taking care to extrapolate precise details from the question.

4. Reach a reasonable conclusion about the liability of the party concerned by reference to this test.

OBLIQUE INTENTION

ESSAY ⟶

You will need to:

1. Explain the role of oblique intention and why it is important in establishing liability for murder.

2. Outline the struggle of the courts to isolate the essence of the meaning of oblique intention.

3. Refer to the line of authority that sought to formulate a test of oblique intention and comment on the progression of the law: *Hyam, Moloney, Hancock and Shankland, Nedrick*.

4. State the *Woollin* test and comment upon whether it has resolved the issues associated with oblique intention.

5. Comment on academic criticism of the current position, in particular following *Re A (Conjoined Twins)*.

Figure 5.5 The different requirements of essays and problem questions[52]

---

52 Finch and Fafinski, *supra* note 50, p. 378.
53 The answer is B: a legal perspective which contends that certain values are inherent by virtue of human nature.

Rather than assessing your analytical skills, MCQs are assessing your applied legal knowledge. To think critically about MCQs, do to not overthink the question! Usually your first instincts of what the answer is are correct. You also do not want to over-complicate the question, as usually the simplest answer is the correct one.

Reflecting on feedback from an exam

As stated in the 'How to use essay feedback critically' section, you generally receive more feedback on an essay than on an exam. However, any feedback you do receive on your work is useful. If you are unable to read or understand the feedback you have been given, ask to speak to your lecturer or tutor so that you know what to do to make your work better next time. See the table that follows for points to consider when reflecting on feedback from your exams.

| TASK TWENTY-SIX | *Reflecting on feedback on your exam*[54] |

Use the following table to reflect upon the feedback you receive on your next exam.

		This is what I did	I would have liked to do this but didn't manage it	I didn't think this necessary	This just was not possible for me	I'll do this next time	This did not apply in this case
1	I read the tutor's comments carefully.						
2	I read my exam again to see how the tutor's comments applied.						
3	I noted things I needed to do before my next exam.						

54 Adapted from Race, *supra* note 37.

		This is what I did	I would have liked to do this but didn't manage it	I didn't think this necessary	This just was not possible for me	I'll do this next time	This did not apply in this case
4	I shared my feedback with one or more other students to see how my commentary compared with theirs.						
5	I considered aspects of my approach on which I would especially ask for feedback next time.						
6	I asked my tutor for further clarification on comments which I didn't understand.						

Suggested reading

- Webley, Lisa (2016) *Legal Writing*. London: Routledge. Chapter 8: Legal Writing in Exams and How to Prepare.
- Campbell, Enid, Richard Fox and Melissa de Zwart (2010) *Students' Guide to Legal Writing, Law Exams and Self-Assessment*. Sydney: Federation Press.

III. Thinking critically about group assessments

The previous parts of the chapter have discussed working autonomously to create critical essay and exam answers. This part of the chapter discusses how you can think critically about group assessments. Group assessments are becoming a more popular way to assess your knowledge and understanding. As well as critical thinking, they provide an opportunity to develop and practice your communication and teamworking skills. Group work is also something you will encounter in the legal (and other) professions. The advantages of group rather than autonomous work is that you get the opportunity to share and develop your ideas with others, which can be social and fun. The disadvantages of group work, however, are that in the delegation process, you lose control of some of the outcomes of your work. This part of the chapter first discusses how to go about planning and preparing to undertake group work and then three main ways your work can be assessed while working as a group. These are first, during group presentations, second, as part of the PBL process and finally, by creating posters.

Group organisation

Brainstorming

Brainstorming is the technique of quickly jotting lots of ideas down in response to a question. You can brainstorm on your own, but the real advantages of the technique come when you are in a group, because that's where other people's ideas can spark new ones among other members of the group.[55] Groups use many different ways to capture the ideas of a brainstorming session, but here are two of the biggies, both of which are led by a co-ordinator:

✓ **Scribe:** Co-ordinators (the scribes) do not so much write (which can be a cumbersome and inefficient process) but rather 'capture' on the board all the ideas that team members call out. They then try to sum up the ideas in an appropriate way, regardless of their own feelings about the merits or demerits of an idea.

✓ **All in:** During these sessions, team members can write on the board their ideas just as they come, or perhaps instead verbally share them with the group. The useful yellow sticky notes can be brought out so that everyone can write their ideas down and then stick them on the board.[56]

Splitting up the tasks involved

Think about ways that elements of your task (be it a presentation, PBL or poster) can be split between the members of your group. Think about the requirements of the task and how these can equitably be delegated to each member of the group.

What to do if a member of your group lets you down

A common issue with working as a group is that different students have different responsibilities and commitments on them, and some take their studies more seriously than others. What should you do, then, if a member of your group lets you

---

55 Cohen, *supra* note 13, p. 149.
56 Ibid., p. 150.

down? What if a member of your group is ill? Or simply does not do the work that is required by the rest of the group? There is a difference between someone not being able to contribute to the group's work and someone who simply does not want to do so. Some modules have an in-built system to report if a student has not contributed to the work of the rest of the group, such as in a reflective statement (see the section in the previous part of the chapter on 'Reflective writing' for a further discussion on this point). Other modules do not take this into account, and although it may seem unfair that a member of a group does not get penalised for their lack of engagement, this is reminiscent of what can happen in the working environment, so having the opportunity to develop your own strategies for overcoming this is a useful process.

Group presentations

Presentations are popular on law courses. Many people who work in the legal field need excellent advocacy skills, because one day they may need to stand in front of a judge in a court of law and present their client's arguments. To be a good advocate, you need to present yourself well. You need to be able to project your voice clearly, present your views succinctly and reason professionally. A few reasons for delivering presentations are provided here. Presentations:

- Encourage you to conduct in-depth research into an area of law.
- Make you actively engage with the law and how it works.
- Help develop many vital skills, from communication skills to research skills.
- Mix together different views, beliefs, concerns, learning styles and experiences.
- Build individual confidence and group comradeship.
- Encourage students to take control of their own learning.
- Are good practice for the real world – your future career and interviews.
- Help you project your thoughts clearly in everyday life.
- Are good practice for when you are a solicitor, a barrister, a legal executive and the like.[57]

Group presentation tips
- Practice, practice, practice!
- If using PowerPoint presentations, Camtasia or other visual aids, use them sparingly.
- Make sure that your group's presentation fits into the time allocated. It is better to be slightly under time than to run out of it!

Problem-based learning (PBL)

As previously stated in the section on PBL, this student-centred approach requires you to work as a member of a group to solve an open-ended issue or problem. Under this approach, it is for you as a group to come up with the arrangements and scheduling

---

57 Cherkassy *et al.*, *supra* note 36, pp. 209–210.

for your work rather than that of a tutor. There are four possible roles you as a member of a PBL group can be involved in. These include:

1   *Project leader*: responsible for proposing the agenda of the meeting, suggests divisions of labour of the tasks and develops the overall project plan.
2   *Facilitator*: describes the process to be followed during the steps of the project plan, determines the appropriate time to proceed with the plan and suggests adjustments to the plan as needed.
3   *Recorder*: takes notes at each meeting and is responsible for making these available to the other members of the group.
4   *Team member*: takes individual notes, participates in the discussions and reviews the resources/materials.

Also present may be a PBL leader or tutor (a member of law staff) who can be involved and consulted during sessions as well as being responsible for marking the groups work.

Posters

Posters require you to demonstrate an ability to give legal advice in lay terms using an effective visual format. They offer an opportunity to disseminate legal knowledge to a wide audience who are not legally trained. You will need to consider carefully how to make best use of a visual medium. Do not crowd your poster with too much written information. At the same time, you need to make your point clearly and without the possibility of upsetting your viewers or of their dismissing or misunderstanding what you are saying.

Suggested reading

O   Barton, Karen and Fiona Westwood (2006) 'From Student to Trainee Practitioner – A Study of Team Working as a Learning Experience'. 3 *Web Journal of Current Legal Issues.*
●   Scallen, Eileen, Sophie Sparrow and Cliff Zimmerman (2014) *Working Together in Law: Team Work and Small Groups for Legal Professionals.* Carolina: Carolina Academic Press.

Key points

The three key points discussed in this chapter were that:

●   Thinking critically about legal essays requires good planning and preparation as well as providing a clear content, structure and language for your work;
●   Preparing critical exam answers can be started right from your note-taking stage so that you are revising, rather than learning information, before your exams start; and
●   As well as helping to develop and practice your critical thinking skills, group work aids your communication and teamworking skills.

The next chapter discusses how to think critically in the workplace and beyond.

Chapter 6

Thinking critically in the workplace and beyond

Chapter aims

The aim of the present chapter is to help you to develop your critical thinking skills in the workplace and beyond. To do this, three key aspects are discussed. These are:

● First, how to think ethically about law;
● Second, thinking critically in the workplace; and
● Finally, how to develop your critical instincts about law as a lifelong skill.

The previous chapters in the second part of TCAL have discussed, in Chapter 4, how you can put your critical thinking skills into practice through your critical reading and writing process, when you are in the classroom and taking part in extra-curricular activities. The previous chapter discussed how to think critically about your assessments, whether they be essays or exams or even as part of group work. Thinking critically is held to be an 'intellectually disciplined process of thought',[1] and although it is predominantly developed and assessed while studying at university, it is a skill that it useful for your career as well as for the rest of your life.

The present chapter combines discussions in those previous to confer how and why it is important to think critically in the workplace and beyond. This is key, because one of the challenges faced by contemporary law students can be coming up with an answer to the questions: what and where next? To discuss these questions, the chapter is structured in three parts. The first part of the chapter discusses the importance of thinking ethically about law. This is important because, as professionals, lawyers have certain duties and obligations to their clients and the courts. To this end, it is desirable that lawyers have clearly defined rules of conduct. The second part of the chapter discusses thinking critically in the workplace, offering tips and guidance on doing so while undertaking work experience and applying for jobs (both inside and outside of the legal profession). The final part of the chapter then discusses ways to develop and hone your critical insights while studying law at university, in the workplace and for your life beyond these environments.

I. Thinking ethically about law

A man asks his solicitor: 'If I give you £400, will you answer two questions for me?'

The solicitor replies: 'Absolutely! What's the second question?'[2]

As illustrated by the lawyer joke, over the centuries, there have been many criticisms of the legal profession stemming from absurdly high lawyer fees[3] and the lack of

---

1 Michael Scriven and Richard Paul (2008) 'Defining Critical Thinking'. *Foundation for Critical Thinking*. Available at www.criticalthinking.org/aboutCT/definingCT.cfm.
2 Lawyer joke from Bonallack and Bishop Solicitors. Available at www.bishopslaw.co.uk/about-us/lawyer-jokes.
3 The Guardian. 'Legal Fees Investigation Reveals Huge Disparities Between Law Firms'. 5 March 2016. Available at www.theguardian.com/law/2016/apr/05/legal-fees-investigation-reveals-huge-disparities-between-law-firms.

diversity regarding gender, homosexuals and ethnic minorities in the profession,[4] as well as cuts to the legal aid system.[5] Due to such criticisms, it is imperative that young lawyers have knowledge and appreciation for the importance of thinking ethically about law. This part of the chapter, first, discusses thinking ethically in theory, and the second part considers legal ethics in practice.

A. Thinking ethically in theory

This section discusses the theory of thinking ethically about law, the difference between legal ethics and the relationship between law and morality and finally, legal ethics in law practice. These elements are now considered in turn.

Legal ethics

Legal ethics is a branch of philosophy that aims to answer the basic question: what should I do in a particular situation?[6] An example for an ethical dilemma is whether it is ever justified to kill another human being. Morally and legally, murder is wrong. Even in the Christian religion, the Sixth Commandment states '[t]hou shalt not kill'. However, is it wrong to kill an enemy on the battlefield? What about suicide, abortion and euthanasia? As indicated by the ethical dilemma of whether it is ever justifiable to kill another human being, our ethics, then, are a process of reflection in which a person's decisions are shaped by their values, principles and purpose rather than their general habits, social conventions or self-interest.

When thinking through an ethical issue, you must be able to identify the ethical principles relevant to the specific ethical situation. Ethical principles, alone, however, do not settle ethical questions. For example, ethical principles sometimes can be applied differently in cases that are ethically complex. Sometimes what is illegal may or may not be a matter of ethics, and what is ethically obligatory may be illegal. There is no essential connection between ethics and the law. Laws often emerge out of social conventions and taboos. What is more, most laws are ultimately made by politicians, who routinely confuse social values with ethical principles.

TASK TWENTY-SEVEN	*Recognising violations of human rights based on universal ethical principles[7]*

One ability essential to sound ethical reasoning is the ability to identify ethical principles relevant to the ethical issue at hand. In this activity, we would like

---

4 For example, see Lisa Webley and Liz Duff (2007) 'Women Solicitors as a Barometer for Problems Within the Legal Profession – Time to Put Values Before Profits?" 34(3) *Journal of Law and Society*, 374–402.
5 Laura Gray. 'Legal Aid Cuts: What Has Changed?'. BBC News. 18 June 2013. Available at www.bbc.co.uk/news/uk-politics-22936684.
6 Anthony Harrison-Barbet (2001) *Mastering Philosophy*. Basingstoke: Palgrave Macmillan, p. 186.
7 Richard Paul and Lisa Elder (2014) *Critical Thinking: Tools for Taking Charge of Your Learning and Your Life*. London: Pearson, p. 367.

you to identify two articles in the newspaper or examples from books in which you believe someone's rights have been violated. This might include the violation of animal rights or human rights. Assume for this exercise that the factual claims in this reading are accurate. Complete the following statements:

1   **The main substance of this article is. . .**

_____

_____

_____

2   **The reason this article suggests to me at least one violation of human rights is. . .**

_____

_____

_____

3   **The universal ethical principle(s) violated is/are. . .**

_____

_____

_____

TASK TWENTY-EIGHT   *Identifying violations of human rights based on universal ethical principles*[8]

Identify a newspaper article that either directly or indirectly implies at least one governmental violation of human rights. Complete the following statements:

1   **The main substance of this article is. . .**

_____

_____

2   **The main reason this article suggests to me at least one governmental violation of human rights is. . .**

_____

8 Ibid., p. 368.

---

3   The universal ethical principle(s) violated is/are. . .

Moral content of law

In comparison to thinking about what you should do in an ethical situation, the relationship between law and morality stems from our communities and cultures. While positivists (such as Hart) recommend the separation of law and morals,[9] liberal laws, for example, attempt to create basic, enforceable standards of behaviour in society. As previously stated (in Chapter 3), in his book *The Morality of Law*,[10] Lon Fuller proposed eight principles which he asserts should be used to decide the decency of legal doctrines. In addition to this, Fuller created a hypothetical case, namely, *The Case of the Speluncean Explorers*.[11] The facts of the case are as follows. In the year 4300, four members of the Speluncean Society (an exploring group) were trapped in an underground cave. Efforts were made to rescue them, at a large financial and human cost (the lives of ten rescuers were lost). On the twentieth day of their entrapment, in light of dwindling resources, the explorers decided they should throw a die to determine which one of them should be eaten in order for the others to survive. Roger Whetmore was drawn as the candidate, although he had withdrawn from the proceedings. Whetmore was killed and eaten, and the remaining explorers were charged with his murder following their rescue. Five judges, sitting in the fictitious Supreme Court of Newgarth, heard the case and provided different decisions to the question: given their extenuating circumstances, should the explorers be found guilty of the murder of Whetmore? A brief overview of each of the five judgments is as follows:

1   **Chief Justice Truepenny:** Finds the explorers guilty of Whetmore's murder but recommends they receive clemency by the executive. He takes the positivist approach that applies the unambiguous wording of the statute to the case.
2   **Justice Foster:** Is a naturalist, who sets aside the explorers' convictions by adopting a purposive approach to the law. States that the defendants were in a 'state of nature', so the statute did not apply to them at the time of Whetmore's death.

---

9 See H.L.A. Hart (1958) 'Positivism and the Separation of Law and Morals'. 71(4) *Harvard Law Review*, 592–629.
10 Lon L. Fuller (1977/2004) *The Morality of Law*. London: Universal Law Publishing Co Ltd.
11 Lon L. Fuller (1949) 'The Case of the Speluncean Explorers' 62 *Harvard Law Review*, 616–645.

3   **Justice Tatting:** Withdraws from deciding the case due to his sympathy for the explorers and feeling of abhorrence and disgust for what they have done.

4   **Justice Keen:** Is a strict positivist who finds the explorers guilty of Whetmore's murder on the grounds that moral considerations are irrelevant in the application of the statute.

5   **Handy J:** Is a realist whose decision rests upon his own common sense, supported by public opinion that the explorers should not be found guilty of the murder.

The ethical dilemma considered in the case of the Speluncean explorers is the extent to which conflicting values (human lives, in this example) can be reconciled. In answer to this dilemma, Justices Foster and Handy find that Whetmore's death was defensible due to the explorers' circumstances, whereas Chief Justice Truepenny and Justice Keen conclude that the defendants were, despite the circumstances, guilty of the victim's murder, and Justice Tatting is unable to come to a decision on the case. As a result, the court is split, and the murder conviction of the defendants is upheld on appeal.

Fuller's hypothetical case of the Speluncean explorers is important because it illustrates the difficulties and complexities of thinking critically about law when making a judgment on an ethical dilemma. Although it is a hypothetical case, the facts are similar to the case of R v Dudley and Stephens.[12] The case concerned two defendants who became shipwrecked in a storm and were stranded on a small lifeboat with two other sailors, including a young cabin boy called Richard Parker.[13] After being stranded for eighteen days, with no food or water, Dudley and Stephens agreed to draw straws to see which one of them would be killed and eaten for the others to survive. The third man did not agree to the process, and the cabin boy (Parker) was too weak to take part in the decision. As the third man had not agreed, the defendants decided to kill Parker, as he was close to death and had no family. They killed the boy, and the three men fed on his body. They were rescued four days later. On their return to England, Dudley and Stephens were charged with and convicted of the boy's murder. It was held that the defence of necessity (which recognises situations of overwhelming urgency that a person must be allowed to respond by breaking the law) was not allowed in this case. The defendants were sentenced to death but granted a pardon by the Crown and only served six months' imprisonment. Upholding the appeal, Lord Coleridge CJ stated that

> [t]hough law and morality are not the same, and many things may be immoral which are not necessarily illegal, yet absolute divorce of law from morality would be of fatal consequence . . . Who is to be the judge of this sort of necessity? By what measure is the comparative value of lives to be measured? It is to be strength, or intellectual or what? It is plain that the principle leaves to him who is to profit by it to determine the necessity which will justify him in deliberately taking another's life to save his own. In this case the weakest, the youngest, the most unresisting, was chosen. Was it more necessary to kill him than one of the grown men? The answer must be 'No'.[14]

---

12   (1884) 14 QBD 273.

13   Recently depicted as the tiger character in Yann Martel (2003) Life of Pi. Toronto: Random House; and (2012) Fox 2000 Pictures.

14   Supra note 12, per Lord Coleridge at p. 287.

Lord Coleridge's judgment illustrates the difficulty in judging ethical dilemmas based on the value of human lives. Although positivists, such as Hart, argue for the separation of law and morals, the naturalists' support of a relationship between the two is necessary in order to preserve human dignity. Lord Coleridge importantly asks the question: who gets to be the judge of who should live or die? How should the worth of human life be valued? It appears that judges are placed in the position to make such (legal) decisions, as shown by the more recent case of *Re A (Children) (Conjoined Twins: Surgical Separation).*[15] The case was concerned with several legal, ethical and religious dilemmas surrounding the surgical separation of conjoined twins named Jodie and Mary. The essential question put to the court was: is it permissible to kill one twin to save the other? As stated in the introductory chapter, during the Court of Appeals decision of the case, Ward LJ stated that this was a difficult case to decide due to the 'seemingly irreconcilable conflicts of moral and ethical values' and lack of existing legal principle.[16] The appeal was dismissed by the court, and it was held that the operation that would kill one twin to save the other could be lawfully carried out by the doctors. In relation to thinking critically about ethical dilemmas or difficult moral situations, consideration of your own principles and values is key.

Tip

Look back at the legal perspectives discussed in Chapter 3 and see which one you think would best help you to act or judge an ethical dilemma, such as the ones faced by the defendants in *Dudley and Stephens* and *Re A (Conjoined Twins).*

B. Legal ethics in practice

Following the discussion in the previous section on the theory of legal ethics, in practice, professional ethics are important for practicing lawyers. They provide guidance for how to deal with dilemmas such as when you have a conflict of interest, confidentiality concerns and pressures from a client. Both the SRA and BSB have their own codes of profession conduct for solicitors and barristers. These are set out in what follows.

Solicitor's Regulation Association (SRA) code of conduct[17]

Ten Key Principles. You must:

1   Uphold the rule of law and proper administration of justice;
2   Act with integrity;
3   Not allow your independence to be compromised;

---

15 [2000] 4 All ER 961; [2001] 2 WLR 480; [2001] Fam 147.
16 *Ibid.*, at p. 155.
17 Available at www.sra.org.uk/solicitors/handbook/code/content.page.

4   Act in the best interests of each *client*;
5   Provide a proper standard of service to your *clients*;
6   Behave in a way that maintains the trust of public places in you and in the provision of legal services;
7   Comply with your legal and regulatory obligations and deal with your regulators and ombudsmen in an open, timely and co-operative manner;
8   Run your business or carry out your role in the business effectively and in accordance with proper governance and sound financial and risk management principles;
9   Run your business or carry out your role in the business in a way that encourages equality of opportunity and respect for diversity; and
10 Protect *client* money and *assets*.

Bar Code of Conduct – Bar Standards Board (BSB)[18]

The general purpose of the code is set out in para 104:

General purpose of the code

104. The general purpose of the code is to provide the requirements for practice as a barrister and the rules and standards of conduct applicable to barristers which are appropriate in the interests of justice and in particular:

(a)   in relation to self-employment to provide common and enforceable rules and standards which require them:

   (i)   to be completely independent in conduct and in professional standing as sole practitioners;
   (ii)   to act only as consultants instructed by solicitors and other approved persons (save where instructions can be properly dispensed with);
   (iii) to acknowledge a public obligation based on the paramount need for access to justice to act for any client in cases within the field of the practice;

(b)   to make appropriate provisions for:

   (i)   barrister managers, employees and owners of Authorised Bodies; and
   (ii)   employed barristers taking into account the fact that such barristers are employed to provide legal services to or on behalf of their employer.

18 Available at www.barstandardsboard.org.uk/media/1353125/word_version_of_full_code_of_conduct___annexes_jan_2012_.pdf.

TASK TWENTY-NINE — *Representing a difficult client*

With the SRA and BSB codes of professional conduct in mind, would you be able to act on behalf of the following client?

Will drafting:[19]
A client asks you to draft a will disinheriting his or her child because of the child's views concerning the war in Iraq. Would you still be able to draft this will?

TASK THIRTY — *Mistake-of-law problem*[20]

Consider how you would react as a practicing lawyer in the UK if faced with the following scenario as well as the questions that follow:

Lawyer X represents the defendant, a large corporation, in a personal injury case arising from an accident in which a truck driven by one of its agents injured a pedestrian – the plaintiff. In the course of extensive negotiation, X realizes that the plaintiff's lawyer is operating under a mistaken assumption about the applicable law. The plaintiff's lawyer thinks that if X proves that the plaintiff was contributorily negligent, this proof will bar the plaintiff's claim entirely. There is a high probability that X can establish contributory negligence. However, a recent statute in the relevant jurisdiction replaces contributory with comparative negligence. Plaintiff's counsel is aware of the statute but mistakenly thinks that it does not apply to this case because the relevant events occurred before its enactment. In fact, the statute applies to all cases filed after its enactment, which would include this case. Plaintiff's counsel has made an offer to settle the case on terms that X believes are more favorable to his client than a fully informed lawyer would recommend to the plaintiff. That is, the offer is outside the zone of minimally probable trial outcomes (appropriately adjusted for likelihood and litigation expense) on the side that favours the defendant. X is highly experienced and is confident of this judgment.

- Should X accept the offer without informing opposing counsel about his mistake?
- Assume that, if X put the issue to the client, the client would decide not to disclose.
- Assume further that neither disclosure nor failure to disclose would subject X to discipline or liability.
- On the other hand, X wants to decide what to do in a principled way so that he could justify his decision.

19 Simon Pepper (1986) 'The Lawyer's Amoral Ethical Role: A Defense, A Problem, and Some Possibilities' *American Bar Foundation Research Journal*, 613–635, p. 618.
20 William Simon (2010) 'Role Differentiation and Lawyers' Ethics: A Critique of Some Academic Perspectives' 23 *Georgetown. Journal of Legal Ethics* 987–1009, pp. 988–989.

TASK THIRTY-ONE   *Sandel's examples*

The following scenarios are taken from Michael Sandel's examples:

Scenario one: Throwing Christians to lions[21]

In ancient Rome, they threw Christians to lions in the Coliseum for the amuse-ment of the crowd. Imagine how the utilitarian calculus would go: Yes, the Christian suffers excruciating pain as the lion mauls and devours him. But think of the collective ecstasy of the cheering spectators packing the Coliseum. If enough Romans derive enough pleasure from the violent spectacle, are there any grounds on which a utilitarian can condemn it?

Scenario two: Is torture ever justified?[22]

Consider the ticking-time-bomb scenario: Imagine you are the head of the local CIA branch. You capture a terrorist suspect who you believe has information about a nuclear device set to go off in Manhattan later the same day. In fact, you have reason to suspect that he planted the bomb himself. As the clock ticks down, he refuses to admit being a terrorist or to divulge the bomb's location. Would it be right to torture him until he tells you where the bomb is and how to disarm it?

Scenario three: The city of happiness[23]

In her story *The Ones Who Walked Away from Omelas*,[24] Ursula Le Guin describes Omelas as a city of peace, happiness and prosperity. She writes,

[I]n a basement under one of the beautiful public buildings of Omelas, or perhaps the cellar of one of its spacious private homes, there is a room. It has a locked door, and no window'. In this room there is a feeble-minded, malnourished, neglected child. Everyone knows the child is there, but '[t]hey all understand that their happiness, the beauty of their city, the tenderness of their friendships, the health of their children . . . even the abundance of their harvest and the kindly weathers of their skies, depend wholly on this child's abominable misery.

Are those terms morally acceptable?

Suggested reading

o   Sandel, Michael (2010) *What's the Right Thing to Do?* New York: Penguin. Excellent examples of moral dilemmas in chapter 2.

●   Herring, Jonathan (2014) *Legal Ethics*. Oxford: Oxford University Press.

21 Michael Sandel (2010) *What's the Right Thing to Do?* New York: Penguin, p. 37.
22 Ibid., p. 38.
23 Ibid., pp. 40–41.
24 Ursula Le Guin (1997) *The Ones Who Walked Away from Omelas*. London: Creative Education.

- Fuller, Lon L. (1949) 'The Case of the Speluncean Explorers' 62 *Harvard Law Review*, 616–645.

II. Critical thinking in the workplace

The previous part of the chapter discussed the importance of thinking ethically about law from both a theoretical and practice perspective. This second part of the chapter moves on to discuss how you can utilise your critical thinking in the workplace. During work experience, when choosing your career path both inside and outside of law and applying for jobs and how critical thinking skills are used in the professions are also discussed in this part.

> In response to the question: what are the essential critical thinking skills wanted by a graduate? Employers commonly assert, something to the effect that, they want to be able to send their best client on a long haul flight sat next to their employee, and that client is still to be their best one when the plane lands.[25]

As indicated by the discussion in TCAL so far, thinking critically about law essentially involves three elements. First, as discussed in Chapter 2, critical thinking relates to highest-order thinking: it requires you to think a little more deeply about a problem or issue. Second, in order to think more deeply about the problem or issue, you need to critically analyse the situation by weighing up its strengths and weaknesses and come to a reflective and creative solution. Finally, as indicated by the discussion in the chapters in the second part of TCAL, the critical thinking process entails a practical aspect. These three steps are also key to preparing for your future career, whatever you decide to do.

Work experience

Legal work experience is a worthwhile experience before, during and following graduating from a law programme. Gaining experience in a legal or professional environment is useful for a number of reasons, from finding the area you want your future career to be in to developing and honing skills for the role you want. Work experiences can include shadowing at a law firm, charity or company. In addition to informal experiences that you may be able to arrange through friends and family or by networking, there is a range of formal experiences, such as vacation schemes, mini pupillages or marshalling. Having work experiences on your curriculum vitae (CV) not only demonstrates your commitment to your career path, it also helps you focus on the practical outcome of your studies: to find a job! Two of the main examples of skills, in addition to critical thinking, that work experience helps you develop are providing you with an awareness of your transferable skills and showing you ways to develop your emotional intelligence. These are considered in the sub-sections that follow.

---

25 Career advisor, Reading.

Transferable skills[26]

A number of studies have been conducted into what employers look for in graduates. The results suggest that the specific facts and skills explicitly taught in most degree courses are relevant to only about fifty per cent of vacancies, and in most cases, recruits require further training; the qualities most sought after are general intellectual and personal skills, which receive relatively little attention in most degree courses.

The ideas that there are general skills which can be acquired and that learning them in one context is transferable to a different context runs contrary to much educational thinking of the recent past, which has instead tended to break everything down into different areas which are artificially separated one from the other.

The distinction between thinking and personal skills is far from sharp, since many things that are usually counted as the latter, as personal skills, are necessary if the intellectual skills are being used effectively. For example, you often have to be able to be patient and persevering to make sense of new information, and you have to be open-minded and tolerant of different opinions before you can evaluate and analyse them accurately. Similarly, it doesn't really matter how brainy you are if you can't communicate your insights and knowledge – as an exercise in public speaking makes clear very quickly!

Transferable skills in law include the following abilities:

- critical thinking;
- conducting research;
- weighing up points and counter them;
- creating logical arguments;
- demonstrating professional communication skills; and
- handling work under pressure.

TASK THIRTY-TWO *Business skills[27]*

You're stressed out about the mountain of work piling up and realise that you can't possibly finish it all. What's the smart way to meet the challenge?

a)   Do the best you can, if necessary working evenings and weekends and skipping meals, to get it all done in some form or another.

b)   Send a note to everyone involved stating clearly that your workload is excessive and you can only do a proper job if some of the deadlines are extended and less work is set.

c)   Recognise that it is your feelings that are the key factor – you feel tired and stressed! Reduce your working hours, take more time off, have proper meals and maybe go somewhere nice at the weekend too.

- See 'Task answers' section for outcome.

---

26 Martin Cohen (2015) *Critical Thinking Skills for Dummies.* Chichester: John Wiley & Sons Ltd, p. 224.
27 Ibid., p. 73.

TASK THIRTY-THREE *Time management*[28]

In your job, you always seem to have several tasks to complete by the end of the week. What's the most efficient way of organising your time?

a) Be linear: Take the jobs one thing at a time, not starting a new task until you finish with the one at hand.

b) Multitask: Tackle everything at once, because this stops you getting bored and some areas overlap, thus immediately saving time.

c) Recognise that the problem isn't your way of working but the amount of time you have. Take a strict look at your daily timetable and clear out all the unnecessary jobs and commit yourself to putting in extra hours until the backlog is cleared.

● See 'Task answers' section for outcome.

Applying for jobs

While also completing your studies and gaining work experience, you may wish to apply for part-time employment as well as researching your future career path. Think critically about your job application:

● Talk to anyone who has worked in a similar position or for the company you are applying for;
● Tailor your covering letter and CV to the job description; and
● Highlight and prioritise the key skills you have for the role.

If you are asked to supply a reference for the position, always seek permission of the person concerned before supplying their contact details. If your designated referee agrees, it is good practice to send a copy of your application and CV to them so that the required information is available to them when they come to write your reference.[29] At an interview, some questions are likely to be on your past career, so be ready to explain how your previous experience gives you a good grounding for the role for which you are now applying. During the interview, try to get across the following messages:

● What motivates you?
● What attracts you to the job?
● What is there in your background or qualifications that make it seem specifically suited for you?[30]

Towards the end of the interview, you will be invited to ask any questions you have of your own. Consider beforehand what you would like to know about the position

28 Ibid.
29 Glanville Williams (2016) *Learning the Law*. London: Sweet & Maxwell, p. 261.
30 Ibid.

that has not been made clear to you already. It is best to ask questions about the work itself. Examples include:

- Is there a training period for the role?
- Can you meet your manager/some of colleagues before joining?
- What are the prospects for promotion?[31]

Legal careers

Many students choose to undertake a legal degree because they want to be a lawyer. There are many reasons for this. Law is commonly viewed seen as a decent, worthy and intellectually stimulating profession. Captivated by images of fictional characters such as Atticus Finch[32] and Harvey Specter[33] or public figures who have law degree such as Barack Obama and Nelson Mandela, it is also seen as a career that is finically rewarding.

> A career in law offers excellent long-term prospects; but the employment scene is a rapidly changing one. It tends to follow the ups and downs of the economy, and to a lesser extent the fluctuations of fashion.[34]

According to the law society, however, in 2016–2017, more than twenty thousand UK and overseas students were accepted to study on law courses. In 2017, the SRA reports that there are approximately 140,000 practicing solicitors in the UK,[35] with approximately five thousand new solicitor traineeships being registered with the SRA in 2016.[36] In comparison, the BSB reported that there were a total of 16,000 practicing barristers in the UK in 2016,[37] with fewer than 1,000 pupillage opportunities available to candidates across the country.[38] You do not have to be a mathematical genius to work out that the number of students undertaking law degrees far exceeds the number of career openings and opportunities in the profession. In addition to the high competition for vacation scheme places and pupillages, course tuition fees for degrees and professional courses, potential changes to the qualifying system itself, stresses on the financial markets and Brexit all contribute to an uncertain future climate in the legal sector. These pressures mean that you need to use your critical thinking skills not only to attain academic success

---

31 *Ibid.*, p. 262.
32 A lawyer who represented an African American defendant in a highly publicised criminal case and a character in Harper Lee's classic (2010) *To Kill a Mockingbird*. New York: William Heinemann.
33 Character in the TV Series *Suits* (2011) Universal Cable Productions.
34 Williams, *supra* note 29, p. 225.
35 For a discussion of the regulated population statistics of practicing solicitors from 2009, see www.sra.org.uk/sra/how-we-work/reports/data/population_solicitors.page.
36 For a discussion of the entry trends into the legal profession, see the Law Society website at www.lawsociety.org.uk/Law-careers/Becoming-a-solicitor/Entry-trends.
37 For an account of practicing barrister statistics from 2010–2016 see the BSB website at www.barstandardsboard.org.uk/media-centre/research-and-statistics/statistics/practising-barrister-statistics/.
38 For an account of pupillage statistics from 2009, see www.barstandardsboard.org.uk/media-centre/research-and-statistics/statistics/pupillage-statistics.

but also to help you to think critically about how you will go about achieving your career goals. Not only do you need to think critically about your future career when applying for jobs, you also need to think critically as a lawyer. This was evident when I asked law graduates what critical thinking means to them and received the following responses:

Lawyers' definitions of critical thinking: critical thinking is

' . . . [t]o be able to analyse different ideas and see their differences and similarities. To be able to see the loopholes in different concepts and be able to find alternative solutions'.[39]

' . . . [e]xpanding in depth into every detail. Thinking outside the "box" and exploring alternative options'.[40]

' . . . [b]eing logical, analytical and thinking about opposing ideas or "outside the box" '.[41]

' . . . [t]hinking outside the box'.[42]

' . . . [a]nalysising to reach conclusions'.[43]

' . . . [a]bility to deeply evaluate an issue considering all possibilities (pros and cons) before coming to a final conclusion'.[44]

Compared with the answers to the question from law students and staff, law graduates commonly responded that thinking critically requires them to 'think outside of the box', thus demonstrating the importance of creative thinking in the legal profession. The other point to note is the variety of careers these law graduates have found themselves in, positions ranging from a corporate tax advisor to a paralegal, trainee advocate and various legal assistants. Although these graduates have diverse roles in the legal sector, ninety per cent reported that they expect newly qualified lawyers to demonstrate critical thinking skills, as shown in Figure 6.1.

In response to the question: how often are you required to think critically in your role? more than half the respondents reported that they 'always' have to think critically in their role. Thirty per cent stated that they 'regularly' think critically in their role, and the remaining twenty per cent reported that they think critically in their role 'sometimes', as illustrated in Figure 6.2.

39 Lawyer at the Office of the Legal Counsel at the African Union Commission, Ethiopia.
40 Corporate Tax Advisor.
41 Paralegal.
42 Pupil in Civil and Criminal Law.
43 Home Office Executive Officer.
44 Assistant Legal Advisor in Civil Law.

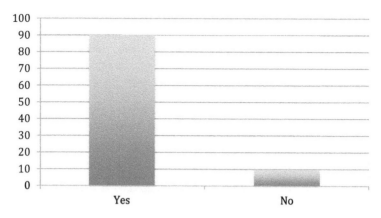

Figure 6.1 Do you have to demonstrate critical thinking in your role?

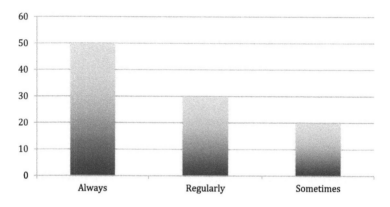

Figure 6.2 How often are you required to think critically in your role?

According to the charts in Figure 6.2, you need to think critically about the career you choose and when you are working in it. The rest of this part of the chapter focuses on discussing the requirements and critical thinking skills required for careers both inside and outside of the legal profession.

Solicitor

In order to qualify as a practicing lawyer, after graduating from your law degree CPE or GDL and completing the LPC, you will need to secure a training contract at a law firm. A training contract is the final stage in the process of qualifying as a solicitor. It provides you with the opportunity to put your academic theory into practice. It can be challenging to find a law firm that provides training contracts. Finding a training contract is a highly competitive process because '[t]here is no system of open competition, and there is no obligation to advertise vacancies'.[45] Three ways to think critically about finding a training contract and becoming a solicitor:

- **Research:** As with writing an essay, you need to research the career you want. Be sure to keep up to date with the latest news for students wanting to become solicitors on the SRA website.[46]
- **Networking:** During your time studying law, your school or department will provide opportunities to meet qualified lawyers at, for example, law fairs, lectures by professionals or other events. Use these as opportunities to talk to people involved in the career and/or area of law you are interested to work in. You may even meet such people through family and friends of your own or by conducting your own work experience.
- **Experience:** Experience in an area of law you are interested in working in can be gained either by your involvement with related extra-curricular activities (discussed in the final part of the previous chapter) or by finding and securing relevant work experience. This will help you find out more about what is involved with a particular area as well as providing key aspects to include on your CV.

As the largest branch of the legal profession, the work of practicing solicitors varies widely. Whether you work for one of the large 'magic circle' firms in the City, a medium-sized firm or for a firm on the High Street, generally, solicitors act as confidential advisors to their clients. Solicitors working in City law firms, for example, may be asked to draft commercial contracts and work alongside colleagues in overseas branches for the firm. You may have assistant solicitors, legal executives and paralegals help you with your work. Trainees in large firms are expected to work at the beck and call of their clients, who can have demanding requirements. If you are thinking about undertaking a career in a large City law firm, you may wish to consider whether you are prepared to make the sacrifices necessary to develop your career. In comparison to a large firm, medium-sized law firms (which have about fifty partners), located in London, tend to specialise in particular areas of law, such as intellectual property, media law or property development. Finally, High Street solicitors are involved with property conveyances, wills and probate as well as divorce law. This type of work entails meeting clients to advise them and preparing contracts of sale or petitions of divorce.

Newly qualified solicitors invariably act as assistant or associate solicitors, working under the supervision of a partner or senior associate of the firm. Under the new professional competence programme, the SRA requires that all solicitors keep up to date with their legal skills and knowledge, offering choice over their learning and professional development needs. Law firms are partnerships, so the ultimate career ambition for most solicitors is to become a partner in a firm. Attaining a partnership means that you transition from being an 'employee' of the firm on a salaried income

---

45 Williams, *supra* note 29, p. 247.
46 Available at www.sra.org.uk/students/students.page.

to being a 'part owner' of the firm, which means sharing in its profits and liabilities. Partnership in a firm no longer means that you are tied to it. Recently, a number of partners have been changing firms to secure higher earnings as well as to develop their practices.

Whether you work for a large, medium-sized or High Street firm, all solicitors require the ability to interview clients to ascertain the nature of their legal problem. This may require you to have specialised knowledge in a particular area of law. On difficult legal questions, however, the opinion of counsel by a barrister may be sought. Critical thinking is an essential aspect of being a solicitor, because three key attributes required by a solicitor are:

- **Communication skills:** Effective communication is key to explain the legal position of your client to a layperson, other lawyer and judge and so forth.
- **Attention to detail:** As solicitors are required to write and review documents, attention to detail is essential to pick up on the fine details of agreements or deals.
- **Teamworking ability:** Includes working with other lawyers on a case or with other supporting staff such as assistants, paralegals and legal secretaries.

Barrister

Similar to the career path of a solicitor, following graduation and gaining at least a second-class honours degree (from either an LLB degree or CPE/GDL), aspiring barristers also require further professional training (in the form of the BPTC) as well as practical training (by securing a pupillage in a chambers). In order to practice as a barrister, you must undertake a pupillage. Pupillage is a one-year 'apprenticeship' with a chambers or other approved organisation (such as the Crown Prosecution Service or Government Legal Service). Barristers are fewer in number than solicitors, and it is more competitive to secure a place in a chambers (for example, approximately 1,800 students undertake the BPTC every year, and there are approximately 500 pupillages offered),[47] although you are able to seek a pupillage for up to five years after completing the Bar Course. Three ways to think critically about securing a pupillage and becoming a barrister are to:

- **Keep up to date:** Make sure to stay aware of any changes for the future ways of qualifying as a barrister on the BSB website.[48]
- **Seek advice:** Talk to barristers in the area of law you are interested to practice as well as seeking advice from career advisors at your college or university. Contact those in the Inns of Temple.[49] Some Inns of Court, for example, offer scholarships to bright candidates.

---

47 See the Inner Temple website at www.innertemple.org.uk/prospective-members/how-to-become-a-barrister?showall=&start=1.
48 Available at www.barstandardsboard.org.uk/qualifying-as-a-barrister/future-bar-training/future-ways-to-qualify-as-a-barrister.
49 For example, the Education staff at the Inner Temple can answer your queries and organise open days and tours.

- **Gain experience:** Look for ways to gain experience of life as a barrister through a mini-pupillage or marshalling for a judge at your local court. Involvement with extra-curricular activities (particularly in moots and mock trials) will help display your passion in advocacy.[50]

In addition to the conventional career path, sometimes it is possible to qualify as a barrister in an alternate manner. For example, qualified solicitors may be exempted from some of the usual training requirements by undertaking the Bar Transfer Test. Following securing and undertaking a pupillage, a barrister's career typically progresses in the following way. Following pupillage, you become a junior barrister and become a 'pupil supervisor' of your own. Many barristers go on to 'take silk', which means 'obtaining the right to wear a silk gown by becoming a Queen's Counsel (QC)'.[51] Gaining the title 'QC' recognises that they have achieved excellence in their profession and appear in the most serious and important cases. Many barristers choose to apply to become judges later in their careers in the high courts, as well as recorders, deputy district judges and tribunal chairs.

In comparison to the security of being employed as a solicitor in a law firm, most barristers are self-employed and operate out of a legal 'chambers'. A chambers is a barrister's office base, which they share with other barristers. Because they are self-employed, barristers do not get a salary. In addition to their everyday living expenses, there are professional expenses to consider when receiving fees. These include the rent of chambers, clerk's commission, travel and the like. The sum of any remaining fees will be subject to further deductions from income tax and national insurance contributions. Fees can take a long time to come in, and some are never recovered. Barristers also have no pension.

Barristers act as legal advisors and courtroom advocates. They put legal arguments to judges, magistrates and juries and cross-examine witnesses and attempt to sway the outcome of a court case to their clients' advantage. According to the Honourable Society of the Inner Temple, being a barrister requires you to think critically in addition to the other following qualities:

- have a high level of intellectual ability;
- are articulate in written and spoken English;
- can think and communicate under pressure;
- have determination and stamina.[52]

If you want to become a solicitor or a barrister, you should not let the negative aspects of the profession discourage you from following your passions and aspirations. Optimistically, after all, people still need to be employed as solicitors and barristers, and why would they not hire you?

---

50 For more information about becoming a barrister visit the Bar Council website at www.barcouncil. org.uk.
51 Williams, *supra* note 29, p. 240.
52 See the Inter Temple website at www.innertemple.org.uk/prospective-members/how-to-become-a-barrister.

> Sometimes things don't go, after all, from bad to worse . . . Some men become what they were born for.[53]

This inspirational speech aside, you do need to have realistic expectations about the work and time and effort you will need to dedicate to actualising your achievements. Your career will not happen overnight; it will take many years of perseverance. You should consider other career options and may find that you end up in the role you want but arrive there a different way from the straight path. You may even come to prefer working in a career that you did not initially consider.

Other legal careers

In addition to becoming a solicitor or barrister, other legal career options include:

- **Solicitor advocate:** It is solicitors, rather than barristers, who conduct many of the cases in the lower courts in the country (such as the county and magistrates courts). Some solicitor advocates work in the higher courts and have developed particular specialties.[54]
- **Legal executive:** Offering specialised knowledge in a particular area of law, legal executives are involved in a large variety of legal work. Legal executives can become partners in law firms, advocates and judges.[55]
- **Paralegal:** Paralegals assist lawyers. Duties vary according to the type of firm and area of law practiced. Generic tasks include: researching and drafting documents, attending client meetings and client management. Generally, candidates are required to have an LPC or completed the CPE/GDL for the role.[56]
- **Legal secretary:** Legal secretaries provide secretarial and clerical support to solicitors, barristers and the law courts. They deal with client correspondence and help prepare documents such as wills, divorce petitions and witness statements. Legal secretaries are specialists because legal documents are composed differently from other commercial documents.[57]
- **Judge:** Both solicitors and barristers can be appointed judges. Judges in England and Wales must be British citizens and should be able to offer a reasonable length of service, usually about five years. Judges need to be able to preside over large amounts of information, scrutinise arguments and deliver judgments containing a clear statement on the law. Appointments of judges are carried out by the Judicial Appointments Commission.[58]
- **Courtroom usher:** Ushers' duties include escorting judges to and from court and preparing and closing courtrooms. They also carry out court duties, such

---

53 Sheenagh Pugh (1995) 'Sometimes' in *Selected Poems*. London: Seren.
54 For more information, see the Solicitor's Association of Higher Courts Advocates at www.sahca.org.uk.
55 For more information, see the Charted Institute of Legal Executives at www.cilex.org.uk.
56 For more information, see the National Association of Licenced Paralegals at www.nationalparalegals.co.uk.
57 For more information, see the Institute of Legal Secretaries and Pas website at www.institutelegalsecretaries.com.
58 For more information, see the Judiciary of England and Wales website at www.judiciary.gov.uk.

as obtaining the names of legal representatives, preparing court lists, maintaining order in the courtroom and handing round exhibits.[59]

- **CPS:** The Crown Prosecution Service (CPS) employs a sizeable number of qualified lawyers (solicitors and barristers in about one hundred branches across the country. The CPS is the government department responsible for about eighty per cent of prosecution in magistrates and crown courts. It is headed by the politically independent Director of Public Prosecutions, who is accountable to the Attorney-General through Parliament.[60]
- **Government legal service:** Lawyers in the government legal service provide legal advice to the government and represent it in court proceedings. It is part of the Civil Service (see the section that follows). Most government departments make appointments from professional lawyers.[61]
- **Local government:** Local government lawyers are qualified solicitors and barristers who act on behalf of and give advice to council staff and local authorities. Most roles require to you already to have trained as a lawyer to handle litigation, advise staff and draft letters and documents on behalf of local authorities.[62]
- **Researcher for the Law Commission:** Working as a researcher for the Law Commission offers a unique and rewarding opportunity to think deeply and work creatively about reforming the law. As a researcher, you will assist Commissioners in conducting legal research, policy analysis and administrative work.[63]

Career options outside of law

If you have specialised in law in your university or college, the knowledge and skills you have acquired will give you a useful background in many walks of life.[64]

In 2012, statistics showed that only forty-five per cent of law graduates were working in the legal sector.[65] That means that more than fifty per cent of law graduates gain employment outside the legal sector. In addition to other roles inside the legal profession, career options outside of the legal sector include:

- **Court Reporting:** The Incorporated Council of Law Reporting (publishers of the *Official Reports*, the *Weekly Law Reports* etc.) employs a number of qualified

---

59 For more information, see the HM Courts & Tribunals Service website at www.gov.uk/government/organisations/hm-courts-and-tribunals-service.

60 For more information, see the CPS website at www.cps.gov.uk/index.html.

61 For more information, see the Government Legal Service website at www.gov.uk/government/organisations/civil-service-government-legal-service.

62 For more information, see the Lawyers in Local Government website at www.lawyersinlocalgovernment.org.uk/about.

63 For more information, see the Law Commission website at www.lawcom.gov.uk.

64 Williams, *supra* note 29, p. 225.

65 See the studies carried out by the Higher Education Statistics Authority at www.hesa.ac.uk.

lawyers to edit law reports, decide what is worthy to report, write accurate summaries in the headnotes *etc.*[66]

- **Journalism:** Journalism involves gathering, interpreting and presenting news and items of topical interest. Unlike the clear educational requirements for jobs in the legal sector, routes into journalism vary. Undertaking work experience or post-graduate or short courses in journalism may help you to network and secure a journalistic role.[67]

- **Civil service:** Civil servants help the government develop and implement its laws and policies. All government departments require the aid of civil servants. The civil service fast stream requires you to have a lower second-class honours degree, at least, in any subject.[68]

- **Police service:** If you enjoy facing challenges and solving problems and would like to contribute to the safety of your community, then it is worth looking at the diverse range of career options in the police. You can start your career out as a Volunteer Police Cadet (ages 13–18 years old) or a Special Constable.[69]

- **Business management:** Business managers typically are responsible for the administrative and supervisory role of increasing a company's profitability and productivity. Roles involve sourcing new clients, creating strategic goals and generating business interest. Business managers are needed in almost every sector.[70]

- **Accountancy:** Quite a number of law students go on to become accountants. Knowledge of law is useful for both the examinations and practice. Accounts can become key advisers in industry and members on the boards of many large public companies.[71]

- **Entrepreneur:** The internet has become a key way for entrepreneurs to become successful. From the creation of social networking sites to mobile application development, small entrepreneurial businesses can connect with more than three billion internet users on a daily basis. A legal degree can be useful to an entrepreneur's understanding of legal issues and regulations as well as policy and policy making.[72]

- **Lecturing:** If you enjoy studying law academically, you may consider a career as an academic lawyer, lecturer or teacher. You are generally required to have a doctorate (PhD) or relevant professional experience to teach law in higher education. In addition, university lecturers are required to conduct research as well as teach, although this is not the case for teaching fellows and assistants. Professional experience may be accepted to teach certain modules or on the LPC or BPTC.[73]

---

66 For more information, see the Incorporated Council of Law Reporting at www.lawreports.co.uk.
67 For more information on careers in journalism, see www.journalism.co.uk.
68 For more information, see the Civil Service Fast Stream website at www.faststream.gov.uk.
69 For more information, see the College of Policing web site at http://recruit.college.police.uk/Pages/home.aspx.
70 For more information, see Reed Recruitment www.reed.co.uk/career-advice/how-to-become-a-business-development-manager.
71 For more information, see the Institute of Chartered Accountants at www.icaew.com.
72 For more information, see www.entrepreneur.com.
73 For more information, see the Higher Education Academy at www.heacademy.ac.uk/individuals.

- **Teaching:** Many law graduates go on to pursue a career in teaching. The Teach First Leadership Development Programme, which includes the Postgraduate Certificate in Education qualification, encompasses training, coaching and work experience in teaching. The skills and experience gained in the classroom offer participants a foundation in leadership, equipping them with skills for a career in the legal profession afterwards.[74]

Suggested reading

- Williams, Glanville (2016) *Learning the Law.* London: Sweet & Maxwell. Chapter 13: From Learning to Earning.
- Cherkassy, Lisa *et al.,* (2011) *Legal Skills.* Basingstoke: Palgrave Macmillan. Chapter 9: Career Planning and Development.
- Maughan, Caroline and Julian Webb (2005) *Lawyering Skills and the Legal Process.* Cambridge: Cambridge University Press.
- Boyle, Fiona *et al* (2005) *A Practical Guide to Lawyering Skills.* London: Routledge.

III. Critical instincts

This final part of the chapter builds upon the previous ones on thinking ethically about law in the workplace to discuss how you can boost your critical instincts in everyday life. As previously discussed (in Chapter 2), it is important that not only lawyers or students but citizens of democratic societies are able to think critically. One reason for this is the rise of concerns surrounding 'fake news' on the internet.[75]

Fake news

Fake news is news stories on the internet that are not true. This could be for two reasons. The first is that a story is deliberately published to make people believe something that is untrue. The second reason is that there may be an element of truth to a story, but it is inaccurate or has been misreported. The main reasons fake news stories are created is to sensationalise an issue so that it becomes popular and easily spread on social media. The problem is that people believe stories that are not based on any truth or reality. Other times, people are being told that a story is 'fake news' when it is a true account in order to make them disbelieve it. The result of these stories is said to have affected the outcome of the US presidential election in 2016, which is a pretty serious claim.[76] Ways to think critically about fake news:

- Can you find other places where the story has been reported (on the internet, in a newspaper or on TV)?

74 For more information, see the Teach First website at http://graduates.teachfirst.org.uk.
75 For example, see Elle Hunt. 'What is Fake News? How to Spot it and What You Can Do To Stop It'. The Guardian. 17th December 2016. Available at www.theguardian.com/media/2016/dec/18/what-is-fake-news-pizzagate.
76 See Hunt Allcott and Matthew Gentzkow (2017) 'Social Media and Fake News in the 2016 Election'. 31(2) *Journal of Economic Perspectives*, 211–236.

- Do you know the organisation that published the story?
- Does the story sound believable?

It may also be worth visiting Full Fact, the UK's independent fact-checking charity.[77] In addition to creating fake news, the goal of most media messages is to persuade the audience to believe or do something. One technique of achieving this is by using the 'language of persuasion', discussed in what follows.

Language of persuasion[78]

Language defines and shapes the world, and language is far from neutral. The experts in the 'language of persuasion' are people who work in advertising, public relations and campaigning.

✓ **Advertisers:** The most straightforward group – they seek to persuade people to buy a product or service. They usually present their message in plain sight – as an advert! – making it much easier to keep a certain critical distance from the message.

✓ **Public relations:** These experts 'sell' positive images – maybe of a political organisation or of a commercial brand on behalf of a corporation, government or other organisation, and they like to do this selling covertly: a certain brand of computer may be used by the hero in a film, or an ambitious politician appears in a TV documentary talking about their love of nature.

✓ **Campaigning (or 'advocacy') groups:** Also want people to 'buy' into particular beliefs or policies, and although they use up-front and straightforward advertisements for their views, they also try to skew debates in their favour so that by the time representatives are actually interviewed on the show or in the press, their views have already been presented to the reader or viewer as 'facts'.

So critical instincts can help you think critically about fake news stories as well as the language of persuasion used by advertisers and public relations and campaign groups. Thinking critically in everyday life requires you to undertake a deliberate intellectual thought process. Spending just an hour a day flexing your critical thinking muscle will lead you to think better not only for your academic studies and in your eventual workplace but as an essential life skill. Ideas of ways to further develop your critical thinking abilities include:

- Watching, reading and listening to the news;
- Making comments on newspaper articles on social networks;
- Contributing to debates on Twitter;
- Using critical thinking on your course forum;

---

77 See https://fullfact.org.
78 Cohen, *supra* note 26, pp. 59–61.

- Starting a student paper about school, local, national or international news reviews; and
- Writing your own student blog.[79]

The etiquette of critical thinking

Finally, bear in mind the usual rules of etiquette used in online forums and face-to-face tutorials. These are important to ensure that you manage to present your view in a positive and friendly way.

- Acknowledge another person's view before going on to challenge it.
- Be constructive in your challenge rather than simply dismissing another's point of view.
- Reflect on what you consider to be the strengths of another person's argument.
- Think about your language and whether you run the risk of being inadvertently offensive before you speak.[80]

TASK THIRTY-FOUR   *Getting into the habit of daily critical thinking*[81]

During the next seven days, document something you do every day that develops your ability to think well. Complete the following statements for each day:

1   **Today I engaged in the following thinking or behaviour that demonstrates my commitment to becoming a critical thinker:**

_____

_____

_____

2   **Before I started learning about critical thinking, I would have behaved in the following way in similar situations rather than in the way described in number 1:**

_____

_____

_____

---

79 For an example of a student blog, see Jenkins Jurisdiction, available at www.jenkinsjurisdiction. wordpress.com.
80 Open University (2008) *Thinking Critically*. Milton Keynes: Open University, p. 27.
81 Paul and Elder, *supra* note 7, p. 413.

3   **My new way of thinking and behaving is better because. . .**

_____

_____

_____

TASK THIRTY-FIVE   _Hunting for sophistry at work_[82]

[R]ead articles in newspapers, news magazines, and similar sources for the purpose of identifying intellectual sophistry at work. Look for situations in which someone deliberately hides or distorts information in pursuing a goal. Note whether the person gets away with the sophistry.[83]

TASK THIRTY-SIX   _Understanding your own biases_[84]

Think about the following questions, write down your answers, if you like:

1   **Do you have any legal prejudices?**
     Think of what you believe about your country, your religion, your family, simply because others – parents, friends, media – conveyed these ideas to you.

_____

_____

_____

2   **Do you ever argue for or against views when you have little evidence upon which to base your judgment?**

_____

_____

_____

---

82 Ibid., p. 16.
83 Examples include: Kate McCann and Tom Morgan. Nigel Farage: £350 million pledge to fund the NHS was a 'mistake'. The Telegraph. 24th June 2016. Available at www.telegraph.co.uk/news/2016/06/24/nigel-farage-350-million-pledge-to-fund-the-nhs-was-a-mistake; and Yochi Dreazen. 'Candidate Trump Promised to Stay Out of Foreign Wars. President Trump is Escalating Them'. 25th August 2017. Available at www.vox.com/world/2017/8/25/16185936/trump-america-first-afghanistan-war-troops-iraq-generals.
84 Paul and Elder, supra note 7, p. 22.

3 **Do you ever assume that your group (your family, religion, nation, friends) is correct (when it is in conflict with others) even though you don't have enough information to determine that is it correct?**

_____

_____

_____

Suggested resources

Books
Lee, Harper (2010) *To Kill a Mockingbird*. New York: William Heinemann.
Orwell, George (1945/2000) *Animal Farm: A Fairy Story*. London: Penguin Classics.
Atwood, Margaret (1996) *The Handmaid's Tale*. London: Vintage.

Films
Chicago (2002) Miramax.
Erin Brockovich (2000) Universal Pictures.
Philadelphia (1993) TriStar Pictures.
Spotlight (2015) Participant Media.
The Paper Chase (1973) Twentieth Century Fox.

Documentaries
Aileen: Life and Death of a Serial Killer (2003) Channel 4.

TV Series
This Life (1996–1997) BBC

Radio Programmes
BBC Radio 4 Law programmes In Action/Thinking Allowed/Moral Maze

Key points

Three key points of this penultimate chapter, are:

- The importance of thinking ethically about law;
- Ways to think critically about the workplace; and finally
- How to further develop your life-long critical instincts.

Concluding remarks about thinking critically about law are discussed in the next and final chapter.

Chapter 7

Conclusion

[D]ubito ergo cogito; cogito ergo sum.[1]

As stated in the introductory chapter, in comparison to other legal textbooks, the discussion in TCAL began by thinking philosophically and theoretically about 'critical thinking' and 'law'. According to the philosophy of Descartes (*'cogito ergo sum'*) we exist *because* we can think. To prove his own existence in the world, Descartes employed a sceptical strategy of doubting everything. When used to the right level, sceptical thinking is a powerful tool that aids critical thought. Used to the extreme, however, skepticism produces uncritical thought(s). Cultivating an inquisitive mind (one that asks lots of questions) whilst studying law is an essential element to attain a first-class law degree (as shown in Figure 1.2 First-class triangle). Not only is this important if you wish to pursue a career in law (as shown by the findings of my study conducted with law graduates, discussed in the previous chapter) but for any professional career. It is also essential that people can think critically, as every generation is faced with its own set of challenges, from killing a woolly mammoth to banning the nuclear bomb and stopping global warming. These challenges are essentially the same (they all threaten human existence), but the particular situations and faces differ.[2] Some of today's main challenges include a rise in media and political propaganda, awareness of fake news stories and the legal challenges to come following Brexit. Due to such challenges, there is the constant need for us to think creatively and self-reflectively about our modern-day legal challenges: to think critically about law.

As discussed in the second chapter, there are a number of different definitions of what 'critical' thinking is. Dictionary definitions differ as to the meaning of the word 'critical' depending upon its context (from meaning 'nearly dead' in medical terms to 'about to explode' in physics).[3] In everyday language, the word 'critical' is associated with providing a 'critique' of something (generally considered to be a negative exercise), whereas this is not what is required in academia. Academics propose many different definitions of the phrase 'critical thinking'. Four academic definitions of thinking critically were set out in Chapter 2. The first was by Richard Paul (founder of the Foundation for Critical Thinking)[4] and Lisa Elder, who state that it is 'thinking about your thinking in order to make it better'.[5] Paul and Elder contend that thinking critically forms part of 'highest-order thinking', which requires 'explicitly reflective' thought that is 'consistently fair': what they call 'strong critical thinking'.[6] It is possible to control and develop our thinking, to move from what Paul and Elder call 'lower-order thinking' or 'weak critical thinking' to the higher levels. As discussed in the preceding pages, highest-order thinking requires you to have an inquisitive mind that is sceptical about the information it receives and attempts to think 'ethically'

1 English translation: 'I doubt, therefore I think; I think, therefore I am'. René Descartes (1644/2016) *The Principles of Philosophy*. London: CreateSpace Independent Publishing Platform.
2 For example, see the moral of George Orwell's tale in (1945/2000) *Animal Farm: A Fairy Story*. London: Penguin Classics.
3 Mike Metcalfe (2006) *Reading Critically at University*. London: Sage Publications, p. 3.
4 See the Foundation for Critical Thinking website at www.criticalthinking.org.
5 Richard Paul and Lisa Elder (2014) *Critical Thinking: Tools for Taking Charge of Your Learning and Your Life*. London: Pearson, p. 1.
6 Ibid., p. 9 and pp. 16–17.

about complex issues (as discussed in Chapter 5). Accepting this definition of thinking critically, you have already achieved some distance along the journey by reading this book! The first part discusses thinking critically about law in theory, and the second part focuses on how to develop your abilities it in practice – from attaining high grades at university to gaining employment and using your skills in the workplace as well as for the rest of your life.

Alternatively, Stella Cottrell provided the second definition of critical thinking discussed in Chapter 2. Cottrell describes thinking critically as a 'cognitive ability'.[7] As it takes place in the mind, I think this is where some of the challenges of critical thought lie. Critical thinking is commonly a difficult term to define (not only because it relates to highest-order thinking, to subjects that do not have a simple 'yes' or 'no', 'right or 'wrong or 'black' and 'white' answers) but because we are unable to know exactly what is going on in another person's head. As contemplated in the second chapter, perhaps thinking critically is a difficult term to define because it is not an experience we all share. Evidence for this hypothesis is provided by the various definitions offered by academics as well as the law students, staff and graduates who participated in the studies conducted for TCAL. As thinking critically appears to differ between students and teachers, schools and departments, universities and HE institutions, the question still remains: what is 'critical' thinking?

Instead of thinking critically being defined as a cognitive ability that requires us to think about our thinking in order to make it better, the Open University asserts that the aim of critical thinking is to maintain an ' "objective" position'.[8] The benefits of objective thought are that it is deemed to be one that is rational, logical and neutral (as it is not influenced by our personal feelings or considerations) as opposed to 'subjective' thought. Objective (or doctrinal) stances of law have, however, been treated with suspicion and distrust by the followers of several legal perspectives that were discussed in Chapter 3 (such as feminists, critical race theorists and legal pluralists). This is because law's seeming 'objectivity' masks the reality of sexism, racism and intuitionalism. In comparison to promoting objectivity, scholars such as Russell Sandberg point to a 'subjective turn' in academia.[9] In line with this, and overcoming the nihilism of postmodernism (the belief that nothing in the world really exists) as well as correlating with the feminist stance of 'positionality',[10] subjective perspectives concede that there is some form of knowledge 'out there' (for example, a legal subject's perspective of law) but that this is open to change, and it depends upon the person being asked. Thus, the potential liberating and creative power of law is realised as it is connected to the imagination of each and every person. Indeed, a Hegelian phenomenological stance[11] towards law (such as a subjective legal pluralist perspective) is one that privileges a legal subjects' elucidation of normativity, holding that law is

---

7 Stella Cottrell (2011) *Critical Thinking Skills: Developing Effective Analysis and Argument*. Basingstoke: Palgrave Macmillan, p. 1.
8 Open University (2008) *Thinking Critically*. Milton Keynes: Open University, p. 7.
9 Russell Sandberg (2014) *Religion, Law and Society*. Cambridge: Cambridge University Press, p. 161.
10 Katherine T. Bartlett (1990) 'Feminist Legal Methods'. 103 *Harvard Law Review*, 829–888.
11 In basic terms, Hegelian phenomenology emphasises the dialectical (discussion of ideas or opinions between people) acquisition of knowledge.

'whatever *we* believe' it to be:[12] in other words, 'law' is a subjective belief. It is not that *each* and *every* person in the entire world will have their own beliefs about what the law is (that there are roughly seven billion legal perspectives); rather, there are sets of established ideas that people draw upon to create their own notions of normativity – as proposed by the structuralist notion of 'discourses' (formal discussions)[13] or what Wittgenstein called 'language games'.[14] Although we each have a unique perspective on the world, our views and experiences do not considerably differ. After all, we are locked into the language we use to communicate to one another as well as experiencing the human condition.[15] As illustrated in the discussions of the seven legal perspectives in Chapter 3 (namely, the doctrinal stances of natural law theory and legal positivism; as well as the critical positions of Marxism, the critical legal studies (CLS) movement, feminism(s), critical race theories (CRTs) and legal pluralism(s)), 'the concept of law which predominates in Western thought is not the only concept of law: law itself is a plural concept, and cannot be reduced to a single perspective'.[16] *All* legal perspectives, from the doctrinal to the critical, are plural: for instance, there is a difference between Austin and Bentham's stances of positivism and those of Dworkin and Hart. There are, however, key attributes that can be bestowed on the perspective of legal positivism (such as the emphasis on the separation between law and morals). The same can be said about feminism(s), for example, as all feminism(s) address 'the woman question' in some shape or form.[17] However, there are three distinct 'waves' of legal feminism(s) that roughly correlate with the perspectives of, first, liberal feminism(s), second, radical feminism(s) and, finally, postmodern and difference feminism(s). Although none of these are totally distinct or isolated from the others, stating that there are different 'waves' of feminism(s) (whilst being a stereotypical approach) is a useful way to start to appreciate the nuances and differences between the various viewpoints. The purpose of Chapter 3 was to provide a basic introduction to jurisprudence and an overview of different legal perspectives, because it is empowering to think theoretically and critically about law. Thus, in contrast to maintaining an objective position, our theoretical and critical thought(s) make us think subjectively. Not subjectively in the sense of establishing independent thought to the exclusion of the thoughts of others (although there are benefits to this to overthrow the pitfalls of, what Irving Janis calls 'groupthink');[18] rather subjective thinking in terms of thinking for yourself and convincing others of your position, in accordance with 'team thinking'.[19] Human beings can hold common objectives, but

12 Amy Codling (2015) 'What Do You Believe? Taxonomy of a Subjective Legal Pluralism' in Russell Sandberg (ed.) *Religion and Legal Pluralism*. Farnham: Ashgate, 199–212, p. 210.

13 Jean-François Lyotard (1984) *The Postmodern Condition: A Report on Knowledge*. Minneapolis: University of Minnesota Press.

14 Ludwig Wittgenstein (1922) *Tractatus Logico-Philosophicus*. London: Routledge.

15 See the work of Hume (David Hume (1738/2017) *Treatise of Human Nature*. London: CreateSpace Independent Publishing Platform) as well as Taylor (Charles Taylor (1989) *Sources of the Self: The Making of the Modern Identity*. Cambridge, Cambridge University Press).

16 Margaret Davies (2008) *Asking the Law Question*. Sydney: Thompson Law Book Co, p. 383.

17 Yavuz Selim Alkan (2012) 'Feminist Legal Methods: Theoretical Assumptions, Advantages, and Potential Problems'. 9(2) *Ankara Law Review*, 157–174.

18 Irving L. Janis (1971). 'Groupthink'. 5(6) *Psychology Today*, 43–76.

19 Martin Cohen (2015) *Critical Thinking Skills for Dummies*. Chichester: John Wiley & Sons Ltd, p. 11.

there is no such thing as an overall 'objective' or neutral stance on law due to our own assumptions, perspectives and biases. On this basis, I contend that thinking critically about law requires us to develop our own 'informed' position or perspective: one that you think reflectively about. Reflective thinking is required so that we consciously consider our own position of an issue, situation or argument. For example, what is required of us at any one time may differ when we are a lawyer, lecturer, judge or member of the public.

Jennifer Moon conveyed the final definition of critical thinking provided by an academic in Chapter 2. She contended that thinking critically requires the ability to consider a 'range of information derived from many different sources' in a 'creative and logical manner', making sure you challenge it to 'arrive at considered conclusions that can be defended and justified'.[20] Following the academic, philosophical and theoretical discussion in the first part of TCAL, how to think critically about law in practice was considered in the second. How to put your critical thinking skills into legal practice was the subject of the fourth chapter. Here practical guidance and tips were provided as to how you can marshal a range of information and think critically about it. A detailed discussion was provided as to how to research and write about legal authorities (legislation, cases and academic opinions). That these should be accurately cited in your assessments (in analytical essays, problem questions in exams as well as during group work, for example) to demonstrate your critical thinking abilities was at the forefront of the discussion in Chapter 5.

As an alternative to the four academic definitions provided in Chapter 2, TCAL's working definition of critical thinking (also set out in Chapter 2) is that

> [t]hinking critically about law is an intellectually disciplined process of thought whereby you develop your own informed legal opinions or arguments on a particular issue.

TCAL's definition of critical thinking is called a 'working definition' because it is to be used to encourage you to develop your own perspective of what 'critical thinking' and 'law' are. As it is unavoidably linked with human cognition, it is easier to contemplate thinking critically in terms of being an 'intellectually disciplined process of thought'.[21] Indeed, rather than being a 'tool', thinking critically can be viewed as an essential 'toolbox'[22] that encourages you to have an inquisitive mind that poses such questions as: *Why? How? Where? So what?* To achieve your own definition of what thinking critically about law is, TCAL outlines that thinking critically involves a two-stage process of thought. The first stage requires you to simply apply your knowledge and research to an argument or situation. You need to know and be able to recall what information is relevant, understand the meaning of it and apply it to the argument or situation at hand. The second stage in the process requires you to be able to analyse the information you remember. This requires you to critically analyse the situation

---

20 Jennifer Moon (2008). *Critical Thinking: An Exploration of Theory and Practice*. London: Routledge, p. 30.
21 Michael Scriven and Richard Paul (2008) 'Defining Critical Thinking'. *Foundation for Critical Thinking*. Available at www.criticalthinking.org/aboutCT/definingCT.cfm; see also Cottrell.
22 Cohen, *supra* note 19, p. 14.

or argument by considering its strengths and weaknesses, then evaluate it thinking about the limitations you have encountered and, finally, create a solution to the problem at hand. As set out in Chapter 4 (in Figure 4.1 'The critical thinking process of thought'), there are five steps in TCAL's critical reading and writing process. First, you need to 'problematise' the question or issue at hand by turning it into a problem that requires a solution. Second, you need to set out the definitions of any key terms or ideas in order to describe them. Third, once the key terms are defined, examine, scrutinise and question the information at hand and weigh up the strengths and weaknesses, pros and cons, of the issue or argument. Fourth, evaluate the validity of the issue or argument, including your own perspective or position. Finally, create either an original or quasi-original solution to the problem. A liberating sense of freedom comes from the ability to think for yourself and create your own solutions to perceived problems or issues.

Indeed, as well as achieving academic success, one of the key challenges faced by contemporary law students can be coming up with an answer to the questions 'what?' and 'where next'? Chapter 6 discussed the importance of thinking critically in the workplace and beyond. It concluded that not only do you need to know how to think critically for your studies and for your career, but you also need to think critically and creatively as to how to achieve your professional goals. Even if you never use your LLB law degree to practice, education is never wasted. The transferable skills, such as thinking critically, you cultivate during your time on the course, as well as the development of your critical instincts, will also stand you in good stead in life in general.

The intention of TCAL is to help you think critically about law. Answers to the questions what is 'critical thinking'? And what is 'law'? are something for you to develop whilst studying for your degree, during your career and over the course of your life. Your answers to these questions may change in different contexts, circumstances and over time. Similar to 'asking the law question', you may find that different stances on what critical thinking is do not considerably differ from one to another. As well as understanding the nuances between our ideas, we may also be able to identify some common themes. In order to begin your journey of thinking critically about law, the questions for you to consider for yourself are:

- Is thinking critically to be important when studying law? If so, why?
- Why is the ability to think critically important for your career?
- What does the phrase 'thinking critically about law' mean to you?[23]

Thinking for yourself summary[24]

Critical thinking skills are an intrinsic element in your study – in your reading, in writing your assignments and in working with others. Look through your course materials

23 Take part in the latest TCAL survey at www.surveymonkey.co.uk/r/J7QRKW2.
24 Open University, supra note 8, p. 28.

for specific guidance on how to apply critical thinking in your discipline, and remember that the sooner you start to develop these skills, the greater the benefit they will bring.

Remember, critical thinking skills involve:

● actively seeking all sides of an argument
● testing the soundness of the claims made
● testing the soundness of the evidence used to support the claims.

You will take these skills with you throughout your student life and beyond into post-graduate study, your career and your personal life. Being able to thinking critically about complex issues is an enjoyable and an exciting skill to have. As you practice and improve your abilities and your thinking becomes more acute and discerning, you will experience the pleasure of becoming a truly independent learner and thinker.

TASK THIRTY-SEVEN   *Articulating your own understanding of critical thinking*[25]

Now you have come to the end of TCAL, complete these statements:

1   **To me, critical thinking means:**

_____

_____

_____

2   **In other words (this should be at least 4–5 sentences):**

_____

_____

_____

3   **I can apply critical thinking to my life in the following ways:**

_____

_____

_____

● Look back at your answers to this task in the introductory chapter and see how they compare to what you have written here.

---

25 Paul and Elder, supra note 5, p. 14.

Task answers

CHAPTER 2: WHAT *IS* CRITICAL THINKING?

TASK FIVE: BRAIN TEASER[1]

The point of this little teaser is that the important information is present in the dull-looking line about the windows all facing south. The house must be at the North Pole, and the furry animal is thus white – a polar bear. It's easy – but unwise – to overlook the dull.

TASK SIX: SCHRÖDINGER'S CAT[2]

One objection would be that cats are conscious too! Maybe they cannot talk, but they can surely tell if they are being poisoned, so that means that if (inside the box) the chain of events was started with the release of the particle by the atom, the cat would not be in a suspended state of being both alive and not-alive anyway – the implausible state that the experiment is supposed to mock.

CHAPTER 4: PUTTING CRITICAL THINKING IN LEGAL PRACTICE

TASK NINE: CAPTURING THE AUTHOR'S POSITION[3]

The author's position is: Is it possible to find a legal job that suits your preferences for court work? The passage provides advice for aspiring barristers on selecting their field according to how much time they want to spend in court.

TASK EIGHTEEN: JUSTICE FOR TV WATCHERS[4]

This is a very confusing question. It seems to be about 'ability to pay', but in fact it isn't. Literally, the argument is those who use a service most should pay most. (If poor people watch a lot of TV – they should pay most!) The only argument here putting that line is argument c), which seems to be saying the opposite: 'Rich people should

1 Martin Cohen (2015) *Critical Thinking Skills for Dummies*. Chichester: John Wiley & Sons Ltd, p. 106, p. 87.
2 Ibid., p. 106.
3 Stella Cottrell (2011) *Critical Thinking Skills: Developing Effective Analysis and Argument*. Basingstoke: Palgrave Macmillan, p. 49.
4 Cohen, *supra* note 1, pp. 88–89.

pay a surcharge on their houses so as to help poor people who maybe don't have a home at all'.

It would be easy to misread the question and plump for argument d) 'Television channels should be paid for by general taxation so that the richer you are the more you pay'. I'd call this almost a trick question.

TASK TWENTY: USING CRITICAL THINKING IN A TUTORIAL[5]

It is likely that the group of students would immediately agree on several words as representing an emotion, for example 'joy'. Even so, they can still debate their reasons for their choices, using this as an opportunity to practice putting forward their ideas, as well as listening and weighing up the ideas of others.

More often than not at a tutorial you will not agree with the views of everyone else. Some students may declare that 'nausea' is an emotion: you may disagree. If you explain why you disagree and give examples to back up your case, then others can state where they differ. They may challenge your original thoughts, forcing you to re-evaluate your own claim. On reflection, you may stick to your original belief, but re-evaluation has helped you state your case more convincingly, or you may change your mind.

CHAPTER 5: THINKING CRITICALLY ABOUT ASSESSMENTS

TASK TWENTY-FIVE: LOOKING FOR THE ROBBER[6]

Given the numbers in the scenario, most people assume that the smart place to start looking for the attacker in the incident is among the indigenous community because of the witness testimony, even though a 'possibility' clearly exists that the witness may have made a misidentification.

But suppose that 10,000 white people live in the city and just 1 'indigenous' person does. The best strategy is then a slam-dunk for the police, isn't it? But then remember that the witness sees 'indigenous people' twenty per cent of the time. The evidence isn't so persuasive now, is it, because the witness will often say someone is indigenous when they aren't. The 'mathematically' correct answer to the original scenario is that a substantially higher probability exists that the villain involved in the street robbery was European rather than indigenous – so the police should be looking for a European robber. Mathematicians use a technique called Bayesian analysis to get an exact figure, but the important thing is to be aware of the general issue. The reliability of the identification of the robber as indigenous is, in this case, forty-one per cent, only about half the eighty per cent reliability people comfortably opted for 'without thinking'.

5 Open University (2008) Thinking Critically. Milton Keynes: Open University, pp. 26–27.
6 Cohen, supra note 1, p. 40.

CHAPTER 6: THINKING CRITICALLY IN THE WORK ENVIRONMENT

TASK THIRTY-TWO: BUSINESS SKILLS[7]

The correct answer is c)! Amazed? But that's the view of most business-skills authorities who offer such questions. In the real world, I suspect answer a) will get you further.

TASK THIRTY-THREE: TIME MANAGEMENT[8]

I think the correct answer is to prioritise – which I didn't put in here! Call it a trick question.

7 Ibid., p. 88.
8 Ibid.

References

Adorno, Theodor and Max Horkheimer (1979) *Dialectic of the Enlightenment*. London: Verso.

Al-Hibri, Aziah Y. (1999) 'Is Western Patriarchal Feminism Good for Third/World Minority Women?' in Susan Moller Okin, *et al.* (eds.) *Is Multiculturalism Bad for Women? Susan Okin Miller with Respondents*. Princeton: Princeton University Press, 41–46.

Alkan, Yavuz Selim (2012) 'Feminist Legal Methods: Theoretical Assumptions, Advantages, and Potential Problems'. 9(2) *Ankara Law Review*, 157–174.

Allcott, Hunt and Matthew Gentzkow (2017) 'Social Media and Fake News in the 2016 Election'. 31(2) *Journal of Economic Perspectives*, 211–236.

Anderson, Benedict (1991) *Imagined Communities: Reflections on the Origin and Spread of Nationalism*. London and New York: Verso.

Anderson, Lorin W. and Krathwohl, David R. (eds) (2001) *A Taxonomy for Learning, Teaching and Assessing: A Revision of Bloom's Taxonomy of Educational Objectives*. New York: Longman.

Andrade, Jackie (2009) 'What Does Doodling Do?' 24(1) *Applied Cognitive Psychology*, 100–106.

Antonaccio, Maria (2001) 'The Virtues of Metaphysics: A Review of Iris Murdoch's Philosophical Writings'. 29(2) *Journal of Religious Ethics*, 309–335.

Aquinas, Thomas (1969) 'Summa Theologica Part II' in Dino Bigongiari (ed.) *The Political Ideas of St Thomas Aquinas: Representative Selections*. New York: Hafner.

Austin, John (1832/2013) *The Province of Jurisprudence Determined*. London: The Classics.

Ayers, A. J. (1936) *Language, Truth and Logic*. New York: Dover Publications.

Balbus, Isaac D. (1977) 'Commodity for and Legal Form: An Essay on the "Relative Autonomy of the Law"'. 11 *Law and Society Review*, 571–582.

Baldoni, John (2010) 'How Leaders Should Think Critically'. *Harvard Business Review*. https://hbr.org/2010/01/how-leaders-should-think-criti.

Bano, Samia (2008) 'In Pursuit of Religious and Legal Diversity: A Response to the Archbishop of Canterbury and the 'Sharia Debate' in Britain'. 10 *Ecclesiastical Law Journal*, 282–309.

Bano, Samia (2012) *Muslim Women and Shari'ah Councils, Transcending the Boundaries of Community and Law*. London: Palgrave Macmillan.

Barnett, Hilaire (1998) *Introduction to Feminist Jurisprudence*. London: Cavendish Publishing Ltd.

Bartlett, Katherine T. (1990) 'Feminist Legal Methods'. 103 *Harvard Law Review*, 829–888.

Bentham, Jeremy (1789/2015) *Introduction to the Principles of Morals and Legislation*. London: CreateSpace Independent Publishing Platform.

Berkley, George (1710/1982). *Treatise Concerning the Principles of Human Knowledge*. London: Hackett Publishing Co.

Berman, Paul Schiff (2007) 'Global Legal Pluralism'. 80(6) *Southern Californian Law Review*, 1155–1237.

Bix, Brain (2009) *Jurisprudence, Theory and Context*. London: Sweet & Maxwell.

Black, Henry Campbell (1979) *Black's Law Dictionary*. St Paul, MN: West Publishing Co.

Blackstone, William (1825/2013) *Commentaries on the Laws of England*. London: Waxkeep Publishing.

Bloom, Benjamin (1956) *Taxonomy of Educational Objectives 1 & 2*. London: Longman.

Bodenheimer, Edgar (1976) 'Hart, Dworkin, and the Problem of Judicial Lawmaking Discretion'. 11 *Georgia Law Review*, 1143–1172.

ButleRitchie, David (2002) 'Situating "Thinking Like a Lawyer" Within Legal Pedagogy'. 1(1) *Cleveland State Law Review*, 29–56.

Buzan, Tony (2009) *The Mind Map Book: Unlock Your Creativity, Boost Your Memory, Change Your Life*. London: BBC Active.

Carty, Anthony (ed.) (1990) *Post-Modern Law: Enlightenment, Revolution and the Death of Man*. Edinburgh: Edinburgh University Press.

Cherkassky, Lisa, *et al.* (2011) *Legal Skills*. Basingstoke: Palgrave Macmillan.

Chiba, Masaji (ed.) (1986) *Asian Indigenous Law in Interaction with Received Law*. London: KPI. Ltd.

Cicero, Marcus Tullius (1928) *On the Republic: On the Laws*. Harvard: Loeb Classical Library.

Codling, Amy (2015) 'What Do You Believe? Taxonomy of a Subjective Legal Pluralism' in Russell Sandberg (ed.) *Religion and Legal Pluralism*. Farnham: Ashgate, 199–212.

Cohen-Solal, Annie (1989) *Jean-Paul Sartre*. Paris: Gallimard.

Cohen, Martin (2015) *Critical Thinking Skills for Dummies*. Chichester: John Wiley & Sons Ltd.

Coke, Edward (1797) *Institutes of the Lawes of England*. London: E & Brooke.

Connerton, Paul (ed.) (1976) *Critical Sociology*. Harmondsworth: Penguin.

Cook, Rebecca (ed.) (1994) *Human Rights of Women; National and International Perspectives*. Philadelphia: Philadelphia University of Pennsylvania Press.

Cotterrell, Roger (1984/2005) *Sociology of Law: An Introduction*. London: Butterworth.

Cottrell, Roger (2011) *Critical Thinking Skills: Developing Effective Analysis and Argument*. Basingstoke, Palgrave Macmillan.

Cowell, Brenda S., *et al.* (1995) 'Coping with Student Resistance to Critical Thinking: What the Psychotherapy Literature Can Tell Us'. 43(4) *College Teaching*, 140–145.

D'Entrèves, Alexander Passerin (1970) *Natural Law*. London: Hutchinson University Library.

Davies, Margaret (2005) 'The Ethos of Pluralism'. 27(1) *Sydney Law Review*, 87–112.

Davies, Margaret (2008) *Asking the Law Question*. Sydney: Thompson Law Book Co.

de Beauvoir, Simone (1949/1989) *The Second Sex*. H. Parshley (ed. and trans.). London: Picador.

de Bono, Edward (1996) *Teach Yourself to Think*. London: Penguin Books.

de Groot, Hugo (1625/2010) *De Jure Belli ac Pacis*. London: Nabu Press.

Dembour, Marie-Bénédict (2006) *Who Believes in Human Rights? Reflections on the European Convention*. Cambridge: Cambridge University Press.

Derrida, Jacques (1990) 'The Force of Law: The "Mystical Foundation of Authority"'. 11 *Cardozo Law Review*, 919–1046.

Derrida, Jacques and Avital Ronell (1980) 'The Law of Genre'. 7(1) *Critical Inquiry*, 55–81.

Derrida, Jacques and Julia Kristeva (1990) 'The Doubly-Prized World: Myth, Allegory and the Feminine'. 75 *Cornell Law Review*, 643–698.

Descartes, René (1644/2016) *The Principles of Philosophy*. London: CreateSpace Independent Publishing Platform.

de Sousa Santos, Bonaventura (2002) *Towards a New Legal Common Sense: Law, Globalization, and Emancipation*. London: Butterworth's.

Dewey, John (1933/1991) *How We Think: A Restatement of the Relation of Reflective Thinking to the Educative Process*. New York: Prometheus Books.

Dewey, John (1966) *Democracy and Education: An Introduction to the Philosophy of Education*. London: Collier-Macmillan.

Dicey, Albert Venn (1885/1982) *Introduction to the Study of the Law of the Constitution*. London: Elibron Classics Series.

Douzinas, Costas (2000) *The End of Human Rights*. Oxford: Hart Publishing.

Durkheim, Émile (1893/1964) *The Division of Labour in Society*. Trans. George Simpson. London: Collier: Macmillan.

Dworkin, Ronald (1977) *Taking Rights Seriously*. London: Duckworth.

Dworkin, Ronald (1986) *Law's Empire*. Cambridge, MA and London: Belknap Press.

Ehrlich, Eugen (1936) *Fundamental Principles of the Sociology of Law*. Trans. W. L. Moss. Cambridge, MA: Harvard University Press.

Elliot, Mark and Robert Thomas (2017) *Public Law*. Oxford: Oxford University Press.

Engle Merry, Sally (1988) 'Legal Pluralism'. 22(5) *Law and Society Review* 869–896.

Faith, Jo, Nick Rossiter and Paul Vickers (2003) 'Understanding Visualization: A Formal Approach Using Category Theory and Semiotics'. 19 *IEEE Transaction on Visualization & Computer Graphics*, 1048–1061.

Falk Moore, Sally (1973) 'Law and Social Change: The Semi-Autonomous Field as the Appropriate Subject of Study'. 7(4) *Law and Society Review*, 719–746.

Fasenfest, David (2016) 'Marx, Marxism and Human Rights'. 42(6) *Critical Sociology*, 777–779.

Felstiner, William L. F., Richard L. Abel and Austin Sarat (1981) 'The Emergence and Transformation of Disputes: Naming, Blaming, Claiming'. 15 *Law and Society Review*, 631–654.

Finch, Emily and Stefan Fafinski (2015) *Legal Skills*. Oxford: Oxford University Press.

Finnis, John (1980) *Natural Law and Natural Rights*. Oxford: Clarendon Press.

Fitzpatrick, Peter (2001) 'Magnified Features: The Undeveloped Law and Legitimation' in Italo Pardo (ed.) *Morals of Legitimacy: Between Agency and System*. Oxford: Berghahn Books, 157–176.

Foucault, Michel (1966/2001) *The Order of Things: An Archaeology of the Human Sciences*. Trans. London: Routledge.

Foucault, Michel (1977/1991) *Discipline and Punish: The Birth of the Prison*. London: Penguin New Edition.

Frank, Anne (1947/2014) *The Diary of a Young Girl*. London: Prakash Book Depot.

Fuller, Lon L. (1949) 'The Case of the Speluncean Explorers'. 62 *Harvard Law Review*, 616–645.

Fuller, Lon L. (1969) 'Human Interaction and the Law'. 14 *American Journal of Jurisprudence*, 1–36.

Fuller, Lon L. (1977/2004) *The Morality of Law*. London: Universal Law Publishing Co Ltd.

Gardner, John (2001) 'Legal Positivism: 5½ Myths'. 46(1) *American Journal of Jurisprudence*, 199–227.

Geuss, Raymond (1981) *The Idea of a Critical Theory: Habermas and the Frankfurt School.* Cambridge: Cambridge University Press.

Gibbs, Graham (1998) *Learning by Doing: A Guide to Teaching and Learning Methods.* London: Further Education Unit.

Gilligan, Carol (1982) *In a Different Voice: Psychological Theory and Women's Development.* Cambridge, MA: Harvard University Press.

Gjesdal, Kristen (2011) *Hermeneutics.* New York: Oxford University Press.

Gramsci, Antonio (1929/2005) *Selections from the Prison Notebooks of Antonio Gramsci.* London: Lawrence & Wishart Limited.

Griew, Edward (1985) 'The Objections to Feely and Ghosh'. *Criminal Law Review,* 341–354.

Griffiths, John (1986) 'What Is Legal Pluralism?' 24 *Journal of Legal Pluralism,* 1–55.

Gruenfeld, Elizabeth (2010) 'Thinking Creatively is Thinking Critically'. 125 *Innovative Practices for Leadership Learning,* 71–83.

Halpern, Diane F. (2009) *Thought and Knowledge: An Introduction to Critical Thinking.* New Jersey: Lawrence Erlbaum Associates.

Harris, Angela (1994) 'The Jurisprudence of Reconstruction Symposium: Critical Race Theory: Foreword'. 82(4) *California Law Review,* 741–786.

Harris, Angela (2000) 'Equality Trouble: Sameness and Difference in Twentieth Century Race Law'. 88 *California Law Review,* 1923–2015.

Harris, J. W. (2004) *Legal Philosophies.* Oxford: Oxford University Press.

Harrison-Barbet, Anthony (2001) *Mastering Philosophy.* Basingstoke: Palgrave Macmillan.

Hart, H.L.A. (1958) 'Positivism and the Separation of Law and Morals'. 71(4) *Harvard Law Review,* 592–629.

Hart, H.L.A. (1961) *Concept of Law.* Oxford, Clarendon Press.

Head, Michael and Scott Mann (2009) *Law in Perspective: Ethics, Society and Critical Thinking.* Sydney: UNSW Press.

Hegel, Georg Wilhelm Friedrich (1807/1976) *The Phenomenology of Spirit.* Oxford: Oxford University Press.

Helman, Gerald B. and Steven R. Ratner (1992) 'Saving Failed States'. 89 *Foreign Policy,* 3–20.

Higgins, Rosalyn (1994) *Problems and Process: International Law and How We Use It.* Oxford: Clarendon Press.

Hill, Mark and Russell Sandberg (2007) 'Is Nothing Sacred? Clashing Symbols in a Secular World'. *Aut Public Law,* 488–506.

Hobbes, Thomas (1651/2017) *Leviathan.* London: CreateSpace Independent Publishing Platform.

Horder, Jeremy (2016) *Ashworth's Principles of Criminal Law.* Oxford: Oxford University Press.

Hume, David (1738/2017) *Treatise of Human Nature.* London: CreateSpace Independent Publishing Platform.

Hunt, Alan (1978) *The Sociological Movement in Law.* London: Palgrave Macmillan.

Huntington, Samuel P. (2002) *The Clash of Civilisations and the Remaking of World Order.* London: Simon and Schuster.

Ishay, Micheline R. (2007) *The Human Rights Reader.* London: Routledge.

Jackson, Amy R. and Dorota A. Gozdecka (2011) 'Caught Between Different Legal Pluralisms: Muslim Women as the Religious "Other" in European Human Rights Discourses'. 64 *Journal of Legal Pluralism,* 91–120.

James, Mark (2013) 'Player Violence and Compensation for Injury: R v Barnes [2005] 1 Cr App Rep 507' in J Anderson (ed.) Leading Cases in Sports Law. The Hague: TMC Asser Press.

Janis, Irving L. (1971) 'Groupthink'. 5(6) Psychology Today 43–76.

Kealy, William A. and James M. Webb (1995) 'Contextual Influences of Maps and Diagrams on Learning'. 20(3) Contemporary Education Psychology, 340–358.

Kearney, Mary Kate and Beth Beazley (1991) 'Teaching Students How to "Think Like Lawyers": Integrating the Socratic Method with the Writing Process'. 64(4) Temple Law Review, 885–908.

Kelsen, Hans (1961) General Theory of Law and State. New York: Russell.

Kelsen, Hans (1967) Pure Theory of Law. Berkley: University of California Press.

Kennedy, Duncan (1982) 'Legal Education and the Reproduction of Hierarchy'. 32 Journal of Legal Education, 591–615.

King, Michael (1993) 'The "Truth" About Autopoiesis'. 20(2) Journal of Law and Society, 218–236.

King, Michael (2009) Systems, Not People, Make Society Happen. Edinburgh: Holcombe Publishing (e-book).

King, Michael and Chris Thornhill (2003) Niklas Luhmann's Theory of Politics and Law. Basingstoke, Palgrave Macmillan.

Kleinhans, Martha-Marie and Roderick A. Macdonald (1997) 'What Is a Critical Legal Pluralism?' 12(2) Canadian Journal of International Law and Society, 25–46.

Knott, P. (2009) 'Thinking Like a Lawyer: An English Interpretation'. 10(3) Transactions: Tennessee Journal of Business Law, 179–188.

Koskenniemi, Martti (1990) 'The Politics of International Law'. 1(1) European Journal of International Law, 4–32.

Koskennieni, Martti (2005) 'International Legislation Today: Limits and Possibilities'. 23 Wisconsin International Law Journal, 61–87.

Kouvo, Sari (2004) Making Just Rights? Mainstreaming Women's Human Rights and a Gender Perspective. Uppsala: Iustua Förlag.

Kuhn, Deanna (1991) The Skills of Argument. New York: Cambridge University Press.

Le Guin, Ursula (1997) The Ones Who Walked Away from Omelas. London: Creative Education.

Lee, Harper (2010) To Kill a Mockingbird. New York: William Heinemann.

Lerch, Carol M., et al. (2012) 'Reflection: A Key Component to Thinking Critically'. 3(1) The Canadian Journal for the Scholarship of Teaching and Learning, 1918–2902.

Leubsdorf, John (1991) 'Stories and Numbers'. 13 Cardozo Law Review, 455–463.

Locke, John (1689/2017) Second Treatise of Government. London: CreateSpace Independent Publishing Platform.

Lukes, S. (1973) Individualism. Oxford: Basil Blackwell.

Lyotard, Jean-François (1984) The Postmodern Condition: A Report on Knowledge. Minneapolis: University of Minnesota Press.

Macdonald, Roderick A. (1998) 'Metaphors of Multiplicity: Civil Society, Regimes and Legal Pluralism'. 15(1) Arizona Journal of International and Comparative Law, 69–92.

Macdonald, Roderick A. (2002) Everyday Lessons in Law. Montreal & Kingston: McGill-Queen's University Press.

Mackenzie, Robin (2010) 'Feminist Judgment of R v Brown' in Rosemary Hunter, Clare McGlynn and Erika Rachley (eds.) Feminist Judgments: From Theory to Practice. Oxford: Hart Publishing. Chapter 14.

MacKinnon, Catharine (1983) 'Feminism, Marxism, Method and the State'. 8 *Signs*, 635–658.

MacKinnon, Catharine (1989) *Towards a Feminist Theory of the State*. Cambridge, MA: Harvard University Press.

Malik, Maleiha (2010) 'Judgment: R (SB) v *Denbigh High School*' in Rosemary Hunter, Clare McGlynn and Erika Rachley (eds.) *Feminist Judgments: From Theory to Practice*. Oxford: Hart Publishing, 336–344.

Mansell, Wade *et al.* (2015) *A Critical Introduction to Law*. London: Routledge.

Martel, Yann (2003) *Life of Pi*. Toronto: Random House

Marx, Karl (1859/2013) *A Contribution to the Critique of Political Economy*. London: The Classics.

Marx, Karl (1875/2009) *The Critique of the Gotha Programme*. London: Dodo Press.

Masek, Alias and Sulaiman Yamin (2010) 'Problem Based Learning Model: A Collection from Literature'. 6(8) *Asian Social Science*, 148–156.

Mazher Idriss, Mohammad (2006) 'Dress Codes, the Right to Manifest Religion and the Human Rights Act 1998: The Defeat of Shabina Begum in the House of Lords'. 11(1) *Coventry Law Journal*, 58–78.

McConville, Mike and Wing Hong Chui (2007) *Research Methods*. Edinburgh: Edinburgh University Press.

McGee, Jeffrey, Michael Guihot and Tim Connor (2013) 'Rediscovering Law Students as Citizens: Critical Thinking and the Public Value of Legal Education.' 38 *Alternative Law Journal*, 77–81.

Melissaris, Emmanuel (2004) 'The More the Merrier? A New Take on Legal Pluralism'. 13(1) *Social and Legal Studies*, 57–79.

Melissaris, Emmanuel (2009) *Ubiquitous Law: Legal Theory and the Space for Legal Pluralism*. Bodmin: MPG Books Ltd.

Menski, Werner and David Pearl (1998) *Muslim Family Law*. London: Sweet and Maxwell.

Metcalfe, Mike (2006) *Reading Critically at University*. London: Sage Publications.

Milgram, Stanley (1963) 'Behavioural Study of Obedience'. 67(4) *Journal of Abnormal and Social Psychology*, 371–378.

Milgram, Stanley (1974) 'The Perils of Obedience'. *Harpers Magazine*.

Mill, John Stuart (1859/2005) *On Liberty*. New York: Cosimo Inc.

Miller, George A. (1956) 'The Magic Number 7, Plus or Minus Two: Some Limits on our Capacity for Processing Information'. 63 *The Psychological Review* 81–97.

Modood, Tariq (1997) '"Difference", Cultural Racism and Anti-Racism' in Pnina Werbner and Modood (eds.) *Debating Cultural Hybridity: Multi-Cultural Identities and the Politics of Anti-Racism*. London: Zed Books.

Moller Okin, Susan (1999) 'Is Multiculturalism Bad for Women?' in Susan Moller Okin, *et al.* (eds.) *Is Multiculturalism Bad for Women? Susan Okin Miller with Respondents*. Princeton: Princeton University Press, 7–47.

Moon, Jennifer (2008) *Critical Thinking: An Exploration of Theory and Practice*. London: Routledge.

Murdoch, Iris (1965/2015) 'On "God" and "Good"' in Marjorie Grene (ed.) *The Anatomy of Knowledge*. London: Routledge Library Editions: Epistemology. Chapter 9.

Murdoch, Iris (1993) *Metaphysics as a Guide to Morals*. New York: Penguin Press.

Naffine, Ngaire (1990) *Law and the Sexes*. Sydney: Allen & Unwin.

Nelken, David (1984) 'Law in Action or Living Law? Back to the Beginning in Sociology of Law'. 4 *Legal Studies*, 157–174.

Norrie, Alan (2010) 'The Coroners and Justice Act 2009 – Partial Defences to Murder (1) Loss of Control'. 10 *Criminal Law Review*, 275–289.

O'Mudd, John (1983) 'Thinking Critically About "Thinking Like a Lawyer"'. 33 *Journal of Legal Education*, 704–711.

Olsen, Frances (1990) 'Feminism and Critical Theory: An American Perspective'. 18 *International Journal of the Sociology of Law*, 199–215.

Parashar, Archana and Vijaya Nagarajan (2006) 'An Empowering Experience: Repositioning Critical Thinking Skills in the Law Curriculum'. 10 *Southern Cross University Law Review*, 219–241.

Paul, Richard and Lisa Elder (2014) *Critical Thinking: Tools for Taking Charge of Your Learning and Your Life*. London: Pearson.

Penner, James E. and Emmanuel Melissaris (2012) *McCoubrey and White's Textbook on Jurisprudence*. Oxford: Oxford University Press.

Pepper, Simon (1986) 'The Lawyer's Amoral Ethical Role: A Defense, a Problem, and Some Possibilities'. *American Bar Foundation Research Journal*, 613–635.

Petersen, Hanne and Henrik Zahle (1995) *Legal Polycentricity: Consequences of Pluralism in Law*. Aldershot: Dartmouth.

Phillips, Anne (2007) *Multiculturalism Without Culture*. Princeton: Princeton University Press.

Plato (2012) *Meno*. York: Empire Books.

Popper, Karl (1957/2002) *The Poverty of Historicism*. London: Routledge Classics.

Pound, Roscoe (1910) 'Law in Books and Law in Action'. 44 *American Law Review*, 12–36.

Race, Phil (2010) *Making Learning Happen*. London: Sage Publications.

Rawls, John (1971/1999) *A Theory of Justice*. Oxford: Oxford University Press.

Raz, Joseph (1979) *The Authority of Law*. Oxford: Oxford University Press.

Reiner, Cedar and Daniel Willingham (2010) 'The Myth of Learning Styles'. 42(5) *Change: The Magazine of Higher Learning*, 32–35.

Riessman, Catherine Kohler (1993). *Narrative Analysis*. Newbury Park: Sage Publications.

Rousseau, Jean-Jacques (1762/2017) *Social Contract, Or Principles of Political Right*. London: Independently Published.

Rudinow, Joel and Vincent E. Barry (2008) *Invitation to Critical Thinking*. Belmont, CA: Thompson Wadsworth.

Russell, Bertrand (1933/2009) 'The Triumph of Stupidity' in *Mortals and Others*. London: Routledge.

Sagan, Carl (2008) *The Demon Haunted World: Science as a Candle in the Dark*. New York: Ballantine Books.

Said, Edward (1978) *Orientalism*. London: Penguin Books.

Sandberg, Russell (2009) 'The Changing Position of Religious Minorities in English Law: The Legacy of Begum' in Ralph Grillo, et al. (ed) *Legal Practice and Cultural Diversity*. London, Ashgate, 267–282.

Sandberg, Russell (2011) *Law and Religion*. Cambridge: Cambridge University Press.

Sandberg, Russell (2014a) *Religion, Law and Society*. Cambridge: Cambridge University Press.

Sandberg, Russell (2014b) 'The What, the Why and the How' in Marie-Claire Foblets et al. (eds.) *Belief, Law and Politics: What Future for a Secular Europe?* Farnham: Ashgate. Chapter 10.

Sandberg, Russell (ed.) (2015) *Religion and Legal Pluralism*. Farnham: Ashgate.

Sandel, Michael (1982) *Liberalism and the Limits of Justice*. Cambridge: Cambridge University Press.

Scriven, Michael and Richard Paul (2008) 'Defining Critical Thinking'. *Foundation for Critical Thinking*. www.criticalthinking.org/aboutCT/definingCT.cfm

Shah, Prakasah (2009) 'Transforming to Accommodate? Reflections on the *Shari'a* Debate in Britain' in Ralph Grillio et al, (eds.) *Cultural Diversity and Legal Practice*. London: Ashgate 73–93.

Shah, Prakash (2005) *Legal Pluralism in Conflict: Coping with Cultural Diversity in Law*. London: Glasshouse Press.

Simon, William (2010) 'Role Differentiation and Lawyers' Ethics: A Critique of Some Academic Perspectives'. 23 *Georgetown. Journal of Legal Ethics*, 987–1009.

Smart, Carol (1989) *Feminism and the Power of Law*. London: Routledge.

Sokolowski, Robert (2000) *Introduction to Phenomenology*. Cambridge: Cambridge University Press.

Steiner, Henry, Philip Alston and Ryan Goodman (2008) *International Human Rights Law in Context: Law, Politics and Morals: Text and Materials*. Oxford: Oxford University Press.

Stern, R. A. (2013) 'Taylor, Transcendental Arguments, and Hegel on Consciousness'. 34(1) *Hegel Bulletine*, 79–97.

Sternberg, Robert J. (ed.) (1999) *Handbook of Creativity*. Cambridge: Cambridge University Press.

Stychin, Carl and Didi Herman (eds.) (2000) *Sexuality in the Legal Arena*. London: Athlone Press.

Tamanaha, Brian (2000) 'A Non-Essentialist Version of Legal Pluralism'. 27(2) *Journal of Law and Society*, 296–321.

Tamanaha, Brian (2001) *A General Jurisprudence of Law and Society*. Oxford: Oxford University Press.

Taylor, Charles (1972) 'The Opening Arguments of the Phenomenology' in Alasdair MacIntryre (ed.) *Hegel: A Collection of Critical Essays*. Notre Dame: Notre Dame University Press, 151–188.

Taylor, Charles (1989) *Sources of the Self: The Making of the Modern Identity*. Cambridge: Cambridge University Press.

Taylor, Charles (1994) 'The Politics of Recognition' in Amy Gutmann (ed.) *Multiculturalism: Examining the Politics of Recognition*. Princeton, Princeton University Press, 25–74.

Teubner, Günter (1992) 'Two Faces of Janus: Rethinking Legal Pluralism'. 13(5) *Cardozo Law Review*, 1443–1462.

Teubner, Günter (1997) 'Global Bukowina: Legal Pluralism in the World Society' in Günter Teubner (ed.) *Global Law Without a State (Studies in Modern Law and Policy)*. Aldershot: Dartmouth Publishing Co.

Thompson, Alan (1987) 'Critical Legal Education in Britain'. 14 *Journal of Law and Society*, 183–197.

Thompson, Mark and Martin George (2017) *Thompson's Modern Land Law*. Oxford: Oxford University Press.

Trubeck, David M. (1984) 'Where the Action Is: Critical Legal Studies and Empiricism'. 36(1/2) *Critical Legal Studies Symposium*, 575–622.

Vakulenko, Antasisa (2007) 'Islamic Dress in Human Rights Jurisprudence: A Critique of Current Trends'. 7(4) *Human Rights Law Review*, 717–739.

von Benda-Beckmann, Franz (2002) 'Who's Afraid of Legal Pluralism?' 47 *Journal of Legal Pluralism and Unofficial Law*, 37–74.

Wacks, Raymond (2009) *Understanding Jurisprudence: An Introduction to Legal Theory*. Oxford: Oxford University Press.

Wallerstein, Shlomit (2009) ' "A Drunken Consent is Still Consent" – Or Is It? A Critical Analysis of the Law on a Drunken Consent to Sex Following Bree'. 73(4) *The Journal of Criminal Law*, 318–344.

Wax, Ruby (2014) *Sane New World*. London: Hodder.

Weber, Max (1954) *Max Weber on Law in Economy and Society*. Trans. Edward Shils and Max Rheinstein. Cambridge, MA: Harvard University Press.

Weber, Max (1968) *Economy and Society: An Outline of Interpretive Sociology* in Guenther Roth and Claus Wittich (eds.) New York: Bedminster Press.

Webley, Lisa (2016) *Legal Writing*. London: Routledge.

Webley, Lisa and Liz Duff (2007) 'Women Solicitors as a Barometer for Problems Within the Legal Profession – Time to Put Values Before Profits?'. 34(3) *Journal of Law and Society*, 374–402.

Wilks Kefer, Matthew (1996) 'Distinguishing Practical and Theoretical Reasoning: A Critique of Deanna Kuhn's Theory of Informal Argument'. 18(1) *Informal Logic*, 35–55.

Williams, Glanville (2016) *Learning the Law*. London: Sweet & Maxwell.

Williams, Patricia (1991) *The Alchemy of Race and Rights*. Cambridge, MA: Harvard University Press.

Williams, Rowan (2008) 'Civil and Religious Law in England: A Religious Perspective'. 10(3) *Ecclesiastical Law Journal*, 262–282.

Wittgenstein, Ludwig (1922) *Tractatus Logico-Philosophicus*. London: Routledge.

Wollstonecraft, Mary (1792/2017) *A Vindication of the Rights of Women*. London: CreateSpace Independent Publishing Platform.

HANSARD

Hansard (3rd November 1997) *Human Rights Bill*.

POLITICAL DECLARATIONS

Jefferson, Thomas, United States of America Declaration of Independence, July 4th, 1776.

GOVERNMENTAL REPORTS

Dearing, Ron (1997) *Higher Education in the Learning Society* (*Report of the National Committee of Inquiry into Higher Education*). London: HMSO.

Independent Report. 'The Browne Report: Higher Education Funding and Student Finance'. *Department for Business, Innovation and Skills*. 12 October 2010. www.gov.uk/government/uploads/system/uploads/attachment_data/file/422565/bis-10-1208-securing-sustainable-higher-education-browne-report.pdf

Joint Committee on Human Rights (2002) 'The Case for a Human Rights Commission'. 6th Report. VI (HL 67; HC 489).

Office for National Statistics. '2011 Census, Qualifications and Labour Market Participation in England and Wales'. 18 June 2014. www.ons.gov.uk/ons/dcp171776_367378.pdf

LAW COMMISSION REPORTS

Law Commission (2004) *Partial Defences to Murder*. Law Comm No 290. London: TSO.

REPORTS BY PROFESSIONAL BODIES

BSB (2015) 'Academic Stage Book'. www.barstandardsboard.org.uk/media/1699477/academic_stage_book_15-16_with_covers.pdf

SRA (2013) 'Training for Tomorrow'. www.sra.org.uk/sra/policy/training-for-tomorrow/resources/policy-statement.page

LEGAL PROFESSION CODES OF CONDUCT

Bar Code of Conduct – Bar Standards Board (BSB) www.barstandardsboard.org.uk/media/1353125/word_version_of_full_code_of_conduct___annexes_jan_2012_.pdf

Solicitor's Regulations (SRA) Code of Conduct www.sra.org.uk/solicitors/handbook/code/content.page

EDUCATIONAL LITERATURE

QAA Publication. 'The Framework for Higher Education Qualifications in England, Wales and Northern Ireland'. August 2008. www.qaa.ac.uk

HIGHER EDUCATION STATISTICS

Higher Education Statistics Authority. 'Destinations of Leavers from Higher Education Longitudinal Survey 2016/17'. www.hesa.ac.uk/data-and-analysis/publications/long-destinations-2012-13

HIGHER EDUCATION STRATEGIES

University of Reading (2013–2018) 'Learning and Teaching Strategy'. www.reading.ac.uk/web/FILES/cdotl/University-of-Reading-Learning-and-Teaching-Strategy-2013-18.pdf

SKILLS GUIDE

Open University (2008) *Thinking Critically*. Milton Keynes: Open University.

THESES

Amy R. Jackson (2012) *What Is Law? Unveiling a Subjective Legal Pluralism*. University of Reading: Unpublished Thesis.

DISSERTATIONS

Amy Jackson (2008) *How Might Legal Pluralist Methods Lead to a Better Understanding of the Role of Other Actors in Public International Law?* University of Sussex: Unpublished LLM Dissertation.

NEWSPAPER ARTICLES

BBC News. 'School Wins Muslim Dress Appeal'. 22 March 2006. news.bbc.co.uk/1/hi/education/4832072.stm

Dreazen, Yochi. 'Candidate Trump Promised to Stay Out of Foreign Wars. President Trump Is Escalating Them'. 25 August 2017. www.vox.com/world/2017/8/25/16185936/trump-america-first-afghanistan-war-troops-iraq-generals

Gray, Laura. 'Legal Aid Cuts: What Has Changed?' *BBC News*. 18 June 2013. www.bbc.co.uk/news/uk-politics-22936684.

The Guardian. 'Legal Fees Investigation Reveals Huge Disparities Between Law Firms'. 5 March 2016. www.theguardian.com/law/2016/apr/05/legal-fees-investigation-reveals-huge-disparities-between-law-firms

Hunt, Elle. 'What Is Fake News? How to Spot It and What You Can Do to Stop It'. *The Guardian*. 17 December 2016. www.theguardian.com/media/2016/dec/18/what-is-fake-news-pizzagate

Johnson, Boris. 'The Shabina Begum Case Never Had Anything to Do with Modesty'. *The Telegraph*. 23 March 2006. www.telegraph.co.uk/comment/personal-view/3623879/The-Shabina-Begum-case-never-had-anything-to-do-with-modesty.html

McCann, Kate and Tom Morgan. 'Nigel Farage: £350 Million Pledge to Fund the NHS Was a "mistake"'. *The Telegraph*. 24 June 2016. www.telegraph.co.uk/news/2016/06/24/nigel-farage-350-million-pledge-to-fund-the-nhs-was-a-mistake

POEMS

Pugh, Sheenagh (1995) 'Sometimes' in *Selected Poems*. London: Seren.

WEBSITES

Shabina Begum. Live dialogue number 569, 17 March 2005. www.islamonline.net/livedialogue/english
Bonallack and Bishop Solicitors. www.bishopslaw.co.uk/about-us/lawyer-jokes
The Foundation for Critical Thinking: www.criticalthinking.org

FILMS

Life of Pi (2012) Fox 2000 Pictures.
Troy (2004) Warner Bros.

TV SHOWS

Suits (2011) Universal Cable Productions.
The Big Bang Theory (2007) CBS.

Index

Note: Italicized page numbers indicate a figure on the corresponding page. Page numbers in bold indicate a table on the corresponding page.